Bella Read.

Mistley in the Days of the Rigbys

Ivan Garwood

First Published by
LUCAS BOOKS 2003

ISBN 1903797-27-6

British Library Cataloguing in Publication Data
A catalogue record for this book is available from the British Libraray

Printed in the UK by
Barnwell's Print Ltd., Aylsham, Norfolk NR11 6ET
Tel: 01263 732767

PREFACE

My interest in the period covered in this book began at an early age, when my grandmother, who lived in a house in Mistley called "Rigby Villa", told me stories which had long circulated in the folklore of the village about the "goings on" at the Old Hall many years before. Many notable and sometimes notorious visitors had come to Mistley Hall in the mid-eighteenth century, to enjoy the parties which often continued throughout the night. The lavish entertainment was provided by Richard Rigby, who owned the whole village and surrounding land. The knowledge of the hospitality Mistley offered spread far and wide; it thus became a convenient stopping place between London and Harwich for the many friends of Rigby at that time.

My interest was further stimulated when some years later I found many documents and letters relating to the Rigby family amongst the deeds of Rigby Villa. These were probably misplaced by an unknown solicitor's clerk who "helpfully" filed anything bearing the name Rigby into one large parcel.

When I commenced my research, which covers a period of nearly 140 years in Mistley's history, I quickly found it would be impossible to write in detail on the hundreds of documents I had to study, so I have confined my story to a selection from those which I found particularly interesting.

I have also tried to show how Mistley and the surrounding lands looked during this period, so that the changes over the years may be seen and compared with the present day features. Many houses built by the Rigbys still remain as carefully preserved listed buildings.

Whilst in compiling my story I have found it helpful to refer to many other interesting accounts about the Rigbys, I have attempted to avoid too much repetition, and as far as possible have confined myself to primary source material gleaned at first hand from the letters and documents I have consulted.

CHAPTER 1

THE VILLAGE UP TO EARLY 1700

Mistley nestles comfortably in a wooded cove on the River Stour some nine miles from the sea at Harwich. In earlier times the Stour, or "Stower", had been the natural border between the East Angles on the north bank, and the East Saxons on the south. Neither kingdom was renowned for its peaceful habits, and it is probable that much fighting would have taken place in and around the river areas.

There is also little doubt that the dreaded Viking ships sailed up the quiet waters of the Stour, and fire and bloodshed would have marked the spots where their occupants landed. The inhabitants of Mitteslea and Chedinghov, which respectively, Mistley and Manningtree were then called, would have been overjoyed when one summer's day in the year 885, the news arrived that Alfred the King of England's army and fleet had captured sixteen Viking ships at Bloody Point at the mouth of the Stour, and killed their crews. They would have been less pleased when in the autumn of 894 it became known that the Vikings had settled round about the nearby River Colne. There is some evidence of Viking influence in many of our coastal areas shown in the place names where they temporarily settled, e.g. Thorpe-le-Soken and Kirby-le-Soken. Despite the violence, which extended over a long period in our history, as the years rolled forward conditions generally became more peaceful. Many changes took place over the next 600 years, as Mistley had numerous owners, until in 1552 King Edward VI gave the lands to Sir John Rainsforth. Sir John had two wives, but no children, and sometime later Paul Viscount Bayning, acquired the property. During the time of the Viscount's ownership the whole estate prospered, the farm lands were developed, and the Estate appears to have been managed in an exemplary manner. After Viscount Bayning's death the estates became the property of his son. On his death they passed to his daughter Anne, who had married Aubrey de Vere, the 20th Earl of Oxford. Unfortunately, following the good stewardship of Viscount Bayning, it is recorded that the Earl of Oxford impoverished his wife's inheritance.

At this time, England was a country of hamlets, and many of its towns, which were naturally smaller than those of today, were on the coast. The population was only $5^1/_2$ million, and indeed in Mistley it was even declining. Communications were poor, and the dirt roads became almost impassable in the winter months. The countryside was still heavily wooded, but much of this was being cleared for improved methods of agriculture, and local industry. The name of the village appears to have changed several times. It was originally known as "Mistle-leigh", which translated as "wood with mistletoe". Later we find "Mistoly" and "Misley", while in 1700 the village is spelt "Missley" in various records.

Apart from the small industrial section, most of the village and surrounds at this time could be described as having an idyllic and pastoral setting. The wide river and grass fields sweeping down to the leafy woodlands alongside were later captured by Gainsborough and Constable in their beautiful paintings of the landscape in the estuary and Dedham Vale close by.

Mistley was connected to Manningtree by a rough roadway alongside the river, passing through the waterlogged Hopping Marsh over a bridge of the same name and crossing a stream which ran into the river. The bridge still retains this name today.

Alongside the river channel was a small wharf, and a hard area on which ships could lie. Here were more than thirty acres of woods and grazing land, known as lands of "le Thorne". At its centre was a green, where some of the villagers lived in small tiled or thatched cottages close to the river.

Towards the east, hills rose steeply, and stretched almost to Bradfield shore. These hills were covered with woodland, and fell away to the river's edge, where they formed hanging cliffs. Below the cliffs there is evidence of sandy beaches, with steps built into the cliff to the waterside below. The woodlands were teeming with wildlife, and abundant with wild flowers, which grew freely in the English countryside at this time.

To the south of the lands of le Thorne lay many woods, and pastureland for grazing cattle and sheep. Further to the south east was more woodland, with farms on the borders of Bradfield and Tendring. In 1700, Mistley had more or less the same boundaries it has today; it was divided into four Manors, with farm lands of more than 1500 acres. Each of the farms had a large manor house or Hall which was managed by a tenant farmer, who paid an agreed rent to the owner of the Estate.

The dwellings of the Mistley villagers were mostly simple cottages scattered throughout the farmlands, where most of their inhabitants worked. Some appear to have been located in the Mistley Heath portion of the estate and others at the hamlet of Horsley Cross. There would have been fewer than thirty houses in the village, and possibly not more than a hundred people.

In spite of the poor sanitation, Mistley appears to have been a healthy place to live. No victims of the dreadful outbreak of plague which afflicted England in 1663 were recorded, although in neighbouring Colchester more than 4500 died.

The church of St. Mary the Virgin at Mistley Heath was built in the 13th century, with an attractive porch added some 150 years later. A few ruins of the old church can still be seen, but there are no remains of the parsonage which stood in the corner of the field on the opposite side of the road. The ancient church had a small steeple in which there were four bells, but by 1700 the building had become seriously dilapidated. The newer porch, however, remained in good condition, built with smooth flints, with two stained glass windows. To the right and left of the doorway there was beautiful stonework in arabesque style. There were merchants' marks and designs in stone and flints, which were placed as tribute to those who gave material assistance to the erection of the porch. The moulding was studded with Tudor rose emblems. From here a spiral staircase rose to the priest's room. The floor was made of glazed tiles, with flagstone surrounds.

The church contained two great pre-reformation altar tops, whose surfaces were etched with five crosses symbolic of our Lord's five agonies. Both were of Purbeck marble; one was rough hewn, and the other had a moulded facing. Over the years many tombs had been constructed, and the body of the church had a massive chancel arch, with buttresses supporting the outer walls.

In 1707 a visitation was carried out, and it was ordered that "the bible be new bound", and that "there be a new pulpit cushion". "The chancel should be repaired, and the east window glazed".

The parsonage house, which was reported as "very ruinous", was to be repaired, and the floor mended, with a carpet provided for the communion table. The ivy and bushes about the church and churchyard were to be "scrubbed" up. Despite the poor state of repair of the church the four bells in the steeple were found to be in good order. The priest in charge was Dr. Alec Burgess, and there is little doubt that his tiny church was sadly coming to the end of its life.

The village school was a large hexagonally-shaped building of wattle and daub, with a thatched roof overhanging a walkway, supported by vertical wooden pillars. It was situated in the area of Mistley known as Pound Corner, and until the building was demolished a few years ago, it was always known as Pound House. The brick-built pound in which a fine horse chestnut tree is growing was probably erected later. No information as to its use is available, and as there is no gate in it, its original use in uncertain.

It is probable that, although scattered, the village community was close knit. Set in peaceful surroundings there were a variety of opportunities for work, principally, of course, in agriculture.

The Pound in upper Mistley with the side of the old thatched schoolroom in the background

CHAPTER 2

AGRICULTURE & INDUSTRY - MISTLEY 1700

In the England of 1700 agriculture was the principal source of occupation, but Mistley's proximity to the River Stour allowed opportunities for a number of small businesses to flourish, with trade coming in and out of the small wharf adjacent to the lands of le Thorne along the riverside.

Agriculture

The village was divided into Manors, and in each of these was a farm bearing the same name. At the turn of the century much land was being recovered from scrub and woodland, adding to the size of the farming areas. At this time many farmers in England were eagerly consulting some of the new scientific knowledge being published. Those in Mistley might well have attended the eight lectures on scientific farming and good husbandry which were held at nearby Manningtree early in 1700. The farmland was being extensively improved by using cargoes of chalk brought from Kent. It was landed at the wharf at Mistley, and other points on hard areas along the banks of the Stour, where it was collected by farmers using their own wagons. Loads of marl and clay were also used to improve the texture of the rather light soil which constitutes Mistley farm land. Probably much to the annoyance of those living nearby, regular shipments of "London muck" arrived and were placed behind the piece of land on which the Towers church was subsequently built. The land is shown on all the old maps as a "depository for manure", and early writers report that it was heaped in "noisome" piles close to the river. The manure was collected by farmers who paid 15/-. per load using their own men to load it into the carts. The men who worked on the ships had a thankless task, using metal tined forks, hand-operated winches and wicker skips to unload the manure.

The farmers had to select the type of crop, which they grew with great care. Because of the soil composition a system of rotation was used, allowing one field to lie fallow every three or four years. The main crops grown were wheat, oats and barley, with potatoes, turnips, clover and beans sharing in the rotation. Some cattle were kept; the Devonshire breed of cows was preferred, as these were considered to be greatly superior to the others. Sheep rearing was also becoming an important part of the agricultural scene following the arrival in England of numbers of spinners and weavers from the continent. There were more than 250 looms within easy reach of the Mistley farms, e.g. at Dedham and other villages to the north. Although hay and straw were required for use on the farms locally, much of it was shipped to London for the many hundreds of horses using the streets of the large city.

There were six main farms in Mistley, each practising different methods. One was engaged almost entirely on daily operations, with some sheep grazing. Three were almost completely arable, and the other two reared cattle and sheep. The many woodlands on the farms were stocked with deer, and the largest farm had a parkland area in which they grazed. Much of the produce went to the London market from the wharf, but the villagers would have had an ample supply of food readily available.

Some of the agricultural workers would not have been employed continuously throughout the year, and much hardship occurred during the winter months when there was little work on the farms. The farm labourer was paid six shillings per week when in work, but the basic wage may have increased at harvest time.

4

Industry & other types of employment.

Other opportunities for work existed in the forms of some of the small industries operating in and around the village. There was a tiny malting near the quayside which would have only been in use during the winter months. Consequently there was an opportunity to work on the land in the summer, and in the malting in the winter. The malt would have been made from barley grown on the local farms, and in the Dairy Farm there was a small Malt Room and Brewhouse; beer would have been brewed here for the personal use of the farmer and his workers. A brewery at nearby Manningtree supplied the few ale houses in Mistley and Manningtree and the surrounding villages. It is possible that some of the malt would have found its way to some of the London breweries, shipped from the small wharf.

In 1705 a bill was submitted to parliament for approval to open a waterway from Mistley to Sudbury; it was declared that the effecting of a passage for horses, barges, boats and other vessels would be beneficial to trade, convenient for the conveyance of coals, and advantageous to the poor. An Act of Parliament was duly passed authorising the construction of the waterway, and this resulted in a vast increase of trade to and from the Mistley Wharf. By 1713 operations under the Stour Navigation (Trust) Co. were in progress; it is interesting to find that in 1780, when a second Act was passed, Golding Constable, the artist's father, and Gainsborough's two brothers, Samuel and John, served on the Commissions. The horse drawn barges became a feature of the upper reaches of the Stour until the arrival of the Railway some 150 years later. The passage to Sudbury took two days, with thirteen locks to be negotiated, and as there were only sixteen bridges, the horses were trained to cross by stepping on the barge, and off on the opposite bank. Produce of every description was transported, which included cereal crops from the neighbouring farms. Goods from abroad were transhipped, together with large quantities of coal, which arrived in Mistley from north-east England. A charge of -/5d. per drum was made for tar, soap and vinegar, and return cargoes of bricks arrived from the brickworks at Ballingdon, near Sudbury. The wage of the lighterman was 24/- per trip from Mistley, out of which he had to pay the horse leader 6/-s.

As trade increased, the wharf became too small to handle the large amount of traffic, and many other barges were loaded at the Wharf at Manningtree. There was an increasing tonnage of coal from the Durham area, and apart from Sudbury, other villages on the Stour took advantage of the barges running past them. In addition to the barge traffic regular shipments were made to London.

A few families living close to the beach had traditionally fished in the river for generations. There were also a few smacks operating from both Mistley and Manningtree, which began to venture far into the North Sea following a conversion which provided small wells in the holds of the vessels. After fish were caught they were kept alive in the wells, which allowed the fishermen to take longer trips to sea. Some of the fish were caught in nets, and others by using rods. Yet another method was to use a very long line on which hundreds of hooks were secured. These were baited and allowed to sink to the sea bed. After a time they were retrieved, and the fish removed from the hooks. Oysters were to be found in one part of the Stour, but these did not develop in the same abundance as those in the Colne. There were, in addition to the oysters, a great number of other shellfish which were regularly collected at low tide. Cockles, whelks and winkles were eaten by the villagers in the vicinity of Mistley. Whiting, cod and bass were also caught, but the main catches were flounders, plaice and eels. The eels were smoked in the fishermen's houses, and sold to the villagers.

Although many of the vessels using Mistley were square rigged, most of the ships were cargo-carrying ketches, schooners and barques, with some sailing barges which later evolved into those we see today. With increasing numbers of vessels coming to Mistley and Manningtree, a great need for ballast for steadying arose which was loaded into the ships' holds, when they left the quay without cargo.

Ballast was dug both for road repairing and shipping requirements, in two parts of Mistley. The smaller pit was dug in land south-east of the Anchor Inn, the larger on the west of the Harwich Road stretching nearly to Furze Hills in the south and School Lane in the west. The digging of ballast from these pits began early in the eighteenth century, ceasing some 150 years later. As these pits were situated in the highest part of Mistley, they contained numerous springs, many of which are still to be seen today. After 1844 this whole area west of the Harwich road was developed and East Mistley created. Three small sloping roadways now run down the side of what was the ballast pit, and California Road runs through the centre of it.

Due to the absence of building stone in this part of the country the manufacture of bricks to replace the wattle-and-daub method of construction had become very important. In the area of the old shipyard at the eastern end of the quay there was brick loam of the highest quality. Kilns were built to dry the bricks, made from these large banks of dark red loam running down to the river. Some of this loam remains today and can be seen in the steep bank on the north of the railway line. The bricks were stored in an enclosure near the river known as the "brickfield", and were sold to the general public for many years.

The need for coal gradually became greater for both industrial and domestic purposes, and a coal yard was constructed near the wharf. At one time there was a great deal of concern when the Sunderland wholesalers raised their prices considerably. Some forty merchants met at Mistley and threatened to charter their own ships, and deal with the collieries direct. After this the prices remained stable, resulting in increased consumption.

Another ancient industry carried out at Mistley and Manningtree was salt making. Apart from its many other uses, salt brine was used to preserve meat and fish, because of the difficulty of keeping fresh food wholesome for even a short period in those days. The east coast of England was found to be one of the best areas for the manufacture of salt. Thanks to the low rainfall, and breezy conditions, the receding water left a residue of salt, which was taken up by the next tide. Due to this ceaseless process the river water became very saline, and when the spring tides were at their highest levels, the salt maker would allow the water to fill a small reservoir. This was usually some thirty-five feet square, and fifteen feet deep, situated in the river bank. Once the sediment had settled the water was pumped by hand into a large wooden tank, where it was allowed to clear, and run into shallow boiling pans made of lead. The water was brought to boil briefly, and was then kept hot for a longer period. As it cooled the impurities rose to the surface. This residue was taken off, using a copper skimmer, which was made specially for this purpose. In due course, crystals continually formed on the surface of the water in the shape of small pyramids. Some would have been as large as two inches square, but most were very much smaller. The crystals which formed on the surface were used for the finest table salt, and those which formed below for pickling, the residue being for agricultural purposes only. After draining, the salt crystals were carefully drawn from the pan, or leddie, using a wooden rake and shovel. Finally the crystals were placed in an oven, and carefully dried to a satisfactory moisture level. Several men would have been engaged in this process, which required workers with a great deal of skill and sound judgement. In addition to the boiling process of manufacture, the rock variety was also converted to fine salt at Manningtree for many years. The villages in which salt was manufactured usually had an Inn nearby called the "Three Cups", the sign of which was the armorial bearing of the Salters Company. It is interesting to find that an inn of this name once stood on the crossroads at the top of New Road, just a few yards to the south-east of the tiny Adam Lodge. The next bend in the road to Clacton is still known as "Cups Corner". The coal for firing the pans and ovens was brought by ship from north-east England, and unloaded at the small quay nearby, which was aptly named Northumberland Wharf, later known as "Coke Quay". This ancient craft did not continue for many more years, giving way to brick making on the same site.

There were at least three blacksmiths' forges to shoe, and to service the harness of the innumerable horses used on the local farms. One was at Horsley Cross, another opposite the Green at Mistley Heath and the third, a larger one, stood at the bottom of Mistley Hill, next to the house now called the Abbey. Repairs of every description were carried out, primarily of an agricultural nature.

On the wharf was a small business mostly engaged in ships' chandlery, together with an office to deal with cargoes arriving for transhipment to Sudbury. There would have been some premises for the customs officers, who superintended some of the goods arriving at the wharf from overseas.

Apart from the agriculture, there was other work carried out in the sparsely populated Thorne portion of the village. Most of this work would have been of a laborious nature, resulting in the necessity for thirst quenching activities! There are records of beer houses in Mistley and the hamlet of Horsley Cross, with several in neighbouring Manningtree.

It should be realised that the estate was owned entirely by a remote member of the landed gentry. A steward would have been engaged in collecting the rents, and managing the estate for the owner. This system of absentee landlords was operating all over England at this time, and it resulted in little security for the village people, who at times would suffer extreme hardship cause by the "laissez-faire" attitude of the landlords and, at times, the bad administration by the Steward.

Changes in ownership would always give rise to anxiety on the part of the inhabitants, and it would be interesting to know what their feelings were when in 1709 they learned that Edward Rigby, a linen draper from London, had inherited their village.

CHAPTER 3

EDWARD RIGBY, 1654-1711

In the year 1709, Edward Rigby could not possibly have foreseen that, as a result of his inheritance of part of the large estates of the late Countess of Oxford, his family would exercise great influence over the village of Mistley, and the people living there, for many years ahead.

Edward was born in 1654, and followed his established family business as a linen draper. Apart from property in Essex, Suffolk and Ireland, he owned a successful linen and cloth establishment in the city of London. He was quite wealthy, and lived with his wife Anne in a large house in the Parish of St. Andrew in Holborn. He had previously lived in Covent Garden, and was a confirmed Londoner, with no desire to live in a country estate in Essex.

His eldest son Richard was born in 1679 and was given a good education, enabling him to engage in a variety of business activities, some in the West Indies. He was not attracted to the

An artist's impression of the wharfe at Mistley Thorne in the 17th Century

family business, and after returning to England from one of his frequent trips he visited Mistley, and became enraptured with the area. It was not long before he realised that, along with the beautiful countryside beside the Stour estuary, there was great potential both for lucrative improvements to the estate, and development of the increasing shipping trade to the small wharf.

Edward's second son James was also well educated, but was of a less ambitious nature, and assisted in the accountancy of the business in London. He had also spent some time on the family plantations, which were mainly situated in Jamaica, with some business in the Windward Islands.

Edward also had two daughters, Anne and Catherine, and a granddaughter bearing five Christian names, Mary, Anne, Isabella, Margaretta and Beatrix, who was the apple of her grandfather's eye! Edward had another daughter who married one John Ashton, but her name is unknown. It is probable that she died at an early age as her daughter was brought up by her grandmother, Anne, and lived with the family in Holborn.

In 1689 Edward Rigby had come into other inheritances, one of which was property at Needham Market in Suffolk. However he rarely visited the property there and there is no evidence that he spent any time at Mistley. It would appear that he had little liking for the place, as in his will, made in 1710, he decreed that the whole estate should be sold.

The Inheritance.

Anne, the Countess of Oxford, had died at an early age, leaving no children, and her husband, Aubrey de Vere, the Earl, had become life tenant of her many estates scattered throughout England. Among these were the manors and farms, together with the village of Mistley, which were managed entirely by an agent for many years With an absentee landlord, the estate had become run down and impoverished. Businesses, such as they were, run by tenants without the freehold of the land they occupied, made investment very risky. Consequently, although there were several opportunities for development in Mistley, the extreme uncertainty of the future acted as a deterrent to trade and industry.

After the death of the Earl of Oxford in 1703, an Act of Parliament granted a reversion of the ownership of the estates, and these went to the four aunts of the late Countess Anne; Cicily, Lady Newark, Anne, Viscountess Bayning, Mary, Countess Anglesea, and Lady Elizabeth Dacres, all of whom were deceased. The inheritance of Lady Newark descended to her two daughters, Lady Anne Rosse, and Lady Grace Pierpont, who were also dead. No records have been discovered concerning the relationship, but the inheritance of Lady Rosse ultimately came to Edward Rigby; it consisted of an eighth of the estates of the late Countess Anne of Oxford.

The Act of Parliament authorising the reversion resulted in five legatees inheriting the estates. By an indenture quinquepartite dated the 24th June 1709, the five legatees agreed to the division of the estates into eight lots. There was a further agreement that two of the legatees would accept lots five, six, seven and eight, leaving the remaining half of the estates to be divided among the three remaining legatees. Of this, Edward Rigby and Grace Pierpont's daughter, Elizabeth, were each entitled to a quarter, and one William Peck to half, through the Countess of Anglesea.

In order to decide upon the division of the lots numbered one to four it was arranged in the quinquepartite agreement that "Israel Harrison, and John Sackfield should make or cause to be made, and seal and sign several writings or scrolls, containing each of them one of the

Family tree showing the principle members of the Rigby, Hale and Pitt Rivers families.
1709- 1845

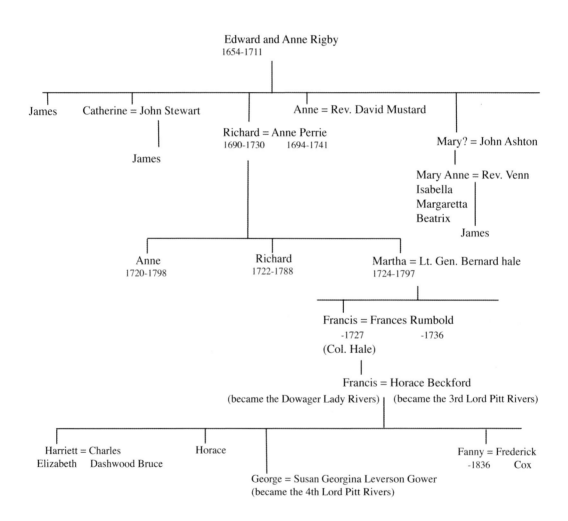

Frances, the Dowager Lady Rivers, the daughter of Col. Hale Rigby became the last owner of the Mistley Estate.
Her son George, the 4th Lord Pitt Rivers and the trustees were reluctantly forced to sell it in 1844.

four first lots written in the schedule". These would be enclosed in two balls of wax, put into a hat or cap, and "those concerned should agree upon some chile, and cause him to put his hand into the hat or cap, and take out the first of the two balls of wax alone, and deliver it to the said Edward Rigby and the remaining ball should be given to William Peck, as and for the fourth part belonging to him...William Peck will then open the first ball of wax delivered to Edward Rigby, and divide the two lots therein...These will again be rolled up, and enclosed into two further balls of wax, and put into a hat or cap...The same chile will take out one ball of wax, and deliver to the same Edward Rigby, as the eighth part or share belonging to him...The remaining ball will be delivered to Elizabeth Pierpont, as and for the eighth part belonging to her."

Upon breaking open the ball of wax, Edward Rigby found it to contain a list of certain manors, farms and quayside property; by this unusual method of allocating the shares, he had become owner of the large estate of Mistley. Thus began the story of the Rigby family, whose presence in the village would extend over a period lasting some 35 years.

Details of the Inheritance.

The lots in the schedule enclosed in the ball of wax are shown below.

1. The Manor of Misley, also Misseley cum Maningtree.
2. The Manor of Newhall in Tendring, (except the scite of the Manor and lands belonging in tenure of Thomas Moore).
3. The Advowsons and the rights of the church of Missley, also Misseley cum Maningtree.
4. And of the Rectory of Bradfield with the great tithes to such of thembelonging.
5. All those tofts, and pieces of waste ground in Misseley cum Maningtree, with the Wharfe there.
6. The Salt house, and the profits of the fair there.
7. The Manor of Sheddinghal, also Shedding Hall.
8. The capital messuage or scite of the said Manor called Sheddinghal farm containing 334 acres.
9. The Manor of Dickley also Dickley Hall.
10. The capital messuage or scite of the Manor called Dickley Hall Farm containing 282 acres.
11. The Manor of Newhall.
12. The capital messuage or scite of the Manor of Newhall Farm containing 279 acres.
13. A farm in the tenure of George Martin containing 136 acres.
14. Several closes called Swan Lands, and Bowling Lands containing 88 acres.
15. Chappell fields and chappell lands containing 7 acres.
16. The several woods and wood ground and the soyle thereof mentioned in the second lot in the deed of partition containing 276 acres, in Misley, Maningtree and Bradfield in the County of Essex.
    (subject nevertheless to the payment of the said 100 pounds per annum to Knowles).

The estate consisted of nearly 1500 acres of farm and woodland, with the small wharf on the bank of the river in the lower part of the village. The difference in the spellings of Mistley and Manningtree in the schedule to the indenture seems very possibly to have been due to the whim of the clerk who wrote the details in longhand.

The Advowson, or right to the church livings, would be commuted at about £400 for each church. The sum to be paid to Edward Rigby was taken from the Rectorial and Vicarial Tithes, from which would be paid about £40 per annum for the curacy, and about £75 for the poor, and other rates. Small charges would be paid for the church repairs, but there was always a substantial sum left over for the beneficiary.

The land in lot 5 was adjacent to the river, and the description "tofts" meant homesteads, and these would have been situated in the area of the green, where some of the villagers and fishermen lived.

The Salt House was worked on the quayside at Manningtree, and housed an important industry which produced a much needed commodity at that time. This factory refined rock salt, and, as I wrote in chapter 2, continued working for more than 100 years.

Newhall Manor and Farm is now almost exactly as it was in 1709, situated on the western side of the Horsley Cross road, and adjacent to Dickley Hall. The farms were separated by Skiphatch Lane, which still runs between the Bromley Road and the Horsley Cross road as a footpath on the local definitive map. Both farms are known by the same names today, but have slightly increased acreages.

The Manor and land of Sheddinghal is not known under this name now, but was almost certainly most of the land of the present Dove House Farm, which stretched to the upper part of Mistley, and on its western boundary would have been bordered by the Horsley Cross road, which separated it from Dickley Hall, as it does today.

On this farm and the parkland surrounding Sheddinghal, was the old Mistley Hall, also known as Sheditting or Sharing Hall. The Manor House, old even in 1709, was in an area of woodland known as the Mountain Plantation. The woodland still remains in part though decimated by Dutch Elm disease and more recently by the 1987 hurricane, and is now known as the Old Mount. It lies a few hundred yards north of the television mast at Gamekeepers Corner on the Horsley Cross road. Beneath the surface on a large knoll at the eastern end of the wood, bricks and tiles are still easily recoverable. Some of the tiles were sent recently to the Colchester Museum, where after examination they were considered to be at least 400 years old. There are two very overgrown pools in the wood, together with a moat which ran round the garden. This would have been crossed by a bridge taking the roadway to the Manor House. The bed of the moat consisted of silver sand, which can be uncovered today beneath a thick layer of leaves and mud. No streams can be seen running either to the pools or the moat, which must have been supplied by spring water. It is mystifying that although they dry up in the winter months there is often a great deal of water there in the summer, even in dry conditions.

This old Manor House must have been the focal point of the tiny group of dwellings situated close by it on the Horsley Cross road, and the others at Mistley Heath close by the ancient church towards which the house faced. Another small pool, surrounded by trees, was a feature of the parkland, some distance between the house and the church. This was an ornamental part of the gardens, and can still be seen today known as the Oak Plantation. Amongst the gardens and the parklands were also numerous fruit trees to which Richard Rigby later planted further extensions.

The site of the old Mistley Hall had remained unknown to Morant and Wright, the early writers of Mistley affairs, who felt that it might have been nearer The Green. Tradition, however, has always reported it to have been situated in the Old Mount, and this is now supported by examination of contemporary maps.

The other small lots shown in the schedule were to the west of the estate at the top of the present New Road; the Swan Lands and Bowling Lands were near the area of Mistley known as Barnfield, and behind the Waterworks. Amongst other areas shown in the schedule, although not names as such, were 38 acres of land and woodland known as "lands of le Thorne". On these lands were some small houses; others were subsequently built when the wharf was developed. Sometime later the village green became known as Mistley Thorne, with its centre at The Green.

It will be noticed in the schedule that a large amount of woodland, consisting of some 276 acres, was scattered within the farmlands. Some of these woods were very extensive, bearing a wide variety of trees. Cooks and Long Woods, totalling nearly 40 acres, were at Dickley Hall; but by far the larger were Overland, Haywoods, Thatchers, Ausserysons and Abbotts which grew on the Sheddinghal farm leading down to the lands of le Thorne. Many of the trees would have been oak or elm, which were widely used in the ship building. It is interesting to note that none of these woods existed some one hundred years later, as future chapters will show, but the farms bore field names where presumably the woodlands once stood. Although great care was taken to preserve them, and to undertake replanting, trees on the estate were later grown in plantations rather than forests. By the year 1800 the acreages of the woodlands had been reduced by half.

The schedule shows that the Manors, farms and land which Edward Rigby had inherited consisted of almost the whole of the village of Mistley. He sadly died only two years afterwards, and was buried in London. In his will he had appointed Francis Annesley and Charlwood Lawton, two of his friends, to be trustees, and decreed that all his estates and businesses should be sold.

The villagers and workers on the estate were again worried about their future, but had they known it, the year 1711 was to herald a period of prosperity for most of them.

Dove House Farm, the home of the deer park keeper. Previously known as Sheddinghal Farm.

CHAPTER 4

RICHARD RIGBY: THE EARLY DAYS

Edward Rigby's wife and family were deeply shocked when he died, especially as he had appeared in fairly good health. He was held in very high esteem by his friends in London, and in other parts of the country. They were particularly saddened because he had not reached a great age, and his eldest son, Richard, was only thirty-two. It fell to him and his younger brother, James, to take over the temporary management of the family business, and deal with their father's scattered estates.

One of the problems which they encountered was that of the provisions which Edward made in his will, placing the responsibility for disposing of the family estates, including the family business, on the trustees. Certain legacies had to be honoured, after which everything that remained went to his wife Anne. It was soon apparent that after selling the London business, and other estates, there would be no problem paying these legacies. Amongst the estates and property sold was a tenement in Devonshire Street, in the Parish of St. Andrew in Holborn, with backhouse stables and coach-house, which had been the family home. Two further houses in Paternoster Row were sold to Mr. Walter Plummer for £700. The family had two pews in the North Aisle of St. George's Chapel, numbered 13 and 19, and these were also disposed of.

Much to Richard's satisfaction it seemed possible that the Mistley estate could remain in the family, and full agreement was reached by all interested parties. The trustees were able to obtain a decree in Chancery, which satisfied the terms of the will, and Richard persuaded his mother that in order to develop his plans for Mistley, careful management of the financial affairs was of prime importance. Some investment was necessary in order to provide sufficient capital to maintain the existing buildings, and begin a construction programme, which would render considerable benefits to the estate from the rents of the greater number of tenants, who would be attracted to Mistley.

During the first few years, Richard devoted much of his time to reorganising the running of the estate, while his brother James attended to the tenancies and accounts. Much work was done at the Old Hall, and its surrounding lawns and gardens. Shrubberies and orchards were planted, and the pools and moat around the Manor House were renovated and cleaned regularly.

The roadways were a constant problem in those early days, especially during the winter months, and pressure was brought to bear on all the tenants and villagers to carry out repairs using ballast from the two pits on the hill. Minor repairs were also undertaken in the village, and the accounts show that the wall to Hopping Bridge was enclosed. The bridge was then made of wood; the one still to be seen was constructed a few years later. The attractive lake, now part of Mistley Park situated to the south of the bridge, did not exist at this time, and was probably created some time after the erection of the brick bridge.

The visitation which had been made to the church some years before had ordered that a considerable amount of work should be carried out. The Earl of Oxford had allowed the ancient church, like everything else on the estate, to fall into serious disrepair. Richard immediately instituted restoration, thus prolonging the life of the building.

Mistley's few inhabitants at this time were soon to realise how many benefits Rigby's arrival brought to the community. Whilst retaining their respect as owner and Lord of the Manor, he was always ready to give help in cases of illness or hardship, which could frequently occur. Over the next twenty years or so that he lived in Mistley, the excellent work he did in improving the estate to his advantage also proved beneficial to the villagers.

Having established the estate on an efficient, businesslike footing, he soon found that, together with the family capital, there was more than sufficient income to keep the family in a lifestyle equal to that of many of the landed gentry at that time. Richard had a keen financial brain, and worked diligently to increase his personal fortune, but the generosity of his personality meant that he was always ready to share his wealth with others. Perhaps because of his obligations towards his mother and the family, together with his heavy responsibilities on the estate, he appears to have had no romantic connections.

In order to carry out other much more costly plans, Richard, and indirectly the village of Mistley, needed a stroke of luck, and this came about through a series of financial transactions which ruined some, but made others very rich. Richard was one of the lucky ones.

CHAPTER 5

THE SOUTH SEA BUBBLE

The South Sea Bubble was the name given to a series of financial transactions which began with the formation of the South Sea Company in 1711, and ended nine years later in disaster, after a mania of speculation. The idea behind the parent scheme was that the state should sell certain trading monopolies in the South Seas in return for a sum of money to pay off the national debt, which stood at £51,300,000 when the scheme started. The idea fascinated the public, seeming to promise fabulous profits, and the price of the stock rose out of all proportion to the earnings of the company. Many dishonest speculative ventures sprang up in imitation, with the inevitable result that thousands of stockholders were ruined. All classes had joined in the scramble, and a committee of secrecy set up by the House of Commons in December 1720 to investigate the state of affairs, proved that there had been fraud and corruption on a large scale in the running of the company. The Prime Minister, Sir Robert Walpole, who had been an opponent of the scheme from the outset, dealt with the crisis.

Richard Rigby had many friends, both in the West Indies and London, and they gave him sound advice on the prospects of the company. Soon after its formation, Rigby invested a great deal of his own capital, with some of his mother's and brother's. The dividends paid were considerable, and with these Richard acquired further investments. The price of the stock continued to climb, and after a period of some years Richard sold his entire stock, making a fortune in the transaction.

Unfortunately for many others, when the stock continued to be sold panic set in, with thousands of sellers but no buyers. The "bubble" had burst. However, the South Sea Company, in possibly a different form, continued to operate, and from an examination of further investments made by Richard, various interesting facts emerge. Very few details of the early investments which brought him his fortune are known, but one of the earliest showed a profit of £502-2-6., from the South Sea Company in Jamaica, due to errors in their book keeping. Later £1151-18-11. was received in an account with Edward Pratter, with whom it seems that Richard had business arrangements, after the crash in stock value. A further transaction of £1300 was invested in shares in the late 1720s, together with the purchase of 3414 shares at a cost of 8/8d. each, in the South Sea Company, in Kingston, Jamaica. Later £1083-6-8. was paid for 5000 shares, which allowed Richard to trade on the Windward Coast.

The Rigby family became so involved with trade and investment in the West Indies that both James and Richard went to Jamaica, spending much time there. Both developed sizeable interests in coffee and sugar cane plantations. These were purchased by Richard, who ran them with the same efficient style as his farms in England. One dividend from the company at this time included the balance delivered in rum, but it failed to arrive! This caused much consternation, and extensive enquiries were made. An amazing illustration of the then value of money in the West Indies is that Richard bought two thirds of a plantation in Antigua for a mere £20-1-3. It would seem however, that most of the business transactions of the brothers were in Jamaica, and to demonstrate how shares rose in price, in 1729 nearly ten years after the crash, just two shares cost £40. Between 1727 and 1730, Rigby invested at least £650, which it has been possible to trace, and a great deal of money was received in dividends, together with the profit from the trading activities of the plantations. It is difficult to imagine the magnitude of the fortune amassed from the investments as comparisons may be misleading. It should be remembered however that a farm labourer's wages for a whole year amounted to £16, while the price of an acre of land was only £10. Based on these values, the Rigbys would, no doubt, have been millionaires today.

Richard came home from the West Indies in 1727 for the last time, and a short lease written by hand shows a sad state of affairs which was common at the time in trading in that part of the world.

The lease read:

> *"To my brother James Rigby"*
> *"At my leaving Jamaica in May 1727, delivered to my brother James Rigby, 20 Negro slaves, which I lent him on lease for three years for £100 Jamaican money perannum, and for which rent and Negroes he is further accountable to me from the time according to the covenant of the lease, and the value of the Negroes and thereto left in the hands of my brother."*

It is perhaps difficult to reconcile the character of Richard Rigby, who although a religious man, and a philanthropist in his own village, was able to engage in business in the evil Negro slave system which prevailed in our colonies for more than 200 years though it is possibly unwise to pass judgement on actions taken so long ago, when slavery was an accepted practice throughout the world. It continued however for a further 80 years, until in 1807 the slave trade was abolished in our colonies.

We may, however, have mixed feelings on the discovery that the establishment of Mistley, in those early days, and the extensive building work which Rigby eventually carried out, was made possible by dubious transactions with the South Sea Company, and the West Indian slave trade.

The Mistley Wharf, very much idealised was probably painted early in the 18th century

CHAPTER 6

THE MISTLEY CHURCHES

In the early 18th century the spiritual needs of the village were provided for in the ancient church of St. Mary the Virgin at Mistley Heath. The already dilapidated church stood on the double bend on the road approaching the Heath from Mistley. The church had probably never enjoyed large congregations, with only a handful of cottages on the farms close by; however, it was still an attractive building set in a rural scene. Some of the villagers lived over a mile away to the north west, and it would have been more convenient for them to use the church at Manningtree.

The burial ground surrounding the church at Mistley Heath was quite spacious in relation to its size, and the brick wall built around it is still in a remarkably good condition. The churchyard was used for many years after the church was eventually demolished.

The parish register shows an entry on 12th August 1647, recording the burial of one Matthew Hopkins. This could be the notorious witch hunter who condemned many innocent women to death, some from Manningtree, but it has never been established beyond doubt that the entry refers to him.

Before the arrival of Richard Rigby the impoverishment of the Oxford estate at Mistley had affected almost every building, causing much inconvenience to the tenants, who were so poor that they found it impossible to carry out even simple repairs. The worst affected building by far was the ancient church, and although Richard Rigby attempted some renovation, it soon became apparent that unless a very extensive repair operation was carried out, it would have to be closed.

In 1719 the then Rector, Dr. Alec Burgess died, and was succeeded by the Rev. David Mustard on 17th November of that year. He had just married Edward Rigby's daughter Anne, where they lived in the old Parsonage, but sadly Anne died after only two years of marriage. The church only survived for a short time, soon becoming so dangerous that it could no longer be used, the north wall began to bulge and due to the rotting timbers the roof collapsed into the well of the church. The Mistley parishioners were without a church for a number of years, and were compelled to use either Manningtree or Bradfield.

At this time the church was well over 400 years old, but its porch still remained in good condition. This porch, incidentally, remained standing for 400 years, until about thirty years ago when the roof timbers fell into disrepair. Neither the Parish Council nor the Church Authorities made any effort to preserve it, and this intrinsic part of Mistley's heritage was demolished and lost forever. The porch, which was officially listed as an ancient monument, along with one other church in north Essex was used as an example of neglect by the advisory board for redundant churches, who declared that the neglect amounted to a grave dereliction of their moral duty by the Mistley Parish Council and the diocese. Some of the stonework bearing merchants' marks and Tudor roses was recovered, however, and taken to the Colchester Museum, together with the Purbeck marble altar tops.

The failure to save this building is particularly sad in that it was here that Richard

Rigby undertook his first building work, or perhaps excavation, underneath the floor of the church and porch. In the early days of his life at Mistley he constructed a large vault penetrating beneath the church, in which he and his family would be interred, with the porch marking the entrance. Another tomb had been built some years before, belonging to the Nunn family. Joshua Nunn became priest in charge from 1693 until 1708, and when he died he was interred in it, as were his family later. The entrance to his vault was to the north of the church, marked by a stone slab. This was taken away a long time ago. The disused graveyard, and ruins of the old church at Mistley Heath, can still be seen today; the former is honeycombed with small vaults, which, in time to come, will reveal their secrets, when brickwork erected hundreds of years ago eventually collapses.

Although Richard Rigby was at this time busily engaged in extensive building work, particularly repairs to the estate farms, this did not prevent him from giving every assistance towards the provision of a new church. Before any building could be done, it became necessary to present a petition to His Majesty King George II for permission to demolish completely the remains of the old church and to re-erect a new one; this was done in 1729. The details of the petition are shown below. The original spelling has been retained, with some attention to the punctuation for the sake of clarity.

This tiny porch remained for 250 years after the church of St Mary at Mistley Heath had fallen down. The entrance to the Rigby vault was inside.

To the King's most Excellent Majesty.

We Richard Comyns, Sergeant at Law, The Hon. Henry Hassau, Sir Edward Smith, Barrt., Anthony Collins, William Petre, John Hill, John Cheveley, George Montgomerie, Thomas Willford, Gabriel Shaw, Thomas Bramston, William Nicholson, Esquires yor Majesties Justices of the Peace for ye County of Essex, assembled at our Central Quarter Sessions of the Peace held at Chelmsford in and for ye said County, on ye thirteenth day of April in ye second year of your Majesties reign, Anno Domini 1729, that it has been made apparent unto us in open sessions upon the oaths as well as of able and experienced workmen viz. Edward Bartholomew, Robert Baron, Edmund Seaborne, Carpenters, and Jeremiah Loam, John Orman and Walter Webb, Bricklayers, do humbly certify unto Your Majesty that ye Parish Church of Misley being an ancient structure built many years agone of a mouldering stone is by time reduced to total decay, and which has been propt up and supported with difficulty above 40 years since (thro' ye povety of ye inhabitants utterly unable to sustain it longer) the whole roof of ye body has by ye bulging of the north wall and ye rot of ye timbersat length performed therein for several years past. And the steeple being likewise cract, and ye whole fabrick in a very ruinous condition which to restore would upon unjust estimate labour thereof cost ye sum of £6979-10s-6d. as by substantially so as to return it to its former state appears unto it is become advisable in ye regard to ye lesning of ye expense therefore is more suitable to us upon ye oaths of ye able and experienced workmen, it has become more advisable unto the low circumstances of ye inhabitants done of equal dimension with ye former structure, and will require upon ye fourteen pounds 2/6 to rebuild ye same, which may be done at a much less expence as hereinafter mentioned viz. the sum of £1914-2s-6d. of equal which dimensions of ye former structure, and appearing to us inhabitants wholly to rebuild the same and that in regard to its being preferable on all accounts to build an entire new church we do hereby further humbly certify to your Majesty that it appears to us that the situation of the present church is at one extremity of the Parish above a mile and a half distance from ye much greater number of ye inhabitants, and consequently was found very inconvenient at all times, and impractible for many of ye winter season (the road being very bad) to repair thither for the worship of God. And foreasmuch as should your Majesty be graciously pleased to allow of removing the church to a feild called ye Thorne feild upon ye River Stower which ye inhabitants are unanimously agree of opinion would be ye most convenient in general if the same it was there erected there and ye steeple raised to a convenient height would be found to prove likewise a very useful sea mark for ye navigation in those parts.

PAGE 2
Mistley Church
April 1729

If your Majesty would be pleased to grant your Royal Licence for such removal. And do further humbly certify to your Majesty that it appears that the number of ye inhabitants of ye said parish within ten years past, and since ye church has lain in ruin near two hundred persons and is likely to go on increasing from ye conveniency of ye scituation for trade and shipping and they must inevitably remain/destitute of a place for the service of God unless their church be rebuilt to ye expense of which/undertaking their condition is in no way proportioned they being mostly seafaring people and/poor and ye whole estates of ye parish which pay to ye church rates amounting to no more than £417 per annum yet so desirous are they to promote to their utmost so pious and necessary a/work that they have voluntarily subscribed at this time upwards of two hundred pounds being more than ten shillings in the pound upon all ye estates in ye parish over and above a rate of two/shillings and sixpence in the pound laid in yo vestry for ye present year and to which they will all cheerfully/submit so long as shall be necessary in case ye compleating thereof be rendred practicble by ye charitable assistant of their christian bretheren that in order to entitule themselves/to your Majesties Royal favour and the charitable assistance of their christian bretheren the inhabitants have now exerted themselves to ye utmost of their/ability and have not only made a rate of 2/6d in ye pound for ye present year amounting to £52-2-6d. towards rebuilding their church to which they are content to submit so long as shall be found necessary but also have made a voluntary subscription among themselves/for the same purpose of £219-13s. which amounts to above 10s.6d. in the pound more than their whole estates for one year and which sums £52-2s-6d. and £219-13s. make together £271-15s-6d being deducted from ye sum of £1914-2s-6d. there remains £1642-7s. which will be wanting to be collected from ye charitable contribution of your/Majesties good subjects in case your Majesty shall be graciously pleased to grant lettres patent to your petitioners ye said inhabitants of Misley for ye asking collecting and receiving ye same, all of which is most humbly submitted to your most excellent Majesty by us ye Majesties justices of the peace.

The new St. Mary's Church.

After some time the King "graciously" agreed to the petition's request, and granted "letters patent" to allow a new church to be erected at Mistley Thorne. Although the building of the church was sanctioned, there remained the problem of raising the necessary finance. The villagers contributed a small amount towards the cost, and Richard Rigby agreed to pay the remainder. The building of the church began in 1730 on a field running down to the riverside on which the monument known as the Towers Church now stands. The plans for the new church had been finalised as early as 1729, but for some reason Rigby decided upon a building of plain secular design.

Before the work could start, a large mound had to be constructed in the field in order to lift the level of the land. It was carefully raised to the roadway in the south, and included the graveyard which was to surround the church. A small roadway below the graveyard to the north provided access to the quayside roads. This roadway is now a public footpath behind the Towers monument. A reinforced brick wall was built at the north to hold up the mound, and the wall was extended at a low level to enclose the graveyard completely, with a wrought iron fence placed on top of it. These features remain to this day, and the mound on which the church was built provides protection then as now against flooding. The high tide in those days was not far from the northern side of the graveyard, but the area has been built up since, and a river wall created. Old records at this time describe the Mistley Thorne Church as built almost on the strand, or river shore.

The church was built of brick, with a shallow pitched roof, and little ornamentation outside. It was not a large building, the nave measuring barely 35' by 60', with the chancel only 14' square. At the western end of the nave was a small recess of similar dimensions, in which was placed a tiny vestry, and staircase to a small belfry above. There does not appear to have been a steeple, and the five bells, probably from the old Mistley Heath Church were situated above the belfry. A gallery was built above either side of the nave, and extending from it, and facing the chancel were seats for fifty children. The gallery was five feet in depth and it is unlikely that any of them would have been able to see over the top. They would most certainly not have been seen from the congregation. On three sides of the recess and the chancel were semi-circular fanlight windows, and the positions of these can still be seen today. Six wide stone steps ran up the entrance door into a small porch leading through into the centre of the church. Two small windows were placed on either side of the porch, with large domed windows lighting the nave. The tiny font which now stands in Mistley Church stood at the western end, with two small pews by its side. An extremely lofty carved wooden pulpit needed ten steps to ascend. The seating in the church was unique; four box pews placed on either side of the pulpit, with another at the north west end of the nave. Most of the remaining seating on each side of the aisle was on double pews, with the congregation sitting back to back leaving only half of them facing the chancel. The church could accommodate 345 persons, many more than the old one it replaced, with some seats set aside for the poorer residents of the village.

The building was considered revolutionary, with its brick exterior, and plain features. It is difficult to understand why Richard Rigby chose a design of this nature, as whilst it was an imposing building, it bore little resemblance to a traditional church. Perhaps it was fashionable in the architecture of the time which valued symmetry and plain, unadorned design. Some forty years later it was completely redesigned; the towers added by Robert Adam which made it an edifice of much architectural merit, but even less like a church than before! It was well attended as Mistley expanded, and following its consecration by the Bishop of London, in 1735, the Rev. David Mustard officiated as rector for more than 40 years.

The villagers worshipped at the Thorne Church of St. Mary for 135 years, and the

Towers still remain as an important part of our Mistley heritage.

Some years after the church was built, frightening stories began to circulate. Superstition was rife in the country villages in those days, and grave robbing was prevalent in parts of the country. In order to deter the disturbance of graves, a dog would sometimes be buried in the churchyard. This gruesome act could have been carried out in Mistley, which resulted in the legend of the Mistley Hound. For more than 250 years a ghost in the form of a dog was often said to have been seen running along The Walls by the river bank, and disappearing into the graveyard. The last reported sighting was in 1953, but there is little doubt that for many years the legend was believed by many Mistley people.

It is sad to relate that Richard Rigby did not live to see the church, which he had planned and financed; as he died a few years before it was completed.

An impression of how the church built in 1735 may have looked.
It later became 'The Towers' church.

The Ruins of the old church of St. Mary at Mistley Heath as they were in 1990.

CHAPTER 7

THE DOMESTIC SCENE

When he came to Mistley, Richard Rigby had expected to live the fairly quiet life of a country gentleman. His ideas and plans for improvements had originally excited him, but he soon became involved in the lucrative financial transactions which were to make him a very rich man. While settling in at Mistley, and the initial reorganisation took some time, his visits to the South Seas delayed for some years much of the work he had intended to do on the estate and in the village. Money seemed to be attracted to him; he was agreeably surprised when it was found that Lord Clarendon had owed his father £1471-11-4. By July 1722, some years after his father's death, his Lordship had paid £600 of his debts, which was divided between the children.

Rigby was very interested in the land he had inherited, and took over part of Sheddinghal Farm for his own personal use. Although having little agricultural knowledge, he had an astute financial brain, and using modern farming techniques, including a frequent and careful valuation of stock to run it, he became a very successful farmer. Upon examination of his account book, it is found that two horses, "Billy" and "Jolly" were valued at £40 each, and two more, "Dragon" and "Stonethorpe", £12 and £8 respectively. Two cows were valued at £6, and on the mechanical side, three pairs of harrows cost £2 each. Agricultural wages had risen to sometimes as high as 8/- per week for a "good" man, but were actually set at 6/-. Barley was sold at 23/- per quarter weighing 448lbs, and oats 15/-. Eight loads of hay were sold for £8, and 27 loads of clover for £246. He was somewhat disappointed to find that the schedule of the survey of the land he had inherited was not entirely accurate, and he was unable to locate either a wood called Little Highwoods, of 20 acres, or a field corresponding to it. He also found that Overland Wood was only 30 acres, whereas according to the survey it should have been 42 acres.

Richard purchased several more farms at Great Bromley, Great Bentley, Tendring, Little Clacton, Thorpe, Wix and Ardleigh, with the result that the estate rose to over 4000 acres in twenty years. In 1729 he purchased Stacies Farm at Lawford from one William Peck, with a mortgage of £3000. He paid interest at $4^1/2\%$, an indication of the very low rates at the time. A year's land rent for Stacies Farm was £4-1-0d.

In addition to Sheddinghal Farm, the Home Farm adjoining it was managed by a bailiff under Richard's control. More than thirty horses were kept on this farm as well as the stables at the Hall. Over the years Richard became both a good farmer and an experienced horseman. He very much enjoyed riding round the estate, talking to the labourers and visiting his tenant farmers, with whom he always had cordial relations.

Dairy House Farm, the buildings of which were until recently used by the Mistley Riding School, was extensively renovated, especially the malt room and brewhouse. The stables were roofed, and the dairy enlarged to deal with an increasing number of cows. A slaughter house was built, enabling meat to be supplied to the public over a wide area.

At this time a Mr. Gardiner was farming at Stacies, and Mr. John Martin at Newhall. Other tenants were Mr. J. Scarfe, George Martin and Thomas Mumms, having worked on the estate for many years under the Earl of Oxford.

After some time, all the farms on the estate began to show good profits. Farmers were becoming accustomed to new methods, paying a great deal of attention to soil composition. Without the fertilisers which are used today yields were very much lower, but prudent farmers practised the rotation methods and made wide use of manure and chalk. Although the hay and straw produced was used on the farms, there was always a surplus for shipment to London, where it helped to feed the thousands of horses working in the great city. Inevitably the manure was returned for use on the farms, and those situated near the ports had a distinct advantage of acquiring large quantities.

The population of the village was increasing, but even though, following Rigby's policies, living standards improved, it is noted that on Lady Day in 1728, twenty-six tenants were in arrears of rent, totalling £190-14-7, which indicated that the village still had many poor families.

Courtship and Marriage

Over the years Richard had been far too busy even to consider marriage, and there is no record that he ever had female companions. It is somewhat surprising, after so many years as a bachelor, that when he met Miss Anne Perrie, a pretty country girl, possibly via his activities with the South Sea Company, with which her father also had business connections, he formed an intimate attachment to her. Little is known of the Perrie family, but Anne was the eldest daughter of her father John, and had a brother Jonathan. Her father died about this time, and in his will he left £500 to Anne, and a messuage in Antigua. She also inherited £2000 from the estate of Major Long, which had already been paid to her father. After the affairs had been dealt with it was found that there had not been enough "got in" from John Perrie's estate to pay the £500, and this legacy was reduced to £319-5-0, together with the messuage in Antigua. By a series of complicated agreements a dowry was paid to Richard upon his marriage to Anne, and it was further agreed that an annuity would be paid to her from the estate in the event of Richard's death.

No details have been found giving an account of the wedding, which took place on or about 27th October 1719, but it was probably held in London, as this was then the fashionable thing to do. Anne, being only in her twenties was much younger than Richard, who by this time was nearly forty years of age. They lived in the old Mistley Hall on Sheddinghal Farm, and a daughter Anne was born in 1720, and a son Richard in 1722. A second daughter, Martha, was born in 1724.

During his marriage, Richard, ever thrifty, took great care over his financial affairs, and kept careful accounts of his expenditure. It is seen from his accounts that £78-6-0. was paid to his wife for housekeeping from 31st March to 30th June 1728. Some savings were made during the next three months, as the expenditure amounted to only £50. Payment to "young Richard", was £1-16-11, and on one occasion there is an entry in the accounts that he had been allowed 4/- pocket money, but later he received only 2/-. Richard arranged for the education of his son at an early age; a payment to his tutor for half a year amounted to £21-18-0.

The Rigbys, husband and wife, attended many local functions together, especially at Colchester, where Richard's mother had gone to live a few years earlier. Both were loved very much by the local people, whom they frequently visited, and helped in cases of hardship. Anne shared Richard's love of the countryside, and being a fine horsewoman, spent much of her time riding on the estate. Richard had always kept several coaches and grooms to service the horses. The large family coach drawn by four horses was used for the longer journeys, and on occasions Anne travelled in it to London, accompanied by the estate coachman and a servant. The journey would have taken all day, with changes of horses on the way by previous arrangement. The roads were tortuous and bumpy, and it is unlikely that this long journey would have been undertaken in the winter months, when some highways were almost impassable. Smaller post chaises were used for the shorter journeys, using either one or two horses. The coaches were always maintained in an immaculate condition by the coachman, who was proud to have sole charge of them.

The happy years covering the births of the children delayed Richard's building programme though he still found time to visit the West Indies. It would appear, however, that he was persuaded by Anne that it was more important to put the family first, and his greatest desire was for a new home. Thus Richard turned all his attention towards the planning and building of a new Manor House nearer the Mistley Thorne village, which he was to call the new Mistley Hall.

The New Home

The spot which Richard and Anne chose for their new home can be clearly identified today. It was built at the top of the present Church Lane, and the buildings which remain there were joined on to it, providing stables and other ancillary quarters. Their choice also took into account the proximity of the Dairy House Farm, which could easily supply meat and dairy products. It also had a small brewhouse and slaughter house, with ample provision for the stabling of horses. The countryside around the new Hall was undulating, with great scope for gardens and parkland, and a beautiful view over the river to the Suffolk shore beyond. Two roads were made leading to the Hall, and one is still used, beginning at the crossroads at what is known as "Lodges Corner" at the top of New Road, and continuing down Green Lane. This was the main road to the new Hall. The second one came from the road on the riverside to the west of Hopping Bridge, running straight to the Hall. Part of this road ran across the present cricket field, where traces of it can be seen today. The Dairy House, only about 300 yards to the south of the Hall, had an abundance of trees around it, and the main roadway was strangely a public highway, which is still used today. Many of the footpaths over the fields and hills surrounding the new Hall were regularly used by the villagers at that time. Their rights were respected by the Rigbys, and these paths have been retained to this day some 260 years later.

In 1855, Joseph Glass, the writer and poet, wrote the following in his book Reminiscences of Manningtree, which described the building of the new Hall.

> *"Talk of the paths and road he made quite new,*
> *And from each point how much improved the view.*
> *In this we found they all could well agree,*
> *That mostly he was cheerful bland and free.*
> *Sir Richard built the Hall on rising ground,*
> *From where delightful views were seen around,*

With undulating lands and hills and vales,
And in the view the broad expanded Stour,
With Suffolk farms, and village church and Tower.
The beauteous fountain too, Sir Richard gave,
That all the villagers should water have.
The swan that in the centre sits so fair,
Supplies what seems her gracious form to bear."

It is strange that many of our early writers, made errors in their publications, especially as they were much closer in years to the events. Joseph Glass was no exception, as neither of the Rigbys was a knight or baronet, and it was the elder Rigby who built the Hall. It was, of course, his son, who, with Robert Adam, built the "beauteous fountain" or "swan", still standing in front of the Thorn Inn.

Richard, as was his habit, recorded carefully the payments made for the materials he used for the building. One record shows 13,500 bricks, purchased at a cost of £12-8-0, and a further 2000 for £2-6-0. Expenses of £610-4-0, and £232 for materials are also shown, together with the sum of £4-15-0, paid for 230 bushels of lime, which would presumably have been used for the mortar for laying the bricks. Over 6000 nails were purchased at 2/- per 1000, and 1600 pantiles.

The Hall, which was magnificently constructed of an elegant design, was a square lofty building, of four storeys in height. It had 26 windows in front, and white bricks were used in its construction. The roof had a shallow pitch, with numerous square chimneys, and ornamental designs ran along the house under the eaves. The dining and drawing rooms were large and spacious, divided by a number of well-appointed ante-rooms. There were eleven guest rooms, mostly with wonderful views over to the park, to the river Stour beyond. At one corner of the Hall was an attractive addition in the form of a bow, or rotunda. This room had tall elongated windows, which, no doubt, served the purpose of a lounge or music room, and enjoyed excellent views. Beneath the Hall were large cellars, in which fuel was stored, and in some racks were fitted for wine. The extensive ancillary buildings stood to the south west of the Hall, and included the laundry, stables and servants' quarters. A spacious courtyard was laid in stone, and this was surrounded by the stables. Accommodation was also available for the stablemen, and other workmen who worked on the estate. A central section of the building was extended several feet forward, which was reached over a small bridge. Shallow steps led from the bridge to the imposing entrance door through into a spacious hall on the first floor. The bottom floor of the building was slightly below ground level which gently sloped down to it. The Hall was furnished in a plain and homely style, with little decoration, and the family were delighted with their new home.

Although the land around the new Hall was pasture, which could easily be made into lawns, Richard decided that he would transplant as much as he could from his old garden into his new one. He paid £3 to replant 300 currant bushes, gooseberry bushes, and numerous small trees and shrubs. Walnut trees were brought from Dedham, and 260 cherry trees were also obtained and planted, together with 109 apple and 128 pear trees. Mr. Ben Baker was paid £11-7-8 for work on the lawns; he laid out several unusual tulip trees, and evergreens were placed in prominent positions in what was to become a very large garden. In many of the fields surrounding the parkland, Richard constructed a number of Kentish Fences, or Ha-has, as they were sometimes called. These were grass lined ditches used to conceal a fence in the bottom. They were usually planted around the woodlands, and by hiding the fences, the views were considerably improved. The remains of one of these can be seen at the eastern end of the present "Laundry Wood", off Green Lane, and there are traces of one at the top of the hill near Bluebell Wood. One of the Ha-has ran a long distance bordering New Road, but all evidence of this has disappeared.

A delightful feature in the parkland was a small lake, with trees and shrubs surrounding it. At the western end a small brick bridge was built with ornamental work on its face. This pool, now overgrown, and the remains of the brick bridge can be seen in the middle of what is now called "Tunnel Meadow". It corresponded to the small "Oak Plantation" near the old Mistley Hall on Sheddinghal Farm. Perhaps Rigby wished to create the same sort of visual effect they had enjoyed before.

Around the Mansion House the hillocks and fields were bisected by streams, which Richard made good use of, creating a number of lakes. The streams were crossed by well-designed brick bridges. The original positions of the crossings are still in existence, and much of the old brickwork has been preserved over the years when repairs have been carried out. By far the most beautiful stretch of water was the large lake to the east of the Hall, which Rigby created between the land now known as Furze Hills, and the hill of the farmland to the south. Grassy slopes descended steeply to it, and numerous trees were planted around it. The lake was stocked with all kinds of fish, and a tiny thatched cottage for a gamekeeper was erected at the eastern end. Two small brick dams were constructed at the western end, with elaborate arrangements for drainage into compartments, also built of brick. The original brickwork can still be seen. The water ran continuously over a weir at the end, falling into a stream in the form of a miniature waterfall. The mere was called "Gull Pond" at that time, but the house was always known as "Keeper's Cottage", and the lake which still remains became known as "Keeper's Pond". The cosy thatched cottage survived until 1955, but being unused for some years, was vandalised, and finally burnt down. The lake is well kept by the Lawford Angling Society, and has been regularly stocked with fish.

All over the hills and dales Richard planted varieties of rhododendrons of different colours. Many of these were planted around the lake, which with the trees surrounding it, became the most beautiful part of the park. Rhododendrons still grow in some profusion at the western end of the lake, and it may be that they have continued to seed from the time when Rigby planted them. A variety of trees were set in the parkland, and some, especially the oaks, survive today around Furze Hills and woodlands to the south and west. The gardens extended up to Lodges Corner, and the lawns descended gently to the river bank.

The Hall and gardens, with the village and river below, must have presented a delightful picture, but it seems that they did not hugely impress the writer, Horace Walpole, who stayed at the Hall with Richard's son some seventeen years later. He wrote from London in 1745:

> *"I have been near three weeks in Essex, at Mr. Rigby's. It is the charmingest place by nature, and most trumpary by art that I ever saw. The house stands on a high hill, on the arm of the sea, which winds itself before two sides of the house. On the right and left, at the very foot of the hill lie two towns; the one of market quality, (Manningtree), and the other, (Mistley), with a wharf where ships come up. This last was to have a church, but by a lucky want of religion in the inhabitants, who would not contribute to building a steeple,*

it remains an absolute antique temple, with a portico, on the very strand. Cross this arm of the sea, you see six churches, and charming woody hill in Suffolk. All this parent nature did for this place; but its godfathers and godmothers, I believe, promised it should renounce all pomps and vanities of this world, for they have patched up a square house, full of windows, low rooms, and thin walls where-ever there was a glimpse of prospect; planted avenues which go nowhere, and dug fishponds where there should be avenues. We had very bad weather the whole time I was there; but however I rode about and sailed."

Richard had died by this time, and did not read the criticism which other writers have continued to report over the years. The imposing mansion he had built was greatly improved in later years, and Mistley Hall would remain the home of the Rigbys and their descendants for 135 years until 1845.

The first Richard Rigby built this magnificent mansion soon after his marriage in 1719.

CHAPTER 8

BUILDING AT MISTLEY

It was 1724 before Richard Rigby was able to seriously begin the ambitious building operations which had occupied his mind for many years. He realised that if he was to be successful in enlarging the village industry, all his plans would have to be organised, and the building work executed simultaneously. An extended programme would only cause further delay in realising the potential of the village. Presumably, by this time, Richard had a comprehensive scheme in mind; all the projects appeared to have equal priority, and were completed by the year 1730. His first undertaking was to build several houses on land behind the wharf. Some of these still remain, and more were added in the years ahead. His strategy was to renovate some of the old property, and to put up new buildings, which covered at least a dozen projects, including the erection of the Thorne Inn, and alterations on the quay.

The estate inherited by the Rigbys had two windmills and a watermill. One of the windmills was located near the top of Mistley Hill on the road to Harwich, adjacent to the old property, still to be seen today, known as "Ye Old Mill House". This building was the home of the miller who operated the windmill under a tenancy from the estate. The channel in the river running north easterly from the quay towards Harwich is still known as "Miller's Reach", and the mill would have been a mark for mariners. The mill was carefully renovated by Rigby, and occupied at a tenancy of £90 per annum.

A lime kiln had been worked on the quay for many years, and in 1727 Rigby decided to improve it. Most of the old kiln was pulled down, at a cost of £11-3-6, and a new design enlarged it considerably. This new lime kiln was built at the bottom of the hill leading to the quay, where the railway bridge is today on the Harwich road, and was to be worked for a further 50 years, after which extensive modifications and repairs were carried out by Rigby's son.

Richard had felt for some time that it was important for the village to have a large posting inn, and he consequently started building the Thorne Inn during 1724. The inn still exists as the Thorn Hotel, and when it was completed in 1725, it included the section now used as a Post Office. A large banqueting hall was included in the design, with well-appointed rooms for visitors. At this time many of the rooms had uninterrupted views across the square in front, and over the wide river beyond. Numerous smaller rooms were provided for a variety of purposes. One was described as a coffee room, and another designated for Captains only. The Inn also provided accommodation for the Customs Officer, and a large bar, which became extremely well used by the many seamen regularly arriving at the port! The Thorne soon became an important staging post between London and Harwich for travellers to the continent. The Inn provided especially well for coaches and drovers, with enough stabling for twenty horses. A post chaise to London would cost £5, and for £2 a mare could be stabled and exercised.

At this time smuggling was widespread, and it was not long before nine gallons of brandy and four and a half gallons of wine were seized outside the Thorne Inn. The smugglers stood trial at Chelmsford assizes, and were given a prison sentence.

Rigby remained owner of the Thorne inn, and a tenant landlord was installed to manage it. The inn remained in the hands of the Rigby family for a further 120 years. In 1727, the rent paid was £6-10-0 per annum, and the inn became very profitable; it was well patronised by both quay workers, and the Captains and crews of the many ships coming to Mistley, with its advertised clean and well-aired beds. It became a very popular venue for parties and public functions. Petty sessions were sometimes held in the largest room, and the stage coaches brought regular business. The inn was finally sold in 1844 to Mr. D.C. Alston, who owned a brewery at Manningtree.

The Coal and Brick Yards

For many years there had been a coalyard adjacent to the wharf, and in 1727 trade, mostly from the Durham coalfields via Newcastle and Sunderland, had increased to such an extent that it became necessary to enlarge it after carrying out repairs. Between 1727 and 1730, three further coalyards were constructed. The coalyards were built of brick in the form of bunkers some twelve feet in height, in which the coal was placed after it had been unloaded from the ships from the wharf. The coal was shovelled into wicker skips in the hold of the vessel, and winched ashore. The men had to wind the winches by hand, a laborious job which could only be performed by the stronger men. The skips were then winched onto a platform, beside which a tumbril would be driven, and the skip would be tipped into the tumbril, which transported and tipped the coal into the bunkers. In 1727, the repairs to the wall of the western coalyard cost £16-15-3, and one built in the east, by a bricklayer, Mr. Webb, cost £17-10-11.

Coal was now widely used as fuel in the villagers' cottages, replacing wood, and also in small industrial undertakings which had sprung up at Manningtree. Deliveries of coal were made by horse and cart to the tiny villages surrounding Mistley, but by far the largest tonnage was loaded into barges and hauled up to Sudbury and other villages on the way.

A considerable amount of the coal coming to Mistley was used in the brick kilns, although later on coke was burned. Most of the brick kilns had been built some years previously, but Rigby added to these. One group of kilns and its accompanying brickfield, was situated on the Harwich road. A great trade developed in Mistley, and many of the bricks made locally were used in the reconstruction which was taking place. There are certain parts of Mistley where loam still exists which is very suitable for manufacturing bricks; a large amount still remains on areas of the quay banks.

With the increasing industrial works at Mistley, more workmen were needed, and all the houses built by Rigby were soon occupied.

Shipbuilding and Fishing.

By the 1720s more sea fishermen had begun to use Mistley and Manningtree as ports in which to keep their boats and unload their catches. The development of smacks with lead-lined compartments on either side of the holds where fish could be kept alive in the water had resulted in fishermen venturing much further into the North Sea. Quite apart from the fishing, the increase in shipping generally meant that many more facilities were needed for the repair and servicing of vessels. During the next few years shipwrights came to Mistley, and a small shipyard was built on the beach below the hanging cliffs. The position of the yard, which initially was used only for repairs to vessels, was immediately below the top of the hill where the road now leads down to the quay near the railway bridge. The yard was later to become a much larger business, from which ships of several hundred tons' capacity were launched. Sheds for the storage of timber, pitch and tar were built, and the shipyard spread, eventually occupying nearly 400' of the beach, and the area behind it. The business of shipbuilding was to last for more than 100 years.

Malting

For a number of years, Mistley had a small malting, in those days called a Malt Office, and in 1728, Rigby decided to build another. The old malting would probably have been constructed of wood and consisted of merely a ground floor. Its kiln would have been built of brick in the same style as the Kentish oast houses. Mr. John Hoare rented the malting at £30 per annum. It had probably come to the end of its useful life, and was demolished. Rigby decided that he would build the new malting entirely of brick, and accounts show that 2200 bricks were purchased, costing £17-16-10 for the new kiln. The malting had only one floor some 18' wide by 70' long, and was built on the quay on the site of the existing one which stands opposite to Mistley station. The steep bank behind it was strongly supported, as the road to Harwich, as now, ran above it. A small granary was built at the western end, in which both malt and barley could be stored. The tank used for steeping the barley was also made of brick, and the roof was covered using grey tiles. The malting floor and kiln were tiled, and those on the latter had a number of small holes, which allowed heated air to pass through in order to dry the malt above.

These early malts were the forerunners of many which were built at Mistley and Manningtree, and the area was often described as the "Home of Malting". At its peak the industry was paying more than £50,000 in malt tax.

The process of making barley into malt for brewing had remained unchanged for hundreds of years. Inside its thin skin the barley corn consists of insoluble starch or carbohydrate containing small amounts of nitrogenous matter. The purpose of malting is to change the starch into a soluble form, which when lightly crushed will partially dissolve in hot water forming a sugar solution which is used for brewing.

In the old days the first part of the process was to shovel the barley into the steeping tank full of water pumped by hand - a lengthy task. The grain remained in the tank for about two and a half days, and during this time the water was drained about four times to freshen it. The rather smelly steeping water ran down a pipe and straight into the river. The steeped barley was then shovelled from the tank into wooden boxes with two handles at either end. Two men would carry the very heavy box on to the germinating floor, empty it, and spread the grain thinly over the surface where it was allowed to germinate for about ten days. During this time the grain was turned using wooden shovels, and raked at least four times daily with a metal bladed implement called a "plough". The head maltster attempted to keep the temperature of the grain, now called a "piece", to about 60°, and ensure the root growth was kept in check. On the tenth day the germinated grain was shovelled into wicker skips, dragged along the floor and hand-winched on to the kiln. The skip was again dragged across the floor, emptied, and levelled using wooden shovels. During its time on the kiln the grain, now malt, was turned with a wooden fork, to allow the hot air from the furnace to pass through it. When the malt was dry, usually after about three days it was shovelled into a wooden bin and allowed to cool. The temperature in the kiln in the later stages reached at least 200°, and the maltsters were smothered with dust when performing this operation. The final stage, the cleaning of the malt, was certainly the most dusty . The grain had to be thrown through a screen with a wooden scoop which extracted the dust and roots, and the finished malt was stored in bins in the small granary. In due course the malt was delivered to the breweries in large hessian sacks, where it was lightly ground in a mill and placed in hot water in a vessel called a mash-tun. After some time the liquid was drained off into another large receptacle called a copper into which hops had been placed. The liquor was then heated, and after it had cooled it had become a sugar solution, which was put into vessels called vats, where yeast was placed on top and allowed to ferment. Finally the yeast was taken off, the wort filtered, and beer was produced.

From this very brief description of the process it is possible to imagine the very arduous nature of a maltster's work. Not only was the work laborious in the extreme, it was performed under very damp and humid conditions on the malting floor, with great heat and clouds of dust on the kiln.

Several men under a foreman would have been employed in the malting, but it is probable that this work would have run alongside other activities in the port.

Thorne Quay

The small wharf at Mistley had been used for many years; before it was built there had been a landing place or "hard", on which the ships were allowed to ground. After the tide had receded carts could be driven alongside ships, where cargoes could be loaded or unloaded. When the small quay was built an area was left alongside which continued to be used as a "hard".

It had been apparent for some years that because of the barge traffic to Sudbury, and the increasing numbers of ships using the port, the wharf was becoming far too small. In addition the quay was set some distance back from the main channel, and a large expanse in front dried out completely at low tide, while there was barely 7' at high tide. It was decided to build the new quay much further forward, up to the low-water mark, which in turn would increase the depth of water at high tide. In consequence, larger vessels could be accommodated operating at more economic freight rates.

The construction of the new quay was by far the most ambitious project Richard Rigby

The first Richard Rigby built this Quay in 1726 with two docks and a granary

was to undertake. The new quay was constructed of wood with piles driven in at intervals, and tied back to posts some thirty feet behind. Mooring rings were provided, and a hard surface of gravel constituted the working area. The very nature of the surface of the quay did produce difficulties in the winter time and during the wet weather the horses and carts turned the quay into a quagmire. As well as the new quay, Rigby decided to build two small docks, in one of which vessels could lie side by side. A granary was built over the second dock, with a small semi-circular opening, under which small barges could enter. The two docks were built with brick and had wooden piles, and measured about 70' by 40'. The granary was four storeys in height, also built of brick, with a pitched slate roof. Doors were built on each floor of the granary facing the quayside, from which sacks of grain could be lowered to the ships or barges below, although grain from the granary was in most cases delivered loose to the barges, running freely into them from the floors above. Barley in sacks, however, was delivered using a heavy rope placed over a grooved wheel set in a spindle protruding from the top of the granary. On the end of the rope was a small chain with a ring on the end called a "snorter". The chain was threaded around the mouth of the sack, and through the ring which was pulled tight. The rope was then threaded around a circular piece of timber called a "cleat", bolted on the side of the doorway. The sack of grain was pushed gently from the doorway, the granary hand steadied the rope around the piece of timber, allowing it to slide slowly, and the sack descended not very fast because of the friction of the rope. After lowering, the rope had to be pulled up to the floor of the granary and another sack attached. Sadly, many accidents occurred using this method of lowering, in which sacks might be pushed from the doorways without the snorter chain being fixed. A workman who had lowered thousands of sacks would only have to forget just once, and men would be killed by being hit by the falling sack. Men fell out of the doorways on occasions, and it was not until many years later that safety straps, secured round the mens' waists, were invented.

The handsome brick building became known as "Rigby Granary", and thousands of tons of grain were destined to pass through it, until it was demolished only a few years ago.

After the quay and docks were completed, and the granary was in full operation, a large trade built up in the handling of grain. Other shipping trade also rapidly increased, and at its peak more than 500 ships were registered at Mistley. The fishing trade was also increasing, and more smacks began to use the new facilities.

By 1730, Rigby had completed his building programme, and installed his tenants on the farms and other properties. The agricultural estate had been much improved, and was efficiently managed. An agent was appointed to administer the vast estate, and collect the rents. There were many opportunities for work, both on land or at sea. Workers were busy in the coalyards, brickfield, shipyard, salt house, maltings and in the new granary on the wharf which Rigby had provided. The population began to increase dramatically, and the industrial village of Mistley Thorne was created.

CHAPTER 9

THE JOY AND THE SORROW

Some time in 1726, Richard had returned to the West Indies, where he stayed for a short period in Kingston, Jamaica, presumably to ensure that his business interests were running smoothly. He spent much of his time with Edward Pratter, his business associate in the West Indies; his brother James also went with him to Jamaica. From this time little is known about James' movements, but it is thought that he remained there managing the plantations. Richard returned home to England in 1727. With his development work under way, he spent much of his time with his wife and family, especially since many months had been spent travelling to and from the South Seas.

As well as the building work which was being undertaken in the village, the gardens

This memorial to the first Richard Rigby orginally hung in the Towers Church. In 1870 it was removed to the present St. Mary's church, where it hangs on the west wall.

at the Hall remained of great interest to him. He had engaged an experienced gardener to oversee the complicated work which was planned. An extensive kitchen garden was situated to the west of the Hall, and occupied an area of nearly four acres. Several under-gardeners were employed on the estate, and even as late as 1730 the gardens were still in course of construction. The walled kitchen garden eventually became the site of the new Mistley Hall built later on in the 19th century, now the home of Acorn Village. Extensive greenhouses were also built, heated by coal burners. In the years ahead these greenhouses were filled with exotic plants and fruit trees from all over the world.

By July 1730, apart from the new church, which remained to be completed, Richard Rigby had finished the work which he had diligently planned since coming to Mistley some twenty years before. When travelling round his estate, or sitting quietly in his magnificent new home, he would, no doubt, have looked with great satisfaction on his achievements. He had built a large mansion, surrounded by lovely lawns and gardens, overlooking the houses he had erected in the village. He had an adoring wife, who had given him three lovely children. He had, in only a short time, turned the farms of an impoverished estate into efficient profit-making units, run by tenants who were also his personal friends. His building programme, remains of which we can see today, created a prosperous new village, with numerous opportunities for employment. In the England of his day, many people were extremely poor, living in squalid conditions. Mistley was, of course, no exception, but Richard Rigby mindful of this, did everything he could to improve the living standards of the people who lived on his estate. He had constructed malts, coalyards, lime and brick kilns, a magnificent granary and a spacious quay. His establishment of a shipyard with improved facilities for fishermen, had added to the importance and the potential of the estate. Mistley Thorne would grow in importance as the years rolled past, but, sad to say, Richard had little time to see the results of all the work he had done.

Little is known of his life from July 1730, and perhaps at this time some deterioration in his health may have occurred, which resulted in the preparation of his will. We are unlikely ever to know, however, as Richard died suddenly on 31st October 1730, at the comparatively young age of 51, leaving a grieving wife with three young children, and causing great sorrow to the villagers of Mistley. The sadness of his death ended a joyous period in the life of the village which he had created. It was left to the agent of the estate, and the trustees of his will, to determine the way forward. His son, also called Richard, who would become the new owner of Mistley, was only eight years of age, and as the estate would not fall to him until he had reached the age of twenty-five, the next years would obviously be a time in which little would happen to change the life of the village as it had evolved over the past twenty years.

Richard became the first Rigby to be interred in the vault he had carefully constructed many years before, under the old church at Mistley Heath. The following epitaph was inscribed on a plaque, and placed in the newly-built church at Mistley Thorne, from where it was later re-sited in the present church. The words exactly describe the character of the man who came to Mistley so long ago, and did so much for the people living there.

"This monument is erected to the memory of
Richard Rigby, Esq., whose body has been
interred in a tomb in the old churchyard
belonging to this parish.
He was a man endowed with many Christian
virtues, which made him a kind husband, a
good father, and a benefactor to all mankind,
particularly to this parish.
He died on 31st October, 1730 in
the 51st year of his age".

CHAPTER 10

THE TRANQUIL YEARS: 1730-1741

The funeral of Richard Rigby was private, and in accordance with his wishes attended only by his family and close friends. A shadow descended over the whole village, where many draped their windows with black ribbon. The grieving widow withdrew for some time to the Hall to be comforted by her family.

It was fortunate that Richard's two sisters, who had come with him from London when the family moved to Mistley, had since married, and lived there. Catherine had married John Stewart, who had business interests with the family in Jamaica, and Anne to the above mentioned Rev. David Mustard, who had become rector of Mistley in 1719.

From this time on, Anne Rigby, surrounded by a caring family and many friends, devoted her whole life to the task of bringing up her three young children.

The Will

Richard Rigby's untimely death caused much uncertainty in the village, as there was concern that the large estate would be placed on the market, particularly as his eldest son was only eight years old. All fears that this might happen were soon allayed by the publication of Richard's will, which he had made in the July of 1730, only three months before he died. A codicil was prepared in the August, and one cannot help thinking that Richard may have been prompted to this action by illness. Everyone would have been relieved to find that two gentlemen well-known in the village had been appointed as trustees to run the estate. One of them was Richard's brother-in-law, Mr. George Marker, and the other was Mr. Charles Gray of Colchester, who was presumably the family solicitor. They were great friends of the family and would have been much comfort to Anne in the trying years ahead. The trustees were charged with the administration of the estate, carrying out any building repairs which were required. They were also instructed to continue to lend every assistance to the building of the new church, and to pay the financial contribution which Richard had promised.

Richard had left the family residence, Mistley Hall, to his wife Anne, together with all the furniture, pictures, plate, outhouses, gardens and stables. In addition to a specified annual legacy to come out of the profits of the estate, he left the sum of £1,000 to be taken from money from the West Indies, so that his wife could finish his plans to make the Hall more comfortable, and to provide any additions to the gardens that she should find necessary. Because of her love of horses, he left Anne his coach, four of the best horses or mares, and two saddle horses of her choice, with all the saddlery and furniture. The dowry Richard had received from Anne on their marriage was to be returned as previously agreed. The tuition of the children was in Anne's care until they were twenty-one years of age; should she die before this time the trustees would have full responsibility.

True to his benevolent nature, Richard left a years wages to his servants, John White and May Merchant. A mourning ring was given to his niece, Mary Anne Ashton, who some years before had married Rev. Venn of Wrabness. Further rings, at a cost of twenty guineas each, were given to his friends Charles Wager, Knight, John Eyles, Baronet, his brother James, his brothers-in-law, John Stewart and George Barker, and his kinsmen, Jonathan Perrie, Edward Platter, of Jamaica, and Charles Gray. The will was very detailed, with carefully outlined provisions of succession should any of the beneficiaries die. Portions of the will would be void should his wife remarry, and any future beneficiary had to assume the surname of Rigby within one year.

The trustees carefully executed all the provisions made in the will, and the villagers would have been relieved when they found that their tenancies had been safeguarded. However, they were not so vigilant in carrying out other matters. A codicil to the will, which was made in August 1730, once again reveals Richard's concern for the welfare of the Mistley villagers. The beginning of the codicil reads:

"and whereas I had fully proposed to build in my lifetime, six alms houses at or near the Thorne in Mistley as some provision for the wants of such or the inhabitants of that place, as may be reduced by age, sickness, or misfortune, the which purpose I have deferred putting into execution for sometime, hoping to effect the rebuilding of the Parish Church at Mistley, near the same place, with intent to build such alms houses in some convenient situation, order and distance from the said church, the which if I should not live to finish according to my design. My will is that I do hereby authorise, and empower my Extrix and Exors for the time being to perform the same in such manner - in such manner, as they shall judge best to answer the intent herein before, and after mentioned, and to employ and expend in the said building out of my personal estate."

The codicil went on at length to authorise expenditure of £800 for building the alms houses, the building of which should not be deferred longer than three years after the church was built. The houses and the site would be given to the Lord of the Manor of Mistley in trust forever, who must nominate "six persons, men or women of the most decayed honest housekeepers at the Thorne at Mistley, who shall have lived as such for three years continuance, to live in them". The codicil went on to say that should the Lord of the Manor fail to nominate persons to live in the alms houses, the Minister and churchwardens were authorised to do so. Rigby was also concerned over the repairs to the alms houses and for the welfare of the parishioners who were to live in them. The codicil went on further to say:

"And I do devise to the Minister and churchwarden or churchwardens of the Parish of Mistley for the time being and their successors for ever, six chaldrons of coal, 24 bushels of wheat, and 24 bushels of barley or malt, which I appoint to be bought yearly and every year by the Lord of the Manor of Mistley, and wherewith he is to be chargeable so long as he continues to be proprietor of the wharf at the Thorne, or else proprietor of such wharf for the time being out of the produce of the wharfage thereof to be delivered to the said Minister and churchwarden or churchwardens for the time being in order to their distribution of same to and among the several inhabitants of the said alms houses for the time being, to wit, to each of them one chaldron of coal, four bushels of wheat, and four bushels of barley or malt the delivery or distribution I appoint it to be made in the respective alms houses at Michaelmas day every year in the manner aforesaid. And I do by this my will subject and charge the wharfage arising from the wharfs I have built at the Thorne aforesaid and constitute the same for a perpetual fund as well as for the purpose of the said coal and grain as aforesaid as for keeping and maintaining the said alms houses in good and sufficient repair from time to time".

The codicil continued by appointing the Minister and churchwardens to be perpetual trustees, giving explicit instructions that they were given the power to enter on to the wharf and take the profits to pay for the alms houses repairs, and the cost of the coal and grain. They were also given power to sue the Lord of the Manor of Mistley should he fail to pay for repairs and purchase the coal and grain. The codicil to the will was approved in the office of the Archbishop of Canterbury by Anne Rigby on 19th November 1730.

Much care and thought must have gone into the explicit provisions of the codicil, as it was clearly a means of ensuring that any rise in inflation, although virtually unknown at this time, was taken into the account. The residents of the proposed alms houses, the codicil mentions, would have benefited in particular; any repairs to the houses were to have been paid for from an amount taken from the profits of the wharf in perpetuity. The cost of the coal, wheat, and barley or malt which would have been purchased for the tenants of the alms houses would have been no more than £12 at the time. It is, however, sad to relate that the trustees, who had carefully carried out all the other provisions in the will, failed to ensure that the alms houses were built, and no charges were made against the wharf. Over a hundred years passed before it was found that provisions made in Richard Rigby's will had not been fulfilled, and the matter was referred to the Charity Commissioners, who ordered that the rent to the value of the coal and grain should be paid annually to the poor of the village from the profits of the wharf. This charity became known as the "Rigby Gift", and in 1845 it amounted to about £15. The value of coal, wheat and barley or malt was established using prices paid at the nearest market, and initially it was administered by the churchwardens of the parish of Mistley Thorne. The annual payment was taken from the profits of what became known as "Allen's Quay", on which the Mistley Workshops now stand. The owners of this portion of the quay were responsible for the payment of the gift. After 1900, the trustees were appointed by the Parish Council, and with little inflation at that time the value remained at £15, and was distributed annually at either the school or the Village Institute.

During the last war the prices of coal, wheat and barley had increased considerably, and by 1944 the Gift should have amounted to nearly £60. Over the years, however, successive trustees had not paid due attention to the provisions of the will and ascertained the prices at the nearest market. The payment of £15 remained the same as when they took over responsibility. In 1944, the trustees inexplicably allowed the company which owned Allen's Quay to buy itself out of its rent charge for a lump sum of £477 for the purchase of £600 worth of 2$\frac{1}{2}$% Consuls, bringing in the sum of £15 per annum, in perpetuity. The trustees appointed by the Mistley Parish Council, together with the Charity Commissioners, frustrated the careful provisions made by Richard Rigby in his will. No reference appeared in the Parish Council minutes of meetings at that time, and the full details of this affair were not discovered until research for this book was being carried out. During the 1960s the then Mistley Rector reinvested the 2$\frac{1}{2}$% Consuls in the Charity Commissioners' personal fund, and the interest, increased to about £35, is now received, although the cost of the coal, wheat, barley or malt today would amount to nearly £750. The charity is still administered by trustees appointed by the Mistley Parish Council, and a small sum is added each year to allow for inflation. It is disgraceful that in 1944 just a few people who were charged with the responsibility of administering the trust deprived less fortunate villagers in Mistley from receiving a benefit bequeathed by Richard Rigby so long ago.

The Village Industry Develops.

Following the industrial development which Richard Rigby had started, tenancies were arranged for the premises he had built. His new granary was full to overflowing, and the small maltings were working to full capacity. By the end of the 1720s, the population of the village was growing, and the demand immediately rose for more services, which were quickly provided. There were already butchers, bakers and fishmongers in Manningtree, but it was not long before they were also operating in Mistley. The Mistley Thorne Inn was extremely busy, in both its residential and stabling operations. Coaches arrived regularly from London, and with increased numbers of ships using the new quay, the consumption of beer rose rapidly.

The New Church.

The construction of the church was obviously delayed somewhat by Richard's death, but the trustees continued to support the project with finances which had been set aside for it. Mistley had been without a church for six years when the work started, and the villagers were delighted when on 6th June 1735, Edmund Gibson D.D., the Bishop of London, arrived to perform the consecration ceremony. He was accompanied by the Rev. David Mustard, and Anne Rigby and her three children were present at the service, along with other members of the family, and a large congregation of Mistley villagers. After the service the Bishop, and many others met the family at Mistley Hall for refreshments.

Following the erection of the church, the village of Mistley Thorne became a close-knit community, where, because of improved opportunities for work, the standard of living rapidly improved for a large number of its inhabitants.

The Children.

Anne, Richard and Martha were aged ten, eight and six respectively when their father died, and of the three it appeared to have the greatest effect on Anne. She became very fond of the church, and regularly worshipped at both Mistley and Bradfield with other older relatives and friends. She was to grow into a quiet, home-loving girl, completely devoted to her family. Her sister Martha was a pretty girl, rather more vivacious than Anne, but, like her, loved her home where they were no doubt much spoiled by their mother.

As the years passed, Richard became a fearless, active young man, with a great love for the river, on which he was taught to sail. His uncle, George Barker, took him under his wing, and he was soon able to ride and drive round the estate. Initially he received his education at home with his sisters. Later he was sent to London where he was a pupil of a Mr. Winnington, a very experienced tutor, who had schooled the sons of many of the country gentlemen at that time. In later years it was said that the chief errors in Rigby's life were due to Winnington's maxims, described as "perniciously witty", and that he had "lived when all virtues were set to notorious sale. He ridiculed false pretences, and thus, was honest enough in avowing whatever was dishonourable". Under this influence at an early age, it was said that Rigby grew to think it sensible to laugh at the "shackles of morality". It is clear that he lacked his father's discipline and guidance, as later chapters will illustrate.

By this time, the family had added to the number of friends who often came to Mistley Hall, Richard especially making many during his education. On reaching his late teens, he regularly visited London, which was more exciting than the rather sheltered life he led at Mistley. He had made plans for some time to undertake the "Grand Tour", the name given to the visits made by most young men of the English gentry to Europe, where they were welcomed by the nobility and upper classes. It would be true to say that at this time, Richard had become restless, with little interest in matters of the Mistley estate. Perhaps his education by Winnington had started him on the path he was soon to tread.

A Second Sadness.

By the year 1740 Anne Rigby could look back over ten tranquil years, though saddened by the loss of her husband, during which she had had to bring up her children without his guidance. Much work had been carried out at the Hall, and the surrounding gardens, the beauty of which became known far and wide.

During the latter part of 1740, when she was only in her forties, her health began to fail. No record is shown of the nature of her illness, but it is suspected that it may have been consumption. Pathetically, in her will which she made on 2nd February 1741, in the presence of her brother George and the family doctor, she described herself as "sound in mind but sick in body". She died a few months later, and was laid to rest beside Richard in the family vault at Mistley Heath. Her three children were left to the help and love of the family and many friends. Her daughter Anne was now 21, and to her fell the responsibility of the running of Mistley Hall, and dealing with the trustees who looked after the estate. She was to perform this duty for many years, managing all the domestic affairs, and entertaining her brother's many friends when they came to see him at Mistley.

River barges were loaded at Mistley and poled up to Cattawade, where they were joined by horse and drawn to Sudbury.

CHAPTER 11

THE SECOND RICHARD RIGBY

DURING THE YEARS 1741-1752

Anne Rigby had been very close to her mother, and quickly accepted that full responsibility for the family would fall upon her until her brother Richard reached the age of twenty-five, and inherited the estate. In her will, her mother had left Anne and her sister Martha, sums of £1000 each. She also left Anne all her wearing apparel, except jewels and rings, "which she could dispose of as she felt fit". She left Richard a third share in a plantation in Antigua, together with its Negroes, horses, cattle, coppers, mills and other implements and utensils. Over the months ahead, with every help from their many friends and relatives, the two girls were able to manage satisfactorily the Hall's numerous domestic affairs. By this time Richard, who had almost finished his schooling, was perhaps revealing a careless streak in his character, as he was determined to embark on his "Grand Tour" of Europe rather than lend support to his sisters, at what must have been a very sad time for them.

The Right Hon. Richard Rigby
1722-1788.
Lord of the Manor of Mistley
Member of Parliament for
Tavistock.
Paymaster General to H.M.
Forces and Privy Councillor

(By kind permission of the
Marquess of Tavistock and the
trustees of the Bedford estates)

Richard's father had always wanted his son to receive his education locally, and had he lived he would have prevented any part of it being given in London; he had always been concerned that a "so-called fine" education amongst the "young bloods", would only lead him into bad ways. His fears were confirmed as Richard's career was often overshadowed by vice and corruption, as the years ahead were to show.

Only a few months after his mother's death, Richard left Harwich on the first stage of his tour, accompanied by a number of his rich young friends. It was said that these journeys formed part of the education of the young gentlemen of the time, and there is no doubt that in Europe they were treated lavishly, and made more than welcome. The ladies on the continent must have seemed especially vivacious and attractive, and many of the rather callow youths lost their hearts to them, and for some, much of their fortune. Alexander Pope, the distinguished English poet, wrote of them:

> *"They sauntered Europe around,*
> *And gathered every vice of Christian ground.*
> *Saw every Court, heard every King declare his*
> *Royal scene of operas or the fair.*
> *Tried all hors-d'oeuvres defined,*
> *Judicious drank, and greatly daring dined."*

Pope was a brilliant satirist, and his poem aptly describes the antics of the young men who enjoyed themselves abroad, and in many cases spent their fathers' money with great abandon.

It is possible that on this tour Rigby may have met Horace Walpole, who was to be his friend for many years. Horace was the son of Robert Walpole, the Prime Minister, and later became the 4th Earl of Orford. Richard also made great friends with David Garrick, the actor, and Henry Fox, the politician. He had many other acquaintances, who were members of the wealthy circle who visited the clubs and coffee houses in London. There is little doubt that most of them would have spent some of their time in Europe.

Richard returned from Europe in 1743, and was almost immediately elected Member of Parliament for Castle Rising. It is thought that Walpole was responsible for getting him elected, as he lived in the area, and had a great interest in the constituency. Bribery was then rife in England, and some candidates gave food and clothes to the voters, in return for their support at the elections. Moreover the Lords of the Manors employed most of the electorate, and could thus tell them in no uncertain terms who to vote for. The election at Castle Rising started Richard Rigby on a political career which would continue for more than forty turbulent years.

He immediately purchased a house at St. James' Place in London, where he could live when attending the House of Commons. He also became a member of both "Brooks" and "Whites", two well-known popular clubs, frequented by the richest gentry in the country. Here fortunes could change hands on the turn of a card, and many irresponsible young men often recklessly squandered thousands of pounds. Most Members of Parliament visited these clubs, as well as "Crockfords" and one with an unusual name, the "Kit Cat". It was their practice to spend their mornings in the London coffee houses, some accompanied by their ladies, most of whom had dubious reputations, with their evenings spent in drinking and gambling.

Sadly Richard became an inveterate gambler, and was regularly seen at the tables with his friends. Horse racing also held a great attraction for him, and at both forms of gambling he invariably lost heavily, and, it was said, "with little grace".

When Parliament rose, Richard returned to Mistley, and carried out his responsibilities as Lord of the Manor, working closely with the two trustees who were successfully running the estate. Unfortunately at that time he did not command the love and respect of the villagers as his father had before him.

Nearly twenty years had passed since Richard's father had died, and Mistley had become an important Port, with increased transhipments of cargo to river barges for Sudbury. The trade in building materials was increasing, and a further brickworks opened at Dickley Hall Farm. The small shipyard on the beach was busily engaged in building using timber cut from the local mostly oak woodlands. Several families of fishermen had moved to Mistley and Manningtree, and their smacks were voyaging further into the northern seas. Fishing could be a dangerous occupation; the lack of accurate charts, and knowledge of possible storms ahead often resulted in ships being caught far from port, and there was considerable loss of life. Many brave men from Mistley and Manningtree lost their lives during this period, sailing round the English shores. Thousands of ships were wrecked, and plundered, despite the efforts of the Customs Officers. Immediately a wreck was reported, the inhabitants of the nearby villages would comb the beaches and take anything they found home. Rigby, a sailor himself, was always concerned over any local shipowners who suffered losses, and often helped personally with financial contributions.

During 1745 he invited his friend Horace Walpole to come to Mistley to stay with him. Walpole considered himself an authority on houses and gardens, and was highly critical of the Hall, the surrounding lawns, gardens, and large shrubberies, which had been the pride of Rigby's father. He made many suggestions, during the weeks he stayed at the Hall, which Richard eventually carried out, at considerable expense to the estate, over the following years.

By 1746, Richard was beginning to make his mark as a Whig, under the Prime Minister, Henry Pelham, despite the fact that his speeches were often coarse, but frank, delivered in a rather vehement manner. It was generally thought, however, that everyone understood what he was saying, even though they may have disagreed with it! He remained an MP for Castle Rising for barely two years, and in 1747 was elected member for Sudbury, conveniently nearer to Mistley. The election was reported in the newspapers to have been very bitterly fought, against a large opposition, and shortly afterwards Richard had to contest the seat again. This time he considerably increased his majority, although he described it as costing him much expense.

Late in 1747, at the age of 25, Richard finally inherited the Mistley estate, and held a magnificent party for his friends in celebration. This was the first of many which would be held at Mistley Hall in the years ahead. Naturally, having complete control of the estate allowed Rigby more freedom with its finances, and from this time he began to lead a life which was both undisciplined and reckless.

In London, like so many of the rich young men of the time, he continued to indulge in irresponsible gambling and bouts of drinking, in which it was said that few could rival him. As well as pursuing certain "ladies of the town" he also found time to sail his yacht single-handed from Harwich to London Bridge because of a substantial bet with Lord Rochford.

Rigby made careful preparations for his journey, taking plenty of food and drink, and discussing the voyage with his fishermen friends at Mistley beforehand. He left Harwich on the rising tide in the early morning having luckily chosen a day with an easterly wind. He was soon round Walton on the Naze, and followed the coast in the deep water of the "Wallet", where he had sailed before. With the fair wind he was able to sail through a narrow channel called the "Spitway", which at that time had a mark for shipping, and entered into the wide channel, which is now called the "Swin", at high tide. His yacht which was gaff rigged, and about 28 feet long, was quite fast, but with the turn of the tide he anchored, probably near Shoeburyness, where he spent the night. He had wisely avoided a night passage, as without navigation marks he would have certainly been hopelessly lost. The next day he made slow passage, past Southend into the Thames, as the wind had shifted and dropped. He ran into great difficulties when arriving in the narrows of the river in avoiding scores of ships using the waterway in both directions. He eventually arrived at the area near Tower Bridge, and tied up at a wharf near Billingsgate, quickly walking to his favourite coffee shop, where a number of his friends were awaiting his arrival. Two of the fishermen from Mistley returned with the yacht, having travelled to London in Rigby's Post Chaise. In due course he collected his wager from Lord Rochford. To sail single-handed to London, with few aids to navigation, was no mean feat, and that he should have attempted it at all shows a fearlessness, not to say recklessness in him.

Richard was a frequent racegoer, and attended many of the courses in England with his friend Henry Fox. His losses at gambling had reached such vast proportions that he was rapidly disposing of the capital which he had inherited with the Mistley estate. In 1747 he became attached to Frederick, the Prince of Wales, and was frequently invited to levees at Leicester House, which was the Prince's home. The Prince always enjoyed gambling at cards, and wisely Richard always lost politely to him. They became intimate friends, and the Prince who had a great regard for Richard, led him to believe that he would be appointed to the position of Lordship of the Bedchamber, which would have brought him a large remuneration and great prestige. Much to Richard's disappointment the Prince did not honour his promise, and instead offered him a sum of money in compensation. Despite the dissipation of his fortune, however Richard refused the payment, and never went to Leicester House again.

Richard's exploits in London were obviously not repeated at Mistley, where his behaviour was more temperate, alone at home with his sisters, attending to the affairs of the household. Walpole's criticism of the hall and gardens had always rankled, so although a great deal of work had been done, he decided to further rebuild sections of the Hall and reorganise the gardens. A portico and bow window were added, and a colonnade was erected, leading from the Hall to the servants' quarters and the stables. The walls of the dining room were hung with pink paper, with black frets around the edges, which was very popular at that time. Pictures of Indian landscapes were hung around the room, and numerous alterations made to the furnishing. In the grounds two small bridges on the estate were improved, incorporating Gothic and Chinese designs. Bearing in mind Walpole's suggestions, the most important alterations were confined to the gardens. He changed his father's quiet simple designs by demolishing entrenchments, and the walls enclosing square gardens .Hundreds of plants were introduced to form bowers, with Kentish fences surrounding the entire Hall and some of the woodlands in the distance. The cost of the alterations was enormous, as Richard employed the most expert gardeners of the time to assist him. The expense incurred on this project, together with his gambling losses, ate into Richard's wealth to such an extent that the only money he had was from the rents of the tenants on the estate, together with some income from the West Indies.

Horace Walpole came to stay with him again in 1748, and naturally claimed full credit for the changes of which he very much approved! He returned in 1749, and in his writings described at great length what Rigby had done to improve his gardens, dwelling on the bowers and Kentish fences, with which he said Richard had "flounced himself". Soon after this, Walpole strongly criticized Rigby's friendship with some of the rather dubious politicians; their friendship cooled, and was never the same again.

During the coming years, Rigby entertained most of his friends and political colleagues at the Hall while ardently pursuing his parliamentary career. His sister Anne continued to manage the affairs at the Hall with great efficiency, and was devoted to her brother, but rather concerned by his gambling exploits, and on occasions by some of the dubious characters with whom he was associated. Both Anne and Martha often went to London, where they were welcomed in the high society of the great city. Martha became friendly with a Bernard Hale, a respected officer in the army who subsequently rose to the rank of Lt. General. They were married in 1752 and General Hale had a very distinguished career in the Army. The couple lived in many places in the country, due to the General's army commitments, but had a house in London near Richard's in St. James. Their son Francis who was born in 1756 would ultimately inherit the Mistley estate. General Hale became a very supportive friend of Richard throughout some of the adversities which befell him.

By the year 1752, as his tutor Winnington had predicted, Richard had "discarded virtues, found nothing he did dishonourable, and laughed at the shackles of morality". In doing so he lost the fortune which his father and carefully husbanded for him. History, however, was to repeat itself, as Richard, like his father before him, had a stroke of good fortune. In the months ahead an incident occurred which gave Richard the chance to retrieve his lost fortune, and keep his estate in the village of Mistley Thorne.

His Grace the 4th Duke of Bedford
K.G.
1710-1771
A great friend of Richard Rigby

(By kind permission of the Marquess of Tavistock and the trustees of the Bedford estates)

CHAPTER 12

THE 4th DUKE OF BEDFORD

No doubt Richard Rigby was very concerned that only five years after he had inherited the Mistley estate he had squandered a great part of his fortune in a short period of wild living. He soon found that he had less to spend on the dubious pleasures in which he had indulged since he had acquired his inheritance. More important perhaps was the lack of adequate finance to cover the cost of necessary repairs from time to time. Having spent a small fortune creating splendid gardens at Mistley Hall, Rigby found it very expensive to keep them to the high standard he demanded. Entertaining the numerous friends he invited to the hall was also very costly, and as time went by a strong possibility arose that he would have to dispose of certain portions of the estate in order to survive. Investigations disclosed that his father's will precluded this as the estate was entailed, settling the estate in persons successively, so that it could not be bequeathed or sold.

Rigby continued with his Parliamentary career, and his friends who were gradually becoming aware of the loss of his fortune regularly invited him to their homes. One of his closest companions, as has already been mentioned, was David Garrick, the actor who, owned a house in London near the theatres where he regularly played. Rigby saw most of his plays and Garrick always arranged a private box for him. He did not stop going to the race meetings, and his gambling, although reduced to lower stakes, was unabated. His favourite course was Newmarket, but late in 1752 he went to a meeting at Lichfield possibly to meet David Garrick who lived nearby. During the afternoon - we will never know why - he followed a path leading away from the main paddock and the racegoers. Upon turning a corner near some trees he found a well-dressed gentleman defending himself against some ruffians who were attempting to rob him. The fearless Rigby immediately drew the sword he always carried with him, and severely wounded the assailants, who quickly fled. After the men had returned to the safety of the racecourse, Rigby discovered that the man he had helped was none other than the 4th Duke of Bedford. Rigby had briefly met the Duke before in the House of Commons and over a welcome bottle of wine the Duke expressed his heartfelt thanks.

This account of Rigby's first meeting with the Duke had been widely reported by many writers, but fifty years later the following passage appeared in the Authentic Memoirs of Richard Rigby, written by a member of the family. Speaking of his attachment to the Duke of Bedford, the memoirs state, "this alliance with that illustrious family did not arise - as the tale absurdly does - from having protected his grace from personal insults on the course at Lichfield races, a circumstance which happened some years after their first acquaintance". Whatever happened, a bond of friendship was established which was to last for nearly twenty years.

The Duke of Bedford was one of the most powerful politicians at this time, due partly to his friendship with the King. Although in some quarters the Duke was hated, Walpole described him as "a man of inflexible honesty and goodwill towards his Country. His manner was impetuous, but he was not aware of it, and was too warm and overbearing for the world to think well of him".

Rigby was invited to the Duke's magnificent mansion at Woburn, where he was able to meet many influential people, some of whom were members of the House of Commons. He still retained his close friendship with Henry Fox, and as the years went by he became a leading member of the group of noblemen who surrounded Bedford which became known as the Bloomsbury Gang. Lord North, Lord Weymouth, and the Earl of Sandwich were also prominent members.

It was not long before the Duke realised that Rigby was somewhat embarrassed in his financial affairs, and persuaded him to accept a large personal loan of £5000. The sum of money which the Duke lent Rigby made it possible to settle the demands made against him, and to continue his lavish lifestyle. This cemented their friendship, and Rigby was regularly seen with Bedford in London. Arrangements were also made by the Duke for Richard to become MP for his own constituency of Tavistock, a position he was to hold for more than thirty years. Anyone who owned a large estate could force his workers to vote for the candidate of his choice. The Duke of Bedford was no exception. It was always said that no candidates were safe in Tavistock, where "his meat was in every mouth, and cloth for the wearing was on every loom". However, Rigby worked vigorously to recruit support for the Duke at every turn and occasion.

The Parliamentary scene in England at the time of George II was stormy in the extreme, with hatred and rivalry between the various counties, large parts of which were owned by an Earl, Duke or another member of the landed gentry. Illustrating the ill-feeling, the Earl of Clanrecard criticized the Duke of Bedford's group, including Rigby, in the newspapers, and insolently challenged him to a duel. The Duke rejected the challenge, but Rigby, being made of sterner stuff, accepted immediately. Following this, the Earl quickly withdrew his challenge, having been prepared to duel with the Duke of Bedford, whom he felt he could beat, but considering that he would have little chance against Rigby. Richard was not satisfied, and forced the Earl to sign a guarantee of security, and then the matter was closed. This second act Rigby performed for the Duke further cemented their friendship, which might have seemed unlikely, for whilst the Duke was a quiet and dignified man, Rigby had a coarse side to his nature, was forthright and feared no one. Because of this, few people dared to insult him and Lord Cornwallis, who criticized him unfairly, ended up as his opponent in a duel in Hyde Park. In the end, no conflict actually took place, Cornwallis backing down, and Rigby thus obtaining satisfaction. This episode added further to his reputation as a resolute and fearless opponent.

The Duke was very anxious for Rigby to have his portrait painted, and accordingly arranged for this to be done by Eccardt, a well known artist of the time. The painting, when completed, was hung in the Hall at Mistley. The Duke also wanted a copy of it, and later a replica was painted by L. Barrett, and sent to Woburn. The author recently saw the portrait at Woburn Abbey; it shows Rigby to be an extremely good looking man with dark blue eyes, and greying light brown hair. The frame holding the painting is extremely worn, but was originally beautifully carved and painted in gold. Because of the interest shown in it, the curator at Woburn has had the 230-year-old paining restored, and photographed, and a copy of it is now in the Manningtree museum. The Duke himself was also painted by Gainsborough, probably some time in the 1750s. Some twelve years older than Rigby, the Duke looks extremely dignified, beautifully attired, and wearing the Order of the Garter. Letters speak of a portrait of the Duke hanging in Mistley Hall, and perhaps a copy was made for Rigby. A photograph of the Duke's picture hangs next to his friend Rigby's portrait in the museum.

Towards the end of the 1760s the Duke was asked to lend support to members in Devonshire, where he had some influence. Rigby went with him, but such was the hatred of the politicians from other parts of England that the Duke was stoned by a mob in Honiton. Later he was hunted from the town by inhabitants using a pack of bulldogs. On travelling to Exeter he took refuge in the cathedral, and when it was known he was there a mob congregated. It was fortunate that the vergers summoned help to protect him. Rigby stood by his side throughout, but there is no doubt that the landowners in Devonshire had a great deal of support, and may possibly have stirred up the trouble which the Duke experienced.

In 1750 George II died after a reign lasting nearly thirty-three years, and his grandson ascended the throne as George III. Rigby and the Duke of Bedford, with their group, supported the King, who began to defy the constitution of Parliament and interfere seriously with the running of the country. The King hoped to restore what he considered to be powers that Parliament had usurped, and rule through a body known as the King's Friends, of which Rigby was one. Many constitutional problems arose, and unfortunately the sinister figures of the Queen Mother, and her lover the Earl of Bute goaded the King into illegal actions. Politicians were changing sides daily, mostly by bribery, and history records that Rigby and the Duke of Bedford were "quite unscrupulous one minute, and blushing with roses the next". It was not long, however before support for the King ebbed away. Rigby and the Duke became involved in other matters of the crown, and for much of this time were absent from London, having less influence in the corrupt events which were taking place.

The friendship between Rigby and the Duke continued throughout the 1760s, but the Duke became increasingly unpopular throughout the country, and malicious and unfounded rumours spread. For example, it was said that he had received foreign bribes, and he was reviled as a skinflint. Rigby fought for him tooth and nail, and described him as a rigid patriot who had always served his country. The jealousies which beset politicians may well have confused the 19th century writers who described the circumstances at the time of George III, and it is felt that the criticism of the Duke was ill founded. In this early period of his political life, Rigby's friendship with the Duke of Bedford was of great help to him, but he also owed much to the support he always received from his other great friend, Lord Holland. Rigby's political appointments in the years ahead were to make him a very wealthy man, and much of his riches would be devoted to Mistley, as his father's had been before him.

From his first meeting, Rigby wrote the Duke many letters, and these are all well preserved and recorded in an extensive book of three volumes, by Lord Russell. The book is in the British Museum, and the letters are kept in the Bedford Archives in London.

CHAPTER 13

THE MYSTERY OF FRANCES RUSSELL

During 1759 a strange chapter of events occurred at Mistley, which became a talking point in the village, and ended in a mystery which was never solved. Had the rumours that were rife at the time been proved to have been true, the result could have been of serious embarrassment to the Bedford family.

It appears that early in the year 1759, Richard Rigby arranged for Mrs. Whiting, a local woman, to visit a large house at St. Mary Axe, in London. She travelled to the city in the coach and four, driven by the estate coachman. Upon arriving at the house, she was taken immediately into the housekeeper's room. As she passed through she was very impressed with the luxury of the furnishings, and decoration of the rooms - the house was owned by very rich people. Amongst other attractive ornaments she noticed a service of gold plate. After she had waited for some time, two ladies, beautifully dressed in white satin, and wearing diamonds, arrived, bringing with them a small child, about three years of age. Mrs. Whiting was asked to take the child into her care, and was told that money would be paid regularly for her maintenance and educations. The next day the little girl was taken back to Mistley by coach, and later went to live with Mrs. Whiting at Wix Lodge, a farm owned by Richard Rigby. No information was given to Mrs. Whiting concerning the whereabouts of the little girl's parents, but she was told that the mother's name was Fanny Russell, and the child's name was Frances. Some years later the little girl went to live at Manningtree with Mrs. Whiting, and was educated at Dedham. A Mr. William Russell, who represented himself as the child's uncle, occasionally called on Mrs. Whiting, and arranged a payment of £40 per annum for her keep. Second-hand clothes, of superior design, were regularly sent from London for Frances to wear.

Three years passed peacefully without incident, and Mrs. Whiting was thus surprised by the unexpected visit of two ladies in a horse-drawn carriage, wishing to see Frances. One of them was the lady whom Mrs. Whiting had met when she went to London to bring Frances back to Wix. The two ladies, who were travelling to Harwich, were the Duchess of Bedford and Princess Amelia. They made a great fuss of Frances, and spent much time talking to her. Later in the year she was taken to London to the same house in St. Mary Axe, where a gentleman dressed in a bright red military uniform came to see her. He kissed her fondly, and took her on his knee, later giving her a two-guinea piece. He asked Mrs. Whiting questions about her care for the girl, whom she had looked after as though she were her own daughter. She felt at the time that he could have been the little girl's father. Frances never parted with the two guinea piece, and was to treasure it for the rest of her life.

When Frances was about eleven years of age, Mrs. Whiting had a letter from Mr. Rigby, requesting her to take Frances to visit another house in London. Upon arriving they were taken to see a lady who was lying in bed, obviously very ill. Mrs. Whiting was told that the lady was Frances' mother, Fanny Russell. During the visit to her mother Frances had a long conversation, but no information was given to her about her father. Her mother put her arms around her, and impressed upon her emphatically, that although she was being brought up by Mrs. Whiting she was born in wedlock. Mrs. Whiting, and a very upset Frances returned to Mistley, never to see her mother again.

Some time later it was learned that Frances' mother had sadly died, leaving her a mourning ring and a gold watch, with a provision "never part with this ring tho' you want bread". The ring was inscribed Margarette de Drusina, died 1769, which seemed to indicate that Fanny Russell may have married and become Mrs. De Drusina; strangely, however, there was no report of a marriage which produced her daughter Frances, or any explanation as to why the little girl had been sent to Mistley.

As the years went by Frances grew into a beautiful girl, with lovely auburn hair, and an exquisite complexion. She was described by a friend as "a sweet, mild, gentle, and modest person, who was purity itself". In 1780 or thereabouts, Frances married Thomas Norman, a merchant from Manningtree. She had seven sons and three daughters, who were thus distantly related to the well-known Norman family who lived in Mistley for many years. She died in 1809, and her husband followed her barely six months later.

During the early days after Frances Russell's arrival at Mistley, rumours and gossip spread around the village. At this time, two of the servants at Mistley Hall had been sent to Woburn to teach the Duke of Bedford's servants how to brew beer. Whilst they were there they were told that Frances Russell's father was the Duke's eldest son, the Marquis of Tavistock. On their return the servants talked, the tale quickly spread, and much credence was given to it, as the family name of the Bedfords is Russell. The story went further, claiming that the couple had fled to Scotland, where they were married. If this was true, it would have caused massive problems for the Bedford family. The eldest son of the Duke, who would eventually inherit the Bedford estate, and title, would never have been permitted to marry someone of low birth. Fanny Russell did not confirm these rumours, but it was strange that her daughter was sent to Mistley, the home of the Duke's greatest friend, Richard Rigby. It is also remarkable that the Duchess of Bedford called to see the child at Mistley, and that Frances made a visit to a gentleman in red military uniform, as the Marquis of Tavistock was an officer in the Bedfordshire Militia, whose uniform was red.

However, as time passed, the gossip about the affair died down, and the Marquis of Tavistock meanwhile formed a more suitable alliance. In 1764, Walpole wrote: -

> *"Lord Tavistock has flung his handkerchief to Lady Elizabeth*
> *Keppel, and they all go to Woburn for the ceremony, as soon*
> *as her brother the Bishop can arrive from Exeter".*

It was with some humour that Walpole also wrote: -

> *"I am heartily glad that the Duchess (i.e.Tavistock's mother),*
> *does not set her heart on marrying me to anybody, I am sure*
> *she would bring it about".*

The Marquis and Elizabeth were duly married, with Richard Rigby one of the principal guests. The couple had two sons, and remained happily married until 1767, when a dreadful tragedy occurred. Walpole wrote in the March of that year: -

"Lord Tavistock, the Duke of Bedford's only son has killed himself by a fall, and a kick from his horse while hunting. He has been twice trepanned. The scull is cracked through. No man was ever more regretted: the honesty, generosity, humility, and moderation of his character endeared him to all the world".

Lady Tavistock did not long survive her husband, and was said to have died of a broken heart. The Duke and Duchess of Bedford, although comforted by Rigby, were devastated by the loss of their only son; it was said that Tavistock's death 'all but killed' Bedford.

Some fifty years later when there were few people left alive who would have any recollection of events which happened between 1759 and 1769, the family of Frances Russell became curious that they had no record of their grandparents. The gold watch, the mourning ring with its inscription, and the two-guinea piece, were there to remind them of the past, and much time was spent trying to obtain proof of their birthright. Despite exhaustive enquiries the name of the father of Frances Russell was never established. A further investigation was carried out as late as 1862, and even a hundred years later the subject came to light again without success.

The name of the father of Frances Russell, whose children became the forebears of a highly respected family, who have lived for generations in the village of Mistley, will forever remain a secret.

At the time of writing this book the morning ring was still being handed down through the female line of the family and was in the possession of the mother of an acquaintance of the author.

CHAPTER 14

RIGBY'S PARLIAMENTARY LIFE

There are many vivid accounts describing the character of Richard Rigby during his years in politics, and I have limited this chapter to a brief outline of his career, including incidents that I have found particularly interesting, amusing and typical of the man. Much of what was written about him was derogatory, though research has shown that some 19th century authors' accounts of 18th century Members of Parliament were often gleaned from statements made by others of an opposite political leaning. These were hardly likely to have been complimentary, and in addition, constant repetition over the years has clouded the issue even further. Sir G.O. Trevelyan, in his book, "Early History of Charles James Fox", wrote, *'In politics of the day few exceeded him in duplicity and craftiness'*. James Turner, in his book *"The Dolphin's Skin"*, alleges that Rigby sat, *'at the centre of the bribery, his wits drowned in hogsheads of claret, and his pockets furnished with emoluments of the Pay Office'*. Horace Walpole, in an astute description in his *"Letters"* shows him as an 'advantageous and manly person recommended by a spirited jollity, that was pleasing, though sometimes roughened into brutality but of the most insinuating good breeding when he wished to be agreeable. A man who was seldom loved or hated in moderation, yet, he, himself though a violent opponent, was never a bitter enemy'. Sir Nathaniel Wraxall wrote in *"Historical Memoirs of my Own Time"* that he was *'corpulent, coarse, rough, frank, bold and overbearing'*.

There is no doubt that Richard Rigby was a profuse drinker, but despite what many writers had to say, he never lacked friends who were prepared to share a bottle with him. Referring to his drinking habits, Burke, the politician observed, 'that in the matter of sobriety, he did not observe the morality of geography; as he drank in Dublin, so he drank in London, and as he drank in London, so he drank in the country'. In the story "Mistley in Days Gone By", written in the church magazine more than a hundred years ago, he was described as living, 'a gay life, with love of play, which, with his electioneering expenses he had become somewhat impoverished'. More than two hundred years ago, because of the many allegations, slanderous and otherwise, which had been made against him, a document was published entitled "The Real Character of Richard Rigby". It referred to the 'unaffected candour, and manly integrity which attended him all the subsequent scenes of his life. His talents were miscellaneous, possessing a sound judgement, a true critical taste, and a turn for general enquiry. It was no wonder that he had few equals in speculative, and practical knowledge. His conversation was forcible and exhilarating, however, if his wit was not the most polished, it was potentially original and seldom misapplied. As an orator, many were superior, but he did not trifle with the time and patience of the House, but always commanded attention'. It is probable that Rigby, who had little regard for his political opponents, and made no secret of it, would have incurred the dislike of many. From all accounts it would be true to say that he was probably no worse than many other politicians of his time, but unfortunately attracted more attention than most through the forthright and belligerent way in which he treated some members of the House. It becomes hard, however, to accept the validity of some of the accounts which paint Rigby so blackly, when it is clear that through most of his political life there were many who respected and supported him.

Little of the personal enmity incurred by Rigby related to his early days in Parliament. He was very young when he represented Castle Rising, followed two years later by the constituency of Sudbury. Although he had leanings towards the Whigs, he also studied carefully the policies of the Tories. At this time he was assisted by Henry Fox, who gave him much advice, and did everything he could to advance his political career. Richard soon established himself in Parliament, and later became a staunch member of the Bedford group, as has already been mentioned.

Business in Parliament at this time was carried out with scant regard for ceremony. Gibbon wrote that he found the Commons *'a very agreeable coffee house'*. Members came in wearing their greatcoats, with boots and spurs, and it was not uncommon to see a member stretched out on one of the benches. *'Some cracked nuts, and ate oranges, there was no end to their comings and goings, after a ritual bow to the speaker'*. Rigby was no exception to this trend, often attending sessions dressed in a court suit of purple cloth with no trimmings. With his sword thrust through his pocket, he must have presented a formidable figure, and it was said that he neither feared nor respected the House.

By 1755 Rigby had become the Duke of Bedford's Chief Councillor and Lord Holland prevailed upon him to return to court to use his influence to try to overthrow the Duke of Newcastle, who was then Prime Minister. By 1756, they had been successful, and the Duke of Devonshire had become Prime Minister. Walpole, Rigby's colleague and supporter, was greatly concerned at the dubious methods which had been used, and probably because of it severed his friendship with him. In 1757, the Duke of Newcastle returned as Prime Minister, and Rigby became MP for Tavistock for the remainder of his life.

Soon after this time he was to attain high office, with his first assignment undertaken in Ireland. The Duke of Bedford had been appointed Lord Lieutenant for Ireland, and immediately requested Rigby to accompany him to Dublin as his personal secretary. Exercising his considerable skill in dealing with people, Rigby did much to advance the Duke's standing in Ireland. The Irish took to both the Duke and the Duchess of Bedford, being much impressed by the Duchess's charming and gracious manner. But the person who influenced them most was secretary Rigby. Ireland was at times in turmoil, but Rigby had success in most quarters. He used his considerable skill to wash away dissatisfaction by 'dispensing floods of vice-regal claret'. There is little doubt that he was able to attract people to him, but equally, there were many who opposed him.

One of those who initially opposed him was a Mr. Perry, a bold, corrupt, and troublesome lawyer, but he and Rigby soon had warm relations, and many problems were solved. On one occasion when Rigby was defeated in the Irish Parliament, and was told he should resign, his answer was, *'What do I care; there is nothing in the world I like better than woodcock shooting and claret drinking, and I have both here in perfection - why should I resign?'* There were, however, riots in Dublin, and Perry became obstructive again when Rigby was appointed Master of the Tolls. This office was not connected with his official status, and the Irish thought that the choice of a man whom some considered had little grace was not decent. On one occasion, a mob assembled, erected a gallows, and was determined to hang Rigby on it. Fortunately, that morning he had gone out of town to ride, and received warning not to return! The matter was eventually smoothed over, and the situation grew calmer.

As time went by, the Duke and Duchess of Bedford became famous for their hospitality, and much credit for this happy state of affairs was given to Richard Rigby. Although he was not a great speaker in Parliament, his joviality captivated the unruly Irish capital, and his social habits lingered in its memory. In 1758 he was appointed Commissioner for the Board of Trade. For some time Rigby carried out his duties most satisfactorily, and eventually the King gave him the Vice-Treasureship, at a salary of £3500 per annum. Rigby eventually returned from Ireland in 1763, and was immediately given a seat on the English Privy Council.

A short time after his return, he learned that the Duke of Cumberland, in alliance with Pitt and Lord Northington, was pressing for the vacant Chancellorship of Dublin University. Rigby quickly set off for Ireland, and using his friendship with Dr. Andrews, the Provost, he was able to get the Duke of Bedford elected. The Duke was astonished, and there is no doubt that this example of Rigby's loyal friendship made a great impression on him. During the remainder of his life, the Duke never acted in matters of either public or private concern, without Rigby's advice.

During these years of Rigby's Parliamentary life he had many more friends than enemies, but his exploits in London society raised many eyebrows. Several of the sons of his contemporaries sought his company, as is often the case of young people endeavouring to obtain notoriety by mixing with elders of dubious reputations. The story of one young man named Hobert, (whom Member of Parliament George Selwyn was trying to keep out of mischief) relates; *"Hobert had unfortunately dined that day with Rigby, who had plied his head with too many bumpers, and made him a present of some Chinese crackers. Armed in this manner, he went to Lady Tankerville's house, where tea was being taken. He gave the twenty-four crackers to Lady Lucy Clinton, and bid her to light them with the candle, which she innocently did. When the first went off she threw the rest on the tea table, and one after the other they went off with much noise and not a little stink!"* Selwyn went on to say, *"Lady Lucy was plentifully abused, and Mr. Hobert had his share. Few women will curtsey to him, and I question if he'll ever lead any lady to her chair as long as he lives"*.

In 1763, the Prime Minister, George Grenville, introduced an Act for trying disputed elections. There were implications of bribery in many cases during the recent election of Members of Parliament, and the Act was designed to make it easier for investigations to be carried out. Rigby, who some years before had entertained two hundred freeholders at the Thorne Inn at Mistley, en route to Chelmsford, to vote for two candidates, Harvey and Houblon, fought very strongly against the bill in the debate. His main objection appeared to be that the Act would prevent people from entertaining the electorate!

Whatever had been said about Rigby, he had made a great impression in Parliament, and the most sought after position was to fall to him. On 14th June 1768, he was appointed by the Prime Minister, the Duke of Grafton, to the position of Paymaster General of the Forces. The appointment carried with it the authority to lend and invest some of the vast sums of money which would pass through the Pay Office. Rigby immediately proceeded to lend a considerable amount of the country's money. Much of this money went to his personal friends, several of whom were ladies, and they paid the interest directly to him The interest on many other loans and investments made was also paid into Rigby's account. He was, of course, responsible for the money that he lent, but many of the recipients immediately spent what they had borrowed, and continued to pay the interest, which was usually 5%. There was a very poor accounting system at the Pay Office, and audits were never carried out. It is doubtful if he knew the full amount of money he was lending, and certainly the accountants failed to record everything accurately. Many people who borrowed money had no intention of paying it back, and some of the loans were merely squandered in gambling. Rigby did not appear concerned at the amount of money for which he was responsible; on one occasion he lent his friend Lord North, who was eventually Prime Minister, the handsome sum of £30,000.

At this time unrest was occurring in the American colonies. Taxes levied in London were disputed, and as the years passed the war of independence began. Vast sums of money were allotted for the defence of this part of the Empire, of which no accurate accounts were kept at the Pay Office. Members of Parliament felt that Rigby had a 'paradise of jobbery', and had contrived to settle himself as a permanent occupant, where he kept house for most members of successive administrations.

In the early days at the Pay Office he found that, whilst he was making enemies, who were jealous of his position, these were outnumbered by many friends, whom he entertained lavishly. Parties were regularly held there after the House had risen for the night, and hogsheads of claret were consumed until many guests lay drunk beneath the tables. Rigby, who appeared to have a capacity for drinking greater than most, presided over these expensive gatherings, much to the annoyance of some of the members of the House of Commons.. There is little doubt that the position of Paymaster General had provided him with the opportunity of making vast sums of money, which enabled him to spend extravagantly. Much of the fortune he was making was lost in gambling, and still more in the entertaining he so much enjoyed, both in London and at Mistley.

Whilst Rigby's appointment as Paymaster General had provided him with wealth and prestige, the occasion was overshadowed by the great tragedy of the death of The Marquis of Tavistock, son of the Bedfords, which had brought much grief to the family. Over the next few years, Rigby was regularly at the side of both the Duke and the Duchess, and gave them every comfort. Unfortunately in 1769, their sadness was exacerbated when the Duke was cruelly criticized by his enemies. The writer Irmins, referring to the Marquis of Tavistock's death in a public newspaper, wrote;

> *"How can we take part in the distress of a man, who we can*
> *neither love or esteem, or feel for a calamity of which he himself*
> *is insensible. Where was his father's heart when he could look for*
> *or find immediate consolation for the loss of an only son, in*
> *consultations and bargain for a place at Court".*

Irmins wrote a further insulting letter in the newspaper on 15th October 1769:

> *"Let the friends of the Duke of Bedford observe that humble*
> *silence which becomes their situation. They should recollect that*
> *there are still some facts in store at which human nature would*
> *shudder. I shall be understood by those whom it concerns when*
> *I say that these facts go further than the Duke".*

The veiled insinuations in this letter would immediately have reminded some people, especially those at Mistley, of the rumours which had circulated some years earlier concerning the Frances Russell affair.

Rigby was infuriated by the accusations, and even though he was approaching the age of fifty, was quite prepared to challenge Irmins to a duel. He was, however, prevailed upon to refrain, and the matter was not commented on by the Duke and his family. In behaving in a dignified manner the Duke and his friends secured the support of many public figures, and the subject was eventually forgotten.

The Duke of Bedford died in 1771, and Richard Rigby, who was the executor of his will, had lost the greatest friend he ever had. His death was mourned by many in both public and private life, and had a profound effect on Rigby. They had been close companions for nearly twenty years, and his loss heralded a change in much of his lifestyle. He turned to other interests in the 1770s, spending more time at Mistley, where he began a building programme of tremendous importance to the village, and whilst he still entertained at the Pay Office, he began to use Mistley Hall for wonderful and lavish parties.

In his will, the Duke had released Rigby from the extensive loan which he had allowed him nearly twenty years before, and gave him a further £5000. The long relationship between the two can be summed up in a letter which the Duke had written to a friend some years before. His words were:

> *"We liked each other well enough not to part till three in the morning, long before which time the company was reduced to a tete-a-tete, except one other drunk, and asleep in the corner of the room".*

Richard continued his friendship with the family for the remainder of his life, and the young son of the late Marquis of Tavistock became the 5th Duke of Bedford. The young man was devoted to Richard, who gave him every help and encouragement as he grew older. Records show that the young Duke came to Mistley Hall in 1784, for the shooting season, and greatly enjoyed his stay.

From 1771, Rigby became associated with Lord Weymouth, Lord Gower and Lord Sandwich, and in the years ahead, he was to become the centre of endless stormy sessions in the House of Commons. Without the Duke of Bedford's support, Rigby was often on the defensive in Parliamentary debate, but there is no doubt he always held his own. He seldom spoke from the Treasury bench, but stood square and sturdy on the Opposition side of the House, patronising the Ministers when they merited his approbation, or taking them to task if they showed signs of weakness or timidity. Sir Nathaniel Wraxall wrote that his manner was:

> *"Neither to fear, nor even to respect the House, whose composition as a body he well knew, and to members of which assembly he never appeared to give credit for any portion of virtue, patriotism or public spirit."*

Always intensely loyal to the throne, he became a powerful supporter of the King, who was, at that time, described as "rowing ineffectively against the tide of life". A number of members hung upon Rigby's words in Parliament, as they truly thought that he was interpreting, for their guidance, the policy and innermost wishes of the Sovereign. They cheered his informal speeches, and most voted as he directed them. Often, when the House rose, the more favoured members marched forward at his invitation for entertainment at the Pay Office.

In 1777, Rigby became heated when questions were asked concerning the amount of the

Civil List. It is reported that he spoke to the Chair in terms bordering on disrespect, and many of his supporters disagreed with him on this occasion. In one session, Lord North, the then Prime Minister, had again answered numerous questions on details of the Civil List. Rigby rose and attacked the opposition violently, as he felt that the questions were a slight upon the King and his affairs. He said he was "astonished that the Noble Lord could waste his time in answering all these trifling questions, which had been put to him". Although Rigby felt it his duty to defend the sovereign, the King wrote to the Prime Minister indicating that on this occasion it would have been better if Rigby had refrained from commenting on the subject!

As he grew older, Rigby became more and more truculent in many of his speeches, and it was often felt that he was going too far. This may have been due to the pressure he was under in his position as Paymaster General of the Forces. He had for many years been drawing interest on the enormous mass of the nation's money which passed through his hands. He was criticised from all quarters towards the end of the war in America, and eventually taken to task by Pitt and Charles Fox. Pitt protested, with disgust, saying that the nation was weary of paying cash to a person who profited more by war than any of the members present. Rigby fought his way out of it by bluster, saying, "I will venture to remark that however lucrative my office may be, it has been held by the fathers of the two honourable members who spoke last, and make little doubt, whenever I am compelled to quit it, those gentlemen themselves may have an eye to getting it".

During the time of the American wars, it was estimated that Rigby made himself £20,000 per annum. Many millions of pounds of the country's money were squandered, and when the war was eventually lost, England was on the verge of revolution. Strong government by Earl Shelbourne, as Prime Minister, followed by William Pitt ultimately prevailed, and Richard Rigby left the Pay Office on 10th April 1882, having made a fortune. Rigby thoroughly enjoyed his full life at the Pay Office but the outcome of the serious mismanagement of his tenure at the Pay Office will be seen in chapters ahead.

Shortly afterwards, Edmund Burke became Paymaster General, and found that Rigby had left the affairs in a very sorry state. He immediately demanded that Rigby should pay back the country's money, which he alleged had been put to his own use over many years. It was felt that no precedent could be found in political annals, in which a vast amount of the country's money could have been allowed to be used privately, undetected by a slipshod accounting system.

During the fourteen years that Rigby had spent at the Pay Office, he had become, by somewhat dubious means, a very rich man, and much of his wealth was spent to advantage of Mistley. For in spite of the very long period of time during which he was engaged in politics, Richard never abandoned the village. He frequently travelled long distances to attend to the affairs on the estate from both Ireland, and his house in London. After a brief spell in the very early days during which the estate had become run down, Richard's fortune came to the rescue, and the village of Mistley Thorne became known far and wide for the hospitality at the great Hall and the industry of its villagers.

CHAPTER 15

THE GROWING ESTATE

The valuable agricultural lands which Richard Rigby inherited in 1747 consisted of a small number of farms adjacent to the village of Mistley Thorne. The total area covered less than 2000 acres, and included nearly 300 acres of woodland. For some years, when Richard was away on his grand tour of Europe, the trustees of his father's will continued to manage the estate, and attended to all administrative matters which arose. These arrangements were to continue for several more years, as Richard's duties as a Member of Parliament curtailed his visits to Mistley somewhat. When the House was sitting most of his time was spent at his home in St. James. However he did spend time in the village whenever possible. After he finally inherited the estate, and had become completely responsible for it, Richard decided to engage a steward, named John Bevan, who, for a number of years, ran the estate and affairs in the village. As he grew older and the village expanded, a more active man was needed, and Mr. John Ambrose was appointed.

The Ambroses

Early in 1770, Rigby was introduced to a comparatively young man named Ambrose. He came from a family of solicitors practising at Colchester and Manningtree, and although he was in his thirties he excelled in accountancy, which, combined with his legal talents, made him an ideal choice for the business of running the estate at Mistley. From his initial appointment, three generations of the Ambrose family were to deal with the affairs at Mistley, and the Rigbys' private business of the estate over a period of nearly seventy-five years. The first Ambrose, John, ably assisted by his wife Frances was a very successful manager, and soon after his appointment, Rigby built a house which he called East Lodge, to be used as a residence and estate office by the Ambroses. When he retired from active work, their son, also named John, was appointed steward, at a salary of £150 per annum. By this time the family ran one of the estate farms, Bradfield Lodge, at a tenancy of £105 per annum.

John Ambrose the elder died in 1805, aged 71 years, followed by his wife Frances in 1812. They had faithfully served the family for more than thirty years, and were highly respected by everyone on the estate and in the village.

The younger John Ambrose, who had gained experience with his father managing the estate, and his wife, Henrietta Ann, had a son in 1797, who was christened John Thomas Ambrose. While keeping the traditional family name, they added Thomas, which served to distinguish the successive generations. By the late 1830s, the second John Ambrose, who had also served as steward for more than thirty years, was suffering from ill-health, and his son became the third generation of the family to be steward at Mistley. His father's health deteriorated, and he finally died in 1846, aged 76 years, and his wife four years later.

The third John Ambrose continued as steward even beyond 1845, when the estate changed hands. He died in 1881, and was buried at the foot of the large pine tree in the graveyard of the present church. On the well-preserved and imposing granite stone marking the grave is inscribed:

"In memory of John Thomas Ambrose, who died on the
22nd day of November, A.D. 1881, aged 84.
Lord thou hast been our refuge from one generation
to another, Psalm 90.1."

Then follow these quaint but well chosen lines:

"Peace may it be, your ashes rest
Near to the spot you loved the best
And the dear home that hailed your birth
O'erlooks you in your bed of earth."

Forty-three years later a plaque was placed in Mistley Church, commemorating the lighting installed in 1924 in memory of John Ambrose, a "lifelong inhabitant and constant worshipper at the church".

The Farms.

The size of the estate hardly altered for a number of years, as Rigby had very little capital. However, that changed when he made progress in politics, especially when he became Paymaster General. With the vast resources which became available to him, Rigby set out to buy every farm which came on the market in the area which is known as Tendring Hundred. It was said at that time that Rigby wanted to ride from Mistley to Walton-on-the-Naze on his own land. It is not certain whether this desire was ever achieved, but from the large number and positions of the farms added to the estate, it might have been possible.

In addition to the Essex farms, he acquired meadowland at East Bergholt and Stratford St. Mary. One of the meadows was in the tenancy of Golding Constable, the father of the famous painter. Further large estates were acquired in Bedfordshire and Warwickshire, of which much was forest. A Manor House in Cornwall with lands and tenements, part of a large estate owned by Earl Bathurst, was purchased for £40,000 in 1779.

By the year 1780, Rigby owned the following farms and land in the Tendring Hundred, and many of these keep the same names today.

Walton Hall	-Walton-on-the-Naze
Thorpe Park	-Thorpe-le-Soken
New Hall	-Horsley Cross
Bradfield Hall	-Bradfield
Wix Lodge	-Wix
Abbotts Hall	-Horsley Cross
Stacies	-Lt. Bromley
Dickley Hall	-Mistley
Nether Hall	-Bradfield
Dairy House	-Mistley
Turners	-Wix
Margerums	-Horsley Cross
Bradfield Lodge	-Bradfield

Ford Farm	-Mistley
Crossmans	-Bromley
Spinnels and Everets	-Wix
Gallops	-Wix
Gulos and Ferry	-Bradfield
Pond Hall	-Wix
Snows, Devereax	-Kirby-le-Soken
Whiteheads	-Tendring Hundred
Hubbards	-Tendring Hundred
Trinity Land and Mills	-Mistley
Slipes	-Bradfield
Dale Hall	-Lawford
Landermere Hall and Wharf	-Beaumont
Hemstals	-Horsley Cross
Chappel Land	-Mistley
Tanterfield	-Mistley
Old Hall	-Mistley
Cliff Field	-Mistley
Thorne Pasture	-Mistley
Heath Farm	-Mistley Heath

All the farms were held by tenants, paying an annual rent directly to the steward. The records were kept by John Ambrose during each farming year and were carefully written in immaculate hand. The rents included a land tax, and were charged in accordance with the size and acreage of the farm. The largest of these was Walton Hall, tenanted by John Bernard, at a rent of £242 per annum.

One Abraham Carrington, at the small farm called Crossmans, with a rent of £60 per annum, fell upon hard times and came to owe £20. The amount continued to show as a debit against him on the accounts on each lady-day, which indicated the kindness shown to the tenants, as no action appears to have been taken to remove him from his farm. The rents varied widely; John Ambrose was paying £80 per annum for his farm at this time, but later the rents were to rise. Nether Hall, on the banks of the Stour, including creeks and a Parsonage House, was let at a rent of £128 per annum. The two farms, Abbotts and Stacies, situated closer to Mistley Hall, were set at £150 each, and rented by Joseph Nunn and John Barton.

A variety of crops were grown, in which there had been little change over the past seventy-five years, and the employment was mainly seasonal. The wage of a labourer was about 8/- to 10/- per week, but some suffered great hardship, as they were not always in full employment. Barley, wheat and oats were grown in increasing quantities, and much of the crop was shipped to London from the Mistley Wharf. Dairy herds were kept on selected farms, and over the years since Rigby's father owned the estates, there was an increase in trade in wool, which fed the extensive spinning trade of the weavers nearby in Dedham.

During the 1770s a programme of maintenance on most of the properties was carried out, many of which had been allowed to fall into some degree of disrepair over the past years. An ongoing problem was the maintenance of the roadways. It became the responsibility of everyone to keep these as level as possible, but sadly many of the highways were almost impassable during the winter months. Fortunately there was ample ballast in the Mistley area, which was widely used on the roads

An excellent relationship was maintained between John Ambrose and the tenants, and Rigby much enjoyed riding over the estate and meeting his tenants. In 1775, Richard entertained all his tenants to a dinner at the Thorne Inn, at a cost of £12-1.0, which seems an incredibly small amount for so many people!

By 1780, the agricultural estate had increased to more than thirty farms and small-holdings which were well run by experienced tenants. Rigby had benefited greatly from his position at the Pay Office, and in true character, as soon as money was available he spent it liberally. To his credit, however, a great proportion of it was devoted to the benefit of others.

Field Sports and Poaching.

The great estate, which had steadily increased in size, provided excellent opportunities for field sports. Rigby hunted regularly, and friends from all over the country enjoyed both the excellent sport, and the lavish hospitality he provided afterwards. Spacious stables were built at Mistley Hall, where experienced grooms and stable lads proudly exercised and maintained hunters of the finest breeds.

There is no evidence that Rigby neglected his duties in government by participating in the sport he loved so much, but it is a fact that some of the 'noble gentlemen' often put their country pursuits before attendance in the House. The Duke of Richmond wrote to Burke in November 1772, saying, "I would not wish to stir from hence till after Christmas, as I have engaged a large party to come here on 1st December to stay a month to fox hunt". It is difficult to understand how the country survived under the easy-going assembly of George III's Parliament, with the many distractions keeping them away from the House. Some were described as, "Meeting just as the first touch of winter suggests to mankind the wisdom of getting together in cities to keep one another warm; breaking off in December for a month's hunting, and finally dispersing to their country-houses in time for the last of the lilacs, and the laburnums". Rigby, on the other hand, managed to combine his love of sport and entertaining at Mistley with his career as an MP in London.

Coursing, too, took place in this part of the country, as the land was especially flat, and hares were plentiful. There is no record that Rigby was much attracted to the sport, but some of the tenants on the farms regularly attended the meetings.

As the estate was well-wooded there was an abundance of game of every variety, especially pheasants and woodcock, and during the winter, shooting parties were held weekly.

The woods in the park at Mistley were also home to large numbers of deer. One area of Dove House Farm is still known as the Deer Park. These animals were preserved for the aesthetic quality they gave to the countryside, as well as being used for venison.

Cottages were provided for the Gamekeepers on various parts of the estate. One was in the park near the lake over the field which is now known as Furze Hills, and another by the side of the wood called Skiphatch, near Horsley Cross, which is situated to the south east of Dickley Hall. At one time a cottage also stood on the bend of the Horsley Cross road now known as Gamekeepers Corner.

In 1780, John Carrington was the senior Gamekeeper on the estate at Mistley. He had long experience in the art of breeding all sorts of game, and returning them to the wild. In fact he The great woodlands provided ideal natural cover and roosting places for the pheasant and woodcock. The small amount of woodland on the farms today has reduced the natural breeding of pheasants, and there are very few woodcock to be found locally. In the 18th century the woodlands at Mistley were alive with birds, and John Carrington was able to arrange the drives of the birds to the best advantage.

Poaching was prevalent at this time. The following humorous reference to the pursuit of game appeared in the local morning paper at Mistley late in the 18th century, entitled *"Statutory Hints"*:

> *"The time is approaching, when the innocent and unsuspicious Partridge, will attract the nose of the sagacious pointer, and fall a victim to the vivid discernment of the expert gunner; hence preparation will daily take place, and for the month of September all other amusements must be laid aside for the manly exercise of the trigger. Then beware, O ye poachers in the neighbourhood of Mistley, hamper not your game, use no subterfuge for qualifications, not even the strong produce of an annuity. Take care of the traps and guns, which are set for detection of the hedge sculkers after the sun is down, Go not in a chaise or cart lest the noise should betray you. Get home before the croaking owl pays her nocturnal visit to the dormouse. For fear the stalking figure of ingratitude should accost you, with menace more fierce and terrible that the hero mouthed, in the renowned engagement with the woman in the gin shop. Say you have sinned against the Holy Ghost. Feed not your servants with the stewed bones of those birds which are not marketable. Peradventure they may impeach, and tell the secrets of the prison house. But should the rude intermeddling hand of justice lay hold of you, it will be necessary to advance something in the strain of insinuation and deception in order to delude and subvest its progress. Say you come from the north near the Tweed, affect to take snuff, talk mightily large of your property. You cannot promise too much. Should you escape your deserved punishment, never resort to poaching in the region of Mistley lest they catch you again".*

Poachers of whom there were many, may well have paid heed to this warning, but some men, with young mouths to feed, felt there was no alternative than to risk the gamekeepers, and the law, in order to provide a meal for their families.

Much of the Gamekeeper's time was spent in combatting the increasing amount of poaching. On some occasions as many as twenty ruffians would travel in carts to a selected area, where they shot everything they could find in the woods, while dogs were used in the fields. The poachers were often intoxicated, and there was very little the Gamekeepers could do under these circumstances. Fortunately for the Rigby estate this type of poaching did not occur very often. A vivid description of multiple poaching is given in the interesting book written by the Rev. Richard Cobbold called *"Margaret Catchpole"*.

A Trial for Poaching at Mistley.

A particularly interesting case involving three local men was tried at the Essex Assize at Chelmsford in 1786.

The case concerned the prosecution of Francis Strango, James Sandors and Richard Smith, before Mr. Justice Gould for "assaulting John Carrington, Gamekeeper to the Right Hon. Richard Rigby, and several other servants of Mr. Rigby, who were in company with the said John Carrington".

The counsel for the prosecution were the Hon. Mr. Erskine and Mr. Adam, with the solicitor Francis Smithies of Colchester.

There were three indictments preferred. The first was against Francis Strango, James Sandors, and Richard Smith, and contained two counts.

> *"First Count; charged that the defendants on 19th November in the 26th year of his present Majesty, at Mistley in Essex, with force and arms, did assemble, and meet together to the disturbance of the publick peace, having so assembled together then and there with force and arms, with certain guns, then and there loaded (to wit) a powder and leaden shot, and slugs and with sticks, which the defendants respectively then in their hands, and have in and upon one John Carrington, in the peace of God, then and there being did make an assault on him and the said John Carrington, did, then and there beat, wound, ill-treat, so that his life was greatly despaired of, with the intent, him, the said John Carrington, then and there feloniously, wilfully, and of malice aforethought to kill and murder, and other wrongs to the said John Carrington, then and there did, to the great damage, etc., and against the peace etc.".*

> *"Second Count; charged the defendants, being so unlawfully, riotously assembled, and met together as aforesaid on that day, with force and arms etc., at the Parish aforesaid, in and upon the said John Carrington did make an assault, to the damage etc., and against the peace".*

Before the defendants (who were in custody) were called upon to plead against this indictment, Mr. Justice Gould asked to look at it, and enquired Mr. Erskine the nature of the prosecution, which Mr. Erskine related to him, whereupon Mr. Gould replied saying *"The indictment was wrong. The defendants ought to have been indicted under the Act 9 Geo. 1st"* (called the Black Act).

Mr. Erskine said *"To be sure they might, but Mr. Rigby preferred the milder mode of prosecution".*

"Well", Mr. Gould said, *"You may try them, but I hate the game laws".*

The defendants were called to the bar, and pleaded not guilty.

Report of the trial by the Clerk to the Court.

John Carrington was called in support of the charges contained in the indictment on the part of the prosecution, and swore that he was the Gamekeeper to the Right Hon. Richard Rigby. On "Saturday evening the 19th November last", as he, together with James Crooks, William Ward, Philip Clark and Richard Young, four other servants of Richard Rigby were going round the Manor of Mistley, they heard a gun go off several times in or near Margerum's wood in Mistley, the property of Richard Rigby (through which there was no path or common way). Upon hearing these guns, the witness and his companions immediately hastened, and having got into the wood saw the flash of a gun going off twice, and in a few minutes came up with the three defendants. Strango and Sandors each had a gun in his hand, and Smith a large stick. As soon as the defendants saw the witness and his companions, (which was not until they were close to them), Strango immediately presented his gun close to the witness' breast, and Smith at the same time struck at the witness with his large stick, and called to Strango, "damn him", "shoot him", "shoot him". At this instant the witness took hold of the muzzle of the gun, and with great difficulty put it out of the direction of his breast, for Strango tried all he could to keep it in a direction of the witness' head or breast, and whilst engaged Strango fired the gun, the witness having the muzzle in his hand, but luckily no mischief ensued, and witness further added that he was sure the gun going off was not occasioned by any struggle between him and the defendant Strango. Witness also swore that he thought he saw defendant Smith at the same time throw something away into the wood, but found nothing that night, being too much engaged in taking and disarming the defendants to look much about. His companions took the gun from Sandors, which was loaded with powder and large shot. The next day the witness with his brother Richard Carrington went into the wood to look for what the witness thought he saw Smith throw away, and there found a pair of bags, with two braces and a half of fresh shot pheasants, and one pheasant wounded and alive. This testimony of John Carrington was minutely confirmed by Crooks, Ward, Clark and Young in all respects, except finding the pheasants the next morning, which was confirmed by Richard Carrington.

Crooks, Clark, Ward and Young all swore positively to their hearing the report of the gun six times, which exactly corresponded with the number of pheasants found in the bag thrown away by Smith.

Examination.

The defendants had no counsel, and Mr. Justice Gould interrogated each of the witnesses in this point, in this manner. "Will you take it upon yourself to swear that the defendants would not have gone about their business without assaulting you, if you had not interrupted them?". They replied in general terms that they conceived it their duty to seize all persons of such description as the defendants whom they may find in the act of destroying game, or assembled for that purpose.

Mr. Justice Gould then summed up the evidence to the jury very briefly, observing it was not in evidence before them that the defendants had assembled themselves for any unlawful purpose but they had offended against the game laws. That offence, however, was not subject to the present indictment, and therefore they must acquit them, but the defendants were still liable to a prosecution for an offence against the game laws. The jury remained for a considerable time considering this charge, without giving a verdict. The Clerk to the Assize asked them if they were agreed in their verdict; they said no, whereupon Mr. Justice Gould told them they must acquit the defendants, as no evidence was before them to pass the defendants guilty of the charges laid in the indictment. The jury consulted again, and reluctantly gave a verdict in favour of the defendants.

The second indictment also contained two counts, and was somewhat similar to the first; *"Defendant Sandors presented his gun directly to the breast of William Ward, and bid him keep his distance. Notwithstanding, Ward went up to the defendant pretty quick who hit his foot on the stub of a tree causing him to stumble whereupon Ward rushed in upon the defendant and seized his gun and took it from him"*. Ward's testimony was confirmed by the other witnesses. Mr. Justice Gould then said to the witness, *'Did not the defendant retreat from you'*, to which Colin Ward replied, *'Yes, for a few paces'*. Mr. Gould then addressed the jury, saying, *"Why d'ye see gentlemen of the jury, so far as these men assembling for the purpose of committing an assault, they would have got away if they could. Gentlemen you must acquit the defendants"*. The jury accordingly gave a verdict of not guilty.

In the third indictment there were also two counts similar to the others, except that in this case the witness, Crooks, swore that on seeing Smith striking at Carrington with a large stick ran up to him and seized him by the collar. The defendant Smith struck a violent blow at Crooks' head, which he caught on his hand, and said that he lost the use of his arm for a considerable time and suffered great pain with it. At this point Mr. Justice Gould interjected and asked Crooks, *"did you not go up to the defendant and seize him by the collar before you received the blow on your hand from the defendant?"* Crooks replied, *"I certainly did go up to the defendant to take him when I saw him striking at John Carrington with a large stick"*. *"Oh then"*, said Mr. Gould, *"I suppose he only struck you on the hand to make you let go your hold, why do you not see, gentlemen of the jury, the prosecution committed the first assault, for if a Gamekeeper seizes a man, because he is illegally taking pheasants he is guilty of an assault, for the law does not warrant a Gamekeeper touching a man for such an offence. He has no remedy but action by information, and the defendants are now liable to a prosecution notwithstanding your verdict to acquit them"*.

The jury gave their verdict of not guilty. This concluded the case against the defendants, and at this point, Mr. Justice Gould addressed the defendants, saying, *"I suppose you had been shooting Mr. Rigby's pheasants, they roost upon the trees of a night, don't they? You should not do these things, for you are liable to a prosecution by a civil action or information, but I hope they will not prosecute you any further"*. At this point a further conversation took place between Mr. Justice Gould, Mr. Erskine, the defendants and Mr. Smithies.

Mr. Gould: *"Mr. Erskine, will you undertake that these poor fellows will not be prosecuted further"*.

Mr. Erskine: *"I've no instructions, my Lord, for such an undertaking"*.

Mr. Gould: *"Will you undertake, Mr. Erskine, if these poor fellows will give me their word that they will never go poaching to Mr. Rigby's woods and park again"*.

Mr. Erskine: *"I cannot undertake, my Lord, I've no instructions"*.

Mr. Gould, to defendants: *"Hark, ye my honest friends, will you promise me that if you are not prosecuted any further that you will never go poaching to Mr. Rigby's again"*.

Defendants: *"Indeed, my Lord, we never will"*.

Mr. Gould: *"Why there, Mr. Erskine, d'ye see, did I not tell you they would give me their word they would not go there again, consult with your solicitors, Mr. Erskine"*.

Mr. Erskine, to Mr. Smithies: *"Well Smithies, you hear what my Lord says, what shall I tell him?*

Mr. Smithies: *"Tell his Lordship that if he will become surety for them, I will consent to such an undertaking, but on no other terms"*.

Mr. Erskine: *"My Lord, the solicitor will not permit such an undertaking"*.

Mr. Gould: *"Mr. Smithies, will you advise Mr. Rigby not to prosecute these poor fellows further"*.

Mr. Smithies: *"I certainly will my Lord"*.

Mr. Gould: *"I daresay, Mr. Smithies, Mr. Rigby will do nothing further in it without consulting you; if he does consult you, will you be so good as to advise him not to prosecute any further"*.

Mr. Smithies: *"I am sorry to differ in opinion with your Lordship in this matter; if my advice should be asked, it will be directly to the contrary"*.

Soon after the trial had finished, Mr. Smithies caused information to be laid before a magistrate against the three defendants, for shooting pheasants in the night, who summoned them to appear before him to show cause why they should not respectively be convicted. Smith only appeared, and not being able to show any cause to the contrary, the magistrate convicted them all. Smith was fined the sum of £10, and Strango and Sandors £20 each.

Mr. Justice Gould obviously had a dislike for the game laws, which was probably responsible for the biassed comments he made during the trial. Rigby, however, felt he had to support his Gamekeeper and other servants, especially as they might have suffered serious injury in loyally doing what they considered was their duty.

Sometime later a Mr. Robert Kerridge was appointed as Gamekeeper on the estate. In his terms of employment it was laid down that he was able to kill game for home use, and take and seize all guns, bows, greyhounds, hunting dogs, lurchers, ferrets, trammels, nets, hare pipes and snares.

The estate became renowned for the well-organised sport provided, in a truly beautiful setting. There is little doubt that the wonderful opportunities for rural sports were matched only by the lavish hospitality given to the guests who were fortunate enough to be invited to Mistley.

The Woodlands.

When Richard Rigby's grandfather inherited the Mistley estate in 1709, the woodlands totalled 276 acres. By the latter part of the century many of these had been cleared and others planted. The fields on which the woods had stood retained the original names. A great many of the trees at this time had been self sown, due to the density with which they covered the countryside, but Rigby practised careful husbandry in which groups of trees or spinneys were planted. Their purpose was to shade the cattle, and many were planted near a spring which would give a pool beneath.

On the Mistley estate there were numerous streams, which ran down the headlands of some of the fields, and through many of the woodlands. Most of these streams and pools are in existence today, running as they did nearly three hundred years ago, and are still able to provide ample water for the farms.

To manage the extensive forests on the estates, which apart from Mistley stretched all over the Tendring Hundred, a wood gardener was engaged at a salary of £15-15-0 per annum. His duties were to keep records, inspect all woodlands regularly, and organise the planting programme. The majority of the trees on the estates were oak, elm, sweet chestnut and ash, but other varieties were also grown. Careful selection was carried out before any of the trees were felled, a considerable number of which were sold to the shipyard on the quay. Workmen cut the timber into specially measured lengths, to the specification requested by the shipbuilders. The majority of the smacks, hoys, barges, and other larger craft built at the Mistley shipyard were constructed from timber from the Rigby estates.

Mr. Paskell, of Wix, (probably an ancestor of the owners of the timber yard of the same name) bought 33$\frac{1}{2}$ feet of maple, and 79$\frac{1}{2}$ feet of plane. Mr. Betts and later Mr. Howard of the Mistley shipyard were continually buying loads of timber, and on one occasion Mr. Betts bought 190 loads at £4-10-0 per load.

Although much felling had been done, the large farms comprising the estate were extremely rich in woodlands and there was a considerable income from the sale of timber for building both houses and ships. The wars against Spain and France resulted in increased timber required for shipbuilding, many forests suffering severe losses towards the end of the 18th century.

In the 1780s Mr. J. Betts built some very fine ships at his slipway at Mistley, and eventually the yard was tenanted by Mr. James Howard, both of whom employed a number of skilled craftsmen from the village.

Rigby's Mistley estate finally increased in size to include twenty large woodland areas varying from 32 acres to just over one. In addition to the woods, each farm had many small plantations, which contained fine individual trees.

The many other large farms owned by Rigby in the Tendring Hundred also had a high proportion of woodland; in the forest of Walton Hall, for example, there were 7872 oak trees, 2476 ash, and 274 saplings.

The largest wood on the entire estate was called Margerum's, and part of it was situated on the New Hall Farm at Horsley Cross. The wood ran to the westward from the right-hand side of the main road, just short of the present Cross Inn. Nearby was Margerum's Hall, which was described at that time as a "lovely attractive Mansion House". It was surrounded by beautiful gardens, and had a few smaller buildings closer to it. It was one of the very old buildings in Mistley, and at one time was lived in by a Mr. Grimson, a well-known gentleman in the Tendring Hundred. The Hall was eventually demolished and an extension built to New

Hall Farm. The position of this ancient mansion is unknown, but it is possible that it stood to the south of the large wood, as maps show an area named Old Hall Meadow. On the other side of the Horsley Cross road was a further extensive area of forest, which was on the Bradfield Farm, not owned by Rigby. This great forest stretched along the Harwich Road almost to the village of Wix. The road ran through it for a distance of several miles, entering it where the Inn now stands at Horsley Cross. There is no trace of that wood now, nor of that known as Margerum's, but there is a field of the same name in the same position at the present New Hall Farm.

All the woodlands had names, and it is interesting to find that the wood on the right-hand side of the present Green Lane to where Mistley Hall once stood, was there in 1775, and known as "Clock Plantation". The present wood on the opposite side of the road was also there, and is still known as the "Round Clump". The number of trees in this wood was recorded in 1775, and consisted of 32 firs, 46 chestnuts, 10 elms, 9 sycamore, and one horse chestnut. A wood of 15 acres ran along the Horsley Cross road opposite to Ford Farm, and was called "Alder Car". Just to the north of the lofty television mast, a wood known as the "Old Mount" is still there in which the old Mistley Hall once stood. This wood consisted in 1775 of 25 oaks, 30 elms and 3 chestnuts. A very different tree composition exists there today, but records show that it existed more than 250 years ago. "Skiphatch Wood" was also there in 1775 and still stands near Dickley Hall, as does the wood known as "Beech Plantation", or "Bluebell Wood" opposite Ford Farm, at the bottom of the hill.

Mistley Hall Park was surveyed in 1775, and the following large number of trees was recorded:

    486 oaks
    343 firs
    97 alders
    512 elms
    116 chestnuts
    23 birch and poplars
    48 ash
    40 beech
    16 plane
    60 lime

Some of these trees in the area of Furze Hills and Gamekeeper's Pond are still growing, but, alas, in rather poor condition.

On the nearby Dove House Farm, which was part of the Deer Park, were growing the following:

247 oaks	8 horse chestnut	10 birch
271 elms	40 alders	4 chestnut

Plantations and forests added a charm to the countryside around Mistley, and the River Stour was tree-lined on both the Essex and Suffolk sides. These extensive woodlands on the estate were Rigby's pride, but sadly disaster was to overtake them; the forests were devastated by a hurricane at the latter part of the 18th century. History has recorded that over the years, the incidence of a hurricane or extremely strong gales often occurred towards the end of a century. The hurricane and succession of gales which occurred in 1795/6 measure up to that of 1987, which also robbed us of a large proportion of our trees.

The dreadful hurricane of the 18th century played havoc with the estates, but by then Richard Rigby was dead. It is reported that in the November of 1795, thousands of buildings were destroyed by storms, and raging tides. The sea banks at Walton Hall were breached in many places, and the Landermere Farm and Wharf suffered much damage. Sums of £30-13-9 and £33-9-4 were spent on repairs to the Soken estate, and £34-13-6 at Walton Hall. Margerum's Wood was very badly damaged, and fallen elm and ash trees were retrieved and cut into 11' lengths. Thirty-two loads were delivered to the shipyard at Mistley Quay at a price of £2-5-0 per load.

There was much damage, too, on the Bedfordshire and Warwickshire estates, and the fallen trees were cut onto the appropriate lengths of $5^1/_2$ feet and sent to Mr. Betts at the shipyard at a price of £4-0-10 per load.

Nature is a great healer however, and the woods were eventually to recover. Many years later, with a regular planting programme, the woodlands at Mistley were returned to their former grandeur.

Rigby's agricultural estate had rapidly grown in size, and the rent roll had increased to more than £5000 per annum. During the years up to the mid 1780s the estate reached its peak, for which much credit must be given to the steward, John Ambrose.

This halcyon period was sadly to draw to a close over the next few years, as circumstances arose which resulted in the disposal of the greater part of the comparatively new estate. These circumstances and their outcome, are dealt with in the chapters ahead.

CHAPTER 16

RIGBY - LORD OF THE MANOR

Mistley was fortunate in being one of the few large estates in which the owner was regularly in residence, and consequently able to manage it on a personal basis with the help of stewards. As has already been said, estates all over England at this time were owned by landed gentry who frequently treated them as remote spots, from which they took rents but seldom visited, and gave nothing in return. A further advantage to Mistley was that Rigby had a fervent desire to serve as Lord of the Manor, and Squire of the village.

From the time of his inheritance of the land and property at Mistley in 1747, despite having responsibilities in London as an MP, he carried out his duties diligently for nearly 40 years. During this time he gave much of his attention to the villagers, and ensured that there was little hardship. After the rather self-inflicted problems of the first few years, which led to the loss of some of his fortune, his great friendship with the Duke of Bedford led to a much improved financial position. Later, with a new found source of wealth, obtained from his position at the Pay Office, he was able to provide additional houses, and enlarge the industries which secured employment for many. While, as Paymaster General, he suffered much criticism from his political enemies, there is little doubt he was a very popular figure at Mistley Thorne.

When he was at home at the Hall, although most of his leisure time was spent in various sporting activities, he also had a great love for the sea. He kept a large yacht at Mistley, which he frequently sailed in the river and beyond. Amongst his numerous friends in Mistley and Manningtree were some of the families of fishermen who regularly risked their lives sailing with their frail craft to the far northern waters. A number of the Mistley mariners, with their professional skills, regularly accompanied him as members of his crew. His personal friends from London also came to Mistley to sail. He enjoyed the carefree life on the water, and with the help of the fishermen often returned with fine catches.

Sporting activities.

In his young days Richard became a very keen cricketer. His introduction to the sport came about through his friendship with the Duke of Bedford, who was no mean batsman. Many of the country's most competent cricketers could be seen at his own famous ground at Woburn. The Mistley cricket field, off the New Road, with its fine pitch, was prepared by the gardeners from the Hall more than 230 years ago. The Duke and other notable people around the country played regularly at Mistley. Some of the games were played for very high stakes, and often as much as a thousand guineas would change hands. A scorebook was found many years ago recording a match between Ipswich and East Suffolk Cricket Club and Mistley, which at the time may have been Rigby's team.

The roadway connecting the Hall to the Manningtree road ran alongside the western end of the cricket field, and is now part of the outfield of the present ground. The then gravel road is now covered by grass, but the outline can be clearly seen running from the New Road to the railway bank when the weather is very dry.

The villagers would have watched this comparatively new sport with interest, and no doubt many of them would have adjourned to the Thorne Inn at the end of matches for a convivial evening.

Amongst other sports at this time, we also find that Rigby was a keen bowls player. He was a member of the Dedham Bowls Club, and although little is known of his playing ability, the Mistley accounts show that he paid a regular subscription.

With the numerous farms stretching for miles into the Tendring Hundred, Rigby enjoyed riding to hounds, and became a very accomplished horseman. At one time he spent many hours shooting wildfowl at Walton, and also Woodcock, which were found in abundance at the Walton Hall forest. His enthusiasm for wildfowling did not last long, as the open marshes were very cold during the shooting season, and offered little cover. In the Hall park at Mistley the game was allowed to roam unmolested, and provided a fine aesthetic effect amongst the trees and shrubberies.

Theatre and Romance.

Richard frequently attended the London theatres, having formed friendships with David Garrick and many other notable actors and actresses of the time. Later, in 1783, he built a theatre at Manningtree, and knowing so many London performers, he was able to entice some of them to Manningtree from Covent Garden. Rigby became patron of the theatre, where most of the performances were played to packed audiences. Four plays were produced soon after the theatre opened, and tickets were eagerly bought from the Thorne Inn, for *School for Scandal, The Padlock, Love Makes a Man, and Cupid's Frolic*. The music was composed by Mr. Tatnal, from the Theatre Royal at Covent Garden, who also conducted the orchestra. The theatre continued to be popular for many years. Long before this, Richard had met many of the most beautiful actresses of the time, and some of these attractive ladies were invited to stay at Mistley Hall to attend lavish parties . It is, then, something of a mystery that Rigby never married, especially when there were so many opportunities presented to him.

An extract from the "Sketch of the Real Character of Richard Rigby" reveals his feelings towards the opposite sex, in these well-chosen words:

> *"Though never married - nor indeed known to have expressed any violent inclination for the bonds of wedlock, he was fond of the society of women - and by his gallantry and attention made a tender impression on some of the proudest female hearts in either Kingdom. His figure was tall, without anything peculiarly graceful - yet his address and manner were elegant and commanding. It has been remarked that in the prime of life, Mr. Rigby sacrificed pretty freely to conviviality - and it were in vain to contradict it when he had left behind him two or three stubborn evidences of the fact".*

One of Rigby's lady friends in the early days was a mantua-maker, named Martha Reay, who was engaged as a milliner in Tavistock Court in London. She had taken small parts in amateur theatricals, and when Richard saw her on the stage, he was much attracted to her. She was soon to be invited to Mistley Hall, and Richard was delighted when she shared his love of the sea. They met frequently, and Richard bought her a small tea shop in a tower at Walton-on-the-Naze. He often rode, or drove, over to see her, and she regularly stayed at Mistley Hall. She shared in the entertainments at Rigby's home, and became very popular with his friends. She eventually married the Earl of Sandwich, who was a great friend of Rigby, and like him an MP. During the 17 years she was married to him she had a number of children. Fate, however, was to intervene. During an oratorio held at Hinchingbrooke Church, she was introduced to Capt. James Hackman, a soldier in the 68th Foot. It is not known if he ever came to Mistley, but it is certain he fell in love with Martha, and pestered her, causing great embarrassment. She was living in London at the time, and found it very difficult to avoid seeing him, and was concerned that he might use violence on her husband, who was by this time in 1770 an elderly man. Hackman proposed marriage, but on being rebuffed by Martha, resigned from the Army and became ordained. For months he endeavoured to see her, but she avoided him at every opportunity. Hackman, finally became completely unhinged, and one evening after drinking very heavily went to Covent Garden. Outside, he waited for Martha to come from the theatre, where she had enjoyed a performance of *Love in a Village*. The wicked Hackman primed his pistols, and shot her dead. Martha, mourned by Sandwich and Rigby, was buried at Elstree, whilst Hackman was hanged at Tyburn. Soon after this tragedy, Rigby added the unique towers to Mistley Thorne Church. He and Sandwich stood together at the dedication ceremony, and it was always said that the reconstruction which Rigby carried out was done as a tribute to Martha Reay, and the happy times he had spent with her at the little tea shop at Walton.

Although Rigby was reported to have been fond of women, and made a tender impression on a number of them little has been discovered of his ventures with the opposite sex in the circles in which he moved in London. It is, however, known that in his early days he had a great favourite who lived at nearby Colchester named Jenny Pickard. She was reputed to be very beautiful and frequently stayed at Mistley Hall where she was always at Rigby's side at the parties he held. She sadly died at an early age, having had a daughter, who was also named Jenny. Rigby made sure that his daughter was well cared for, and arranged for her education. She never married, and in his will, Rigby left her £100 per year, to be taken from the profits of the estate. Some time later, Rigby met Mrs. Sarah Lucas from Ipswich. Sarah was a widow, and for several years she and Richard were inseparable. She bore him a daughter, also named Sarah who became much loved by Richard's unmarried sister, Anne, spending a large part of her life with her. On reaching her twenties, she married the Rev. Newman, who was Rector of Little Bromley Church. Sarah and Richard remained close friends for many years, and it will always be a mystery why they never married. Perhaps she was considered to be socially inferior, an important consideration in those days among the landed gentry. Late in her life she married Isaac Fisher, a farmer from Wherstead near Ipswich. In his will, Rigby left her £1000, and a further £5000 to the daughter she had borne him.

True to his character, Rigby had accepted his responsibilities and made provision for his children, whom he saw regularly when he was at Mistley.

The Population Increase.

By the 1760s, because of the expanding industry, many more people wished to live at Mistley, and so Richard completely reorganised Mistley Green, which had always been an open grassy space. He built twelve houses on the northern side, which are still there, with a small road in front, and a fine brick wall at the western end. The rents for the twelve houses totalled £62 per year; they were soon let to some of the older families in the village. Rigby advised John Ambrose, the steward, to be selective in his choice of tenants, and under no circumstances allow any of them to be inhabited by rough seamen. To complete the enclosure a number of horse chestnut trees were planted behind the wall. The trees grew into magnificent specimens, and survived until approximately 30 years ago, when they became dangerous and had to be felled, a large branch of the northernmost tree having collapsed on to the roof of the end house, causing a great deal of damage. Other properties were constructed at the eastern end of the green, and included a tiny school and a custom house. Mr. Ambrose, the steward, lived in the beautiful East Lodge, and when the estate was eventually sold, Mistley Green was left to him, with the provision that the residents could have the use of it, and strict regulations were imposed in order to keep it private. East Lodge was completely isolated from the Green by a tall brick wall, which is still there, and had a magnificent garden, with a wonderful view over the park to the Hall above. A number of lofty oak trees lined the paddock, which were eventually felled in order to create the railway bank where the Eastern Union line to Harwich was constructed in 1850.

With the growing population, the congregation at the village church grew. Rigby regularly attended the services with his sister Anne, together with other members of the family when they were staying at the Hall. Sadly, Richard's uncle, the Rev. David Mustard, died in 1775. He had been the priest in the village for more than fifty years, having been the last to officiate at the old church at Mistley Heath. He was succeeded by the Rev. Richard Daniell, who with the curate, the Rev. Mather Thompson, was in charge during the reconstruction of the church in the 1770s. The Rev. Thompson became the rector in 1779 and held the post for a further 27 years.

After the building of the houses, Mistley Thorne was centred around the Green, and became a close-knit community, most of the members of which worked on, or were connected with the estate. Inevitably however, a number of the elderly residents were quite poor, and in 1775 the accounts show that Richard Rigby gave a sum of £20-1-6 to the poor of the village at Christmas.

Richard began spending more time at Mistley in the 1770s in order to oversee the large building programme which had occupied his mind for some years. At this time his sister Anne decided to leave the Hall, and purchased the nearby Lawford Place. She spent £610, turning it into a palatial home. She often attended the church at Lawford, and also became very friendly with the Rev. Newman of Little Bromley Church. Although it is not certain, it is believed that it was there that Rigby's daughter, Sarah Lucas, met the Rev. Newman and romance blossomed.

Rigby's Involvement in the South Seas.

Over the previous years, Rigby had acquired so much additional property, that he had gained an increased income from the estate rents of nearly £6000 per year. This, compared with his father's time, shows the rent roll had increased over fivefold. He had also enlarged his property in the South Seas, in Antigua, Grenada and Jamaica. The trade in sugar had prospered, and the income from the cane fields had risen dramatically. He had many business partners in the West Indies, and worked very closely with a Robert Mackreth, and William and John Dawes, who managed a large estate called Tufton Hall. They had most of their trade in cocoa and coffee in Jamaica. In 1776 they sold 50 bags of cocoa for £85-6-1, and 17 casks of coffee for £458-17-5. The plantations were worked by hired Negro slaves, which for a year's work cost £220. During this year, Rigby's share amounted to £234-7-5. The accounts also show that the slaves were given cheese and beer which cost the estate £4-13-2 and £4-18-0 respectively. The cocoa and coffee came to England from the estate, and were shipped in four sailing vessels, named "Friendship", "Rebecca", "Janny" and "Polly", employed on regular passages to and from the West Indies. There is no record that Rigby ever sailed to the South Seas to see his estates, as his father had done before him, and the business operations were probably carried out by a resident manager. The trade from the West Indies flourished, and Rigby's share in the sale of coffee, cocoa and sugar brought him a considerable income for many years.

Work and Play.

At Mistley, splendid dinner parties were given for the tenants of the estate, where they discussed many aspects of agriculture. Although Richard had a manager on the Mistley Park Estate, he had become an experienced farmer himself, and enjoyed his work on his personal farm. He had managed to perform most of the work which the labourers undertook, and was never found to shirk the hardest tasks.

Amongst his many activities, he found time to become a Justice of the Peace, and regularly sat at the quarter sessions. In this capacity he signed an estimate of repairs for Cattaway Bridge, as it was then known. He was also on a committee to discuss Ramsey Bridge. He reported to a committee on the state of the roads between Wix, Great Oakley and Harwich, which were at times in such a bad state of repair that they became impassable. The inhabitants of the villages had been put to much inconvenience, and complained that proper servicing of the turnpike roads was not carried out. The committee acted on Rigby's report, and the roadways were improved. For many years, in his capacity as a magistrate, it is reported that he acted in a very fair manner; although it was said that on occasions his stern countenance put fear into many who were brought before him. Most of the cases he would have heard would have involved stealing by persons who were poor, and in some cases completely without the means to support themselves.

His family was regularly seen at the Hall, and always attended the social events he arranged. His sister Martha had married Brigadier General Hale, and Richard was very fond of their son Francis who grew into a fine young man, and served with distinction in the army, where he reached the rank of Lt. Colonel. Francis later married Frances, the beautiful daughter of Sir Thomas Rumbold, who had for many years served as Governor of Madras.

For nearly forty years, Rigby carried out his responsibilities as Squire of Mistley Thorne in an energetic manner. During this time he made a great deal of money, of which a large proportion was spent on improving the village. Most of the houses he and his father built still remain, and his policy of encouraging business developed Mistley into an important industrial village, which it has continued to be to the present day.

It would be true to say that when he was away from the village in the early days of his political career, a great deal of his fortune was squandered on wild living in London and Ireland. His entertainment at the Pay Office, where the wine flowed like water also continued unabated. His behaviour at the Pay Office gained him much notoriety, and was detrimental to his political career. The entertainment, and gambling losses, ate up a large portion of his income, and were exploited by his opponents in the years ahead. Nevertheless, he enjoyed his life at his home at Mistley, and the following chapters will reveal the lasting memorials for which his name will be forever remembered.

CHAPTER 17

LIFE AT MISTLEY THORNE from 1750

In the years after the death of the first Richard Rigby in 1730, life in the village slowly improved with the opportunities for employment he had provided. Some twenty years later, further efforts for the increase of industry were undertaken by his son. The population gradually increased as the years passed, and towards the end of the century there were just over eighty houses in Mistley, and some at the outlying farms. These housed just over 550 people, with males exceeded by females by over 10%. Some years before, in order to accommodate the increasing population, the elder Rigby had built some houses near the quay close to the green; this was very convenient, as the shipping trade was expanding and most of the inhabitants worked there, or on other connected duties. For the time, the standard of dwellings was excellent, proven by the fact that 200 years later, many of them are still standing in the lower part of Mistley.

The Thorne Inn had become the focal point of the village, and many functions were held in its spacious ballroom. William Leech was the Landlord from 1754 for over twenty-four years, at a rent of £45 per annum. The consumption of beer was prodigious, especially when Scrivener Allsopp, a prominent brewer of the time, imported fine Ringwood Beers from Hampshire. It is remarkable that beer was being brought from such a long distance, but it had attained great popularity in London earlier, and finally went to all parts of the country. Considering the poor conditions of the roads it is incredible that vast quantities of beer could have been sold at a price which would have been profitable. Most of the local inns were at Manningtree, and it is reported that the "Prince Eugene" always stocked 3000 gallons of beer.

Other activities also occurred at the Thorne Inn. Public meetings were regularly held there, and on occasions a magistrate sat to conduct enquiries. A Lamb Fair took place outside, and drew crowds of farmers and spectators. With the great number of ships using the port, and crews of all nationalities congregating in the public bars, there was much

The villagers of Mistley Thorne drew drinking water from a pipe leading into this cavity over 200 years ago

Mistley Street with some of the houses built by Rigby in the 18th century

An early photograph of Mistley Green shows one of the magnificent Horse Chestnut trees planted by Rigby when the houses were built.

Mistley Green with the twelve attractive red brick houses built by the second Richard Rigby well over 200 years ago.

rivalry, especially as some of the sailors were very rough characters. This sometimes resulted in fighting, which probably upset the village people! One of the bars at the Thorne was set aside as a private room for captains, and when trouble occurred they would use their authority to maintain order. However, although Mistley came in for its share of disturbance, Manningtree by night was far worse!

Customs officers used the Thorne Inn for examination of cargo and checking of the manifests and bills of lading; on several occasions smuggling was discovered, and goods confiscated. The culprits were usually brought to justice, and invariably a prison sentence was given after a trial at the assizes.

Horses and carriages were kept by the landlord, and a post chaise to London cost £5. Post chaises were also used for journeys to Ipswich, Harwich and Colchester, and on regular services to other villages and towns in the area. Stagecoaches travelled between London and Manningtree; a daily coach left the Spread Eagle in Gracechurch Street at 6:45 a.m. calling at Aldwych at 7:00 a.m. The coach carried about twenty people, with only six travelling inside and the remainder having to brave the elements, sitting outside. Coaches travelled from other parts of the city to Manningtree, and some to the Thorne Inn.

With the flourishing trade in the village, there were many jobs, but most of these involved hard labour in the maltings or on the quay. There was, unfortunately, always some hardship amongst the farm labourers, as in the winter months they were often not required on the farms. Some of the men in the village had to walk to farms some distance from Mistley, in an effort to obtain work, and some became very impoverished. Very little could be done to deal with these problems, which were prevalent throughout England in the 18th century, but in order to help alleviate distress in Mistley, the second Richard Rigby built a workhouse. This institution was almost certainly at Mistley Heath, or Bradfield Heath, as the area was known at that time. The piece of land on which the workhouse is believed to have stood, was on the area of the allotments, just before reaching the Heath, on the right-hand side of the road. A fairly large building appears on the early maps, but it did not seem to exist in the 19th century; when Dove House Farm was sold in 1844 this portion of the farm was named Workhouse field.

Later on in the century, another problem arose, in that although men were able to obtain employment, their wages were so low that they were unable to buy sufficient food for their families. Rigby, as squire of the village, was very concerned, and was instrumental in arranging a special meeting of the magistrates, after which an overseer was appointed. This was held at the Thorne Inn, where various regulations were set in place to alleviate the poverty. Payments were made to some poor families, but these did not satisfy everyone. Later on, after further directions by the magistrates in an order signed by John Ambrose, further provisions for the poor were made, in a statement which read:

"It is resolved that rules and regulations for the guidance of overseers be adopted, viz., that (when wages were not sufficient), they do provide each person in every family, (in addition to the earnings), with the means of procuring half a peck of best bread flour per week, together with 1/3d. per head for other necessities, if two only, 1/-d. per head, if three, -/11d., if four, -/10d., if five, -/9d., if six, -/8d., if seven, and -/7d. if more than seven".

It is apparent that even in those days, there was much care and concern for the welfare of the less well-off.

Apart from some drunken brawls amongst the sailors, there appears to have been little crime in the village, although one isolated case occurred, when Mary Aldgate, on 24th

February 1774, stole money from Elizabeth Wallis. She was taken to court on 7th March, and sentenced to a term in prison. Only a small amount of money was taken, but the severity of the sentences was intended to keep crime to a low level. Throughout the county crime was actually quite high, and extreme sentences did little to prevent it. This sort of punishment for minor crimes was a national abuse, but was rectified by the mid-nineteenth century.

In 1774 building on a large scale began on the quay, resulting in many workmen coming to Mistley. Most of these were lodged in the village, and some stayed after the building work had been completed.

In 1730 the rebuilding of the wharf had provided deeper water alongside the quay. Since this time, with its enlarged storage facilities, Mistley's shipping trade had steadily increased. From the small wharf the river barge trade en route for Sudbury had increased. Manningtree was also loading barges at its small quay, but the narrow channel and shallow water did not allow the passage of the larger ships arriving at Mistley.

Towards the end of the 18th century, there was great annoyance in Mistley, when the Commissioners for the Essex Turnpikes erected a tollgate between Mistley and Manningtree. After much argument, a petition was presented to the Commissioners at their General Meeting at Harwich. It read:

> *"We, whose names are hereunto subscribed, being Merchants,*
> *Hoymen, and Traders, at the Ports of Manningtree and Mistley*
> *Thorne, beg leave to inform the Gentlemen Commissioners that*
> *the Tollgate erected between Mistley Thorne and Manningtree is*
> *exceedingly injurious and detrimental to our trade, insomuch*
> *that, in many instances we are obliged to pay the toll at the said*
> *gate, or we cannot get our corn, and other commodities, to and*
> *from the said Ports. We, therefore, humbly hope that you will*
> *take the matter into consideration, and totally dismantle, and*
> *remove the said gate to some other place, where it will be less*
> *injurious to the trade of the said Ports".*

The petition was signed by twenty-seven traders, including Mr. James Betts, who operated the shipyard. The debate went on for a long period of time, and eventually the Commissioners ruled in their favour, and the Tollgate was dismantled as requested. The position of the tollgate is not known, but it was probably on the river road between Mistley and Manningtree where the main road joined it near Hopping Bridge.

With the population continuing to grow in both Mistley and Manningtree, the services expanded to cope with the demands for food and clothing. Eventually, in this small area, there were seven butchers, six grocers, twenty-three bakers, and fifteen other shopkeepers. In case of illness, there were two surgeons, and twelve coal merchants supplied the surrounding villages. Twenty-six beer houses and inns served the more thirsty inhabitants, and three maltsters, and two brewery companies supplied the ale and beer. Much of the corn grown on the farms surrounding Mistley and Manningtree went to the maltsters, and a considerable quantity was shipped to London facilitated by eight corn merchants, who regularly arranged sales in a large building at Manningtree, which served as a Corn Exchange.

Later on, two banks were opened at Manningtree, trading as Alexander & Co., and Nunn and Co.

The Excise Officer was a Mr. Barton, who worked long hours collecting the duties which were paid on some of the cargoes arriving at the port from abroad. Messrs. Strutt, Stammers, Frost, Norman and Golding Constable all had coal yards at the port, and Constable had a warehouse, for which he paid £13 for a year's rent. The coal was loaded in the yards after arrival by thousands of colliers, which sailed to Mistley from the north-west of England. Mr. Alston, the Manningtree brewer, had a small granary on the quay, and a Mr. Folkard had a carpenter's shop in the garden of a house alongside the quay. This house and yard were eventually used by a Mr. Ladbrooke, who was well-known in Mistley until a few years ago. There was a second carpenter's yard behind the houses on the eastern end of The Green. A small warehouse and smithy stood at the bottom of the hill about fifty yards east of the Thorne Inn, kept by a blacksmith called Stribling. This property remained until after the last war, when it was demolished and a garage erected. The old blacksmith's forge and premises was joined to the attractive brick and stone wall, a section of which still runs down to a house called the Abbey, next to the Post Office. Another blacksmith was a Mr. Quilter, whose forge was at Mistley Heath; a third stood on a small piece of ground on the north side of the present railway bridge, on Mistley Hill. A fourth forge was in operation at Horsley Cross, tenanted by a Mr. Scrivener, and stood on the site of the present inn. A very old beer house, demolished just after the war was called the Shant, and the new inn, the Wheelwright's Arms, was erected. The name perpetuated the position of the smithy, but the inn is now known as Hedgerows. Mr. Stribling also had an ironmonger's shop on the opposite side of the road to his forge, and these premises were eventually owned by a Mr. Baxter, of the well-known family, which still lived in the village some 100 years later. The Baxter family was followed by a Mr. Mussellwhite who bought the ironmonger's premises in 1912, where he lived until after the second world war. The small house and shop was demolished soon after and a large brick building now occupies the place where paraffin oil was sold, providing the main source of light for the village. The house had a pretty tree-lined garden, with a small lawn, with steps leading down to the shop.

Most of the shops were in Manningtree, but a small number were situated in Mistley street, only one of which now remains. The houses in the street are still as they were more than 200 years ago, but regrettably some have been spoiled by the covering of the original brickwork with coloured paints and several have fallen into disrepair. Mr. Siser was the butcher, with his shop on the south side of the street, and next to him was the bakery tenanted by a Mr. Hurring. Mr. Thomas Hammond had a grocer's shop in the same premises which are at present still being used. Other cottages contained very small businesses, which explains the large numbers of bakers listed at that time. Two shoemakers had shops in the street, one occupied by a Mr. White, with a tailor's workshop third from the end on the south side, and a barber's opposite to it on the north. Messrs. Mason and Rogers were plumbers and painters, Mr. Whiting was employed as a bricklayer, and amongst this hive of activity the area was blessed with three straw hat makers! As I have shown, the district was well-served with shops of every description. Most of the services listed were trading about thirty years before the end of the 18th century in Mistley and Manningtree, following the increase in trade initiated by Richard Rigby some years earlier.

With the increasing population the congregation at the church grew. Mistley's church was of Anglican denomination, and for some time there had been a small movement towards Methodism. In 1789, John Wesley came to Mistley, where he preached one of his

40,000 sermons! A few were converted to the comparatively new religious movement, and eventually the Wesleyan School was built in west Mistley.

Mistley was unusual in being a small village whose inhabitants were mostly living in virtually new houses, and with industries belying its size. A few of the families working in the village were to benefit a few years later by having the opportunity to buy the houses and premises they occupied, although some, because of financial restraints were unfortunately unable to do so. In general, however, the villagers made the most of their good fortune, and with much merrymaking at both the Hall and the Thorne Inn, these must have been fairly good days for Mistley Thorne. It should, perhaps, not be forgotten that the standard of living in those days was very poor for some of the families.

Dock built in 1726, and strengthened with brick and stone fifty years later.
It was filled in only a few years ago.

CHAPTER 18

BUILDING MISTLEY'S INDUSTRY

A great deal has been written about the life of Richard Rigby, little of it complimentary. Much criticism has been levelled at him over his gambling habits and bouts of heavy drinking. His position at the Pay Office caused much vilification, because of the immense sums of money he was able to acquire, through a custom long practised by others. Rigby was, of course, responsible for the money he lent to his friends, but he could collect large sums of money in interest. In addition he received a very high salary in his position as Paymaster General, quite possibly as much as £30,000 per annum.

As a result of his reputation as "a parliamentary rogue, with little moral character", early writers did not give him credit for the excellent building work he carried out at Mistley, regarding the money he spent on this as being dishonestly gained.There is little doubt that most of the money he spent on ventures in Mistley was obtained from his position at the Pay Office.

By 1770, Mistley had grown into a close-knit community, presided over by Rigby, in his capacity as squire and Lord of the Manor. Although trade in the village was booming, he still felt there was room for improvement, and during the next ten years embarked on an extensive building programme, which would further benefit the inhabitants

The improvements and building works which his father had initiated some fifty years earlier now required repair, with some buildings needing to be demolished. In 1772, Rigby began an ambitious programme which was to cost thousands of pounds, but was to prove of great benefit to the village. Much of this work remains today, a lasting memorial to Rigby.

Although the initial plans were formulated by Rigby himself, he enlisted the aid of some of the foremost architects and engineers in the country to advise him on the methods of construction. Most of the building appears to have been completed in less than eight years.

The following nine projects of an industrial nature were completed, and in addition Rigby was busily engaged in other schemes, which will be described in detail in the chapters ahead.

The Salt Works.

The process of producing salt from boiling sea water had been carried out at Mistley for some years, but it was found that refining rock salt was more economic. The former method was discontinued at this time, and the plant was demolished. The refining of rock salt continued at a site at Manningtree which subsequently became a timber works on the quay. This proved to be a very lucrative business, and repairs and alterations were carried out at the salt house, and the plant carefully renovated.

The Maltings.

For many years Mistley's two maltings had been working to full capacity, but by 1770 they were coming to the end of their lives. These were very tiny buildings and only capable of steeping small quantities of barley. In 1775 one was demolished, and Rigby built another of more modern design, alongside the river behind the church. It was constructed entirely of brick, and two lofty kilns were provided on which to dry the malt. The malting thus had a far greater capacity than the two it replaced. Extensive malt rooms were constructed, adjoining the kilns, which provided adequate storage space for both malt and barley.

Although some improvements were incorporated in the design of the new plant, the conversion of barley into malt remained a most laborious occupation, requiring strong and very fit workmen. The maltsters worked seven days a week in extremely hot and dusty conditions on the kilns, alternating with the dampness and humidity on the germinating floors. This system prevailed in the scores of maltings constructed locally, until the old process was abandoned barely twenty years ago. Malting in those days was an art and not a science, and over the years thousands of local men trod the tiled floors, and sweated on the fiery kilns, producing the fine malt for which Mistley became renowned, and widely known as the "Home of Malting". Rigby's malting lasted 127 years, and was not demolished until 1902, when a new malting known as number 9 was constructed. This building was demolished only a few years ago on the site known as Rigby Quay on which new warehouses have now been constructed.

The Water and Windmills.

Rigby owned two windmills and one water mill which were leased on annual tenancies. By 1770 the one standing at the top of Mistley Hill near the present Old Mill House had been in a poor state of repair or some years. The great sails had become damaged in the strong winds which had blown for two whole days in 1766, and costly renovation had to be carried out. It was, however, made safe to operate, and the old Mill lasted several more years until it eventually had to be demolished. The mill house was divided into three cottages, which are still standing today, one of which is inevitably called "Ye Old Mill House".

Another of the windmills occupied a spot in the Parish of Lawford on top of the hill to the west of the watermill. Although both mills were in reasonable condition, a great deal of money had to be spent on maintaining them. An agreement was made with Mr. William Tomlins, a baker of Redcross Street, London, for a year's hire, which included a house, gardens, and two grass fields of eight acres. Mr. Tomlins was to keep the mills in repair at his own expense, but was provided with timber for the sails. He was also responsible for the tithes, the poor, the church, and highway rates and duties. The rents were £20 for the watermill, and £15 for the house, garden and fields. The windmill was let for £20 per year, and Mr. Tomlins supplied the nearby villagers with freshly ground flour for bread for many years. Strangely the cost of hiring the mills had been considerably reduced during the previous 40 years, when £90 had been charged.

The water mill was situated on the present site of the Tendring Hundred Waterworks, and was operated by the water flowing from the stream which passes through Manningtree en route for the river.

The Shipyard

The shipyard which had existed on the beach for at least twenty years, was in 1775 being successfully operated by Mr. James Betts. He had launched scores of small ships from the slipway, but Rigby, after discussion with him, decided to enlarge it so that ships of up to 1000 tons could be built, and the necessary modifications were put in hand on the slipway, and ship-supporting timbers. Ancillary warehouses were built, and provision made for a boathouse, and storage for sails, pitch and tar. Mr. Betts ran the shipyard for nearly 25 years, during which time he launched many fine ships, some with a capacity of more than 900 tons.

An artist's impression of the wharf at Mistley Thorne in the 17th century.

A photograph taken some 100 years later shows the semi-circular opening beneath the granary under which the water flowed.

Coal and Deal Yards.

With an increasing tonnage of coal arriving from the north of the country, and large cargoes of timber from Scandinavia, it became necessary to provide more storage space. Part of the quay was set aside for the storage of the timber, until it could be shipped by barge to Sudbury or sold locally. A completely new coal yard was built, with reinforced bunkers, in which the coal was stored before delivery. New coal and deal yards were completed in 1778, at a cost of £259-17-11d., and were placed on an open land on the right-hand side of the church. It is also noted that a further small coalyard was constructed at Mistley Heath, at a cost of £4, adding to the nine already in operation on several parts of the quay.

The Lime Kiln.

Richard's father had a lime kiln built several years before, which urgently required extensive repairs. The kiln and premises were practically rebuilt; the building was artistically designed to look like a fort, with ramparts and slit windows. In order to carry out the improvements, piles supporting the old kiln had to be drawn, and 192 yards of earth removed, the work costing £13-8-0. The brickwork was skilfully done by Mr. Whiting, the village bricklayer, and to complete the effect, a flagpole was placed on the building at a cost of 12/-

The Brick Kilns.

The main ovens which were completely renovated and practically rebuilt, and the brickfield, were situated at the eastern end of the quay. The trade in bricks was good, with most of them at this time being used in the building work on the quay. The brickworks employed several men from the village. The loam used at this time came from the small cliffs which still sweep down to the river below the present Anchor Inn. A brick-kiln was also built at this time at Dickley Hall Farm, and remained in operation for a number of years.

Grain Warehouse and Docks.

Some fifty years before, the first Richard Rigby had built the two docks at the western end of the quay, one of which was below the large granary. The two docks and a small wharf, 172' in length had long been known as the "Rigby Quay". These docks had been used continuously for many years, and repairs had become necessary to the granary. During the repairs, the granary was substantially altered, providing more space for grain, and reinforcing the floors. This building was to last until the 1960s, when it was demolished by a company of property developers. The docks were filled in about eighteen years ago, when a wall was constructed in front of them providing additional quay space over the top. Hundreds of thousands of tons of grain were loaded into the Rigby granary over a period of nearly two hundred years. For part of this time the grain was dropped onto small river barges which floated beneath it. Later the granary became hidden by the ugly corrugated iron provender mills built on Mistley Quay, but although part of it was demolished, it continued to be used, and stood the ravages of time, while the area around it became a neglected eyesore.

The New Quay.

In 1773, there was a small quay adjoining the docks to the east, and extending to a "hard" alongside, which had been constructed at the same time as the docks and granary by Richard's father in 1727. This section of the quay was becoming too small to deal with the increasing number of ships coming into Mistley. The only alternative was to construct a completely new quay in front of it, and also to enclose the hard. There would be a considerable gain in the working area on the quay, and it would provide ample space for the cargoes carried in the largest ships.

Rigby had, for some years, been a close friend of the Duke of Bridgwater, an expert in the construction of quays and canals in the Midlands; indeed some of the canals he designed are still in use today. Rigby took advantage of his professional expertise and asked him to design the new quay.

After much consultation, designs were prepared, and it was agreed to construct the quay to a length of 540' mostly of brick and stone. It would extend to the line of low water following the curve of the channel, where the tide would provide the deepest water. The western end would abut the east wall of the two docks, which also followed the channel to the north, known as Thorne Reach. The proposed quay would, therefore, extend in a slight curve from "Thorne Reach" in the west, to the part of the channel known as "Millers Reach" in the east, with the large area of the river known as "Seafield Bay" in front. Much thought went into the name by which the quay would be called, and with Thorne Reach to the north, and the Thorne Inn standing behind, the name of "Thorne Quay" was finally agreed upon, as it remains today.

The most difficult part of the whole operation of the construction of the dock was preventing the work becoming swamped by the tide, which would rise twice daily to a height of more than ten feet above the foundations. Before any work would begin, the area in front had to be made and kept dry. To keep out the tide, and ensure dry working conditions, it was necessary to build a "caisson" or "cofferdam". The cofferdam was probably constructed by setting large wooden piles deep into the river bed, and shored back against the weight of the tide. Attached to the piles were timbers nailed on each side, leaving a cavity between, extending well below the bed of the river. This would have been lined with stout canvas or skin, and clay would be rammed tightly into it, thus providing a tight seal which would prevent the water leaking through. Hand-operated pumps were constantly in use in the cofferdam, and there is little doubt that erosion, and rain seeping through, would have allowed some water to accumulate in the bottom of the works.

In order to raise the levels to the height of the old quay and the land behind, it was necessary to build up an area of nearly 400sq. ft., which consisted of the hard and some beach. Thousands of tons of sand and shingle were used as infill to raise this section, thus providing a level surface. The face of the quay was planned to be 15' to the river bed, so that vessels of over 10' draught could be accommodated. At the extreme end of the proposed quay the channel curved, and a section of curious design some 60' in length was to be built to follow it. The height of the quay here was barely 8' constructed of brick and stone,incorporating a section six feet wide over which the water flowed at high tide. At the rear, a sloping section of brick was to be placed with steps built into it. The top of the sloping section was to be constructed level with the top of the main quay. To the east of the quay ran a steeply sloping beach extending 1300' along the channel, of which sixty feet or more was covered at high tide, stretching from where the present maltings stand, along to a point, far below, but in line with the Anchor Inn. The cliff above it was extensively wooded, through which ran a track to the beach, now the present quay hill. Several buildings existed at the rear of the beach abutting the cliff, at the top of which ran the main turnpike road to Harwich. In the middle of this area of the beach were the shipyard and storage areas.

In the construction of a quay this size, secure foundations were vital. Firstly, a large trench some ten feet deep and eight feet wide was dug, into which trimmed oak tree trunks were placed, carefully cut so that they fitted closely. The tops were flattened, and formed the foundations on which the bricks were laid. It takes little imagination to realise how difficult it must have been to manipulate the tree trunks into the trenches; all this work being performed by hand, although horses were used to drag the trunks, and drop them into position.

Mr. William Hindle, a surveyor, was engaged to take charge of the building operations. His initial survey done some months earlier had cost £15. A Mr. Wallis was appointed to be in charge of labour, and it was his responsibility to engage and control the men on the day-to-day building operations. Most of the labour was brought in from outside the village; the majority of the men being bricklayers and masons. The numbers of men varied during the months ahead, and on some days as many as fifty were employed. The operation appears to have begun during the year 1774. On 19th October that year, 41 labourers, carpenters, and masons were paid £30-6-4d., and later the numbers were increased to 47 men, earning £38-13s. On 3rd March 1775, Mr. Stribling, the blacksmith, was paid £14-1-10^1/2d, for ironwork on the quay, and Mr. Whiting, the bricklayer, earned £2-5-7^1/2d, for his work. . Large copings of Portland Stone were placed along the top of the quay, having arrived by ship early in the 1770s. The unloading of these massive pieces of stone using a hand winch was a laborious and difficult task. These large pieces of stone extended over the whole length of the quay. Similar blocks of stone ran lengthwise in sections between the bricks, and other stone buttresses were built into the brickwork, at regular intervals. The complete structure was tied back every twelve feet, using strong chains secured to the tree trunks set some five feet below the surface, and about thirty feet to the rear. Wooden piles were placed against the tree trunks to stop them moving and to support the quay. In 1778 Messrs. Yeall and Co. supplied 52 piles, and a further 60 were purchased from Flowers and Co. Iron mooring rings, some ten inches in diameter, and at least three inches thick were placed at suitable intervals along the top of the quay, to which ships could be secured.

As has been said, much of the construction work involved heavy lifting of the large blocks of stone and timber. This involved the use of block and tackle, and to assist in the lubrication a sum of £12-5s. was paid for hogs lard. William Schollar provided the 72 tons of Portland stone, which was delivered by ship at a cost of £52-10s. A number of these large slabs of stone can be seen on the approach road to Mistley Quay. Thousands of tons of sand were used during the construction, both for mortar between the bricks, and infill behind the quay, using large quantities from the ballast pit at the top of the hill. In addition six shipments of sand arrived from Langfort Fort at Felixstowe between January and March 1777, carried by a vessel called the "Good Intent", which illustrates how long the quay was taking to construct. Supplies of sand were seriously depleted in the ballast pit, and 164 tons were brought from the river at the end of Millers Reach. A port hand buoy now marks the spot from which this was excavated, and is a marker where ships turn to run up the channel to Mistley Quay. From that time this part of the river has always been known as "Ballast Hill". One surprising cargo consisted of 143 bushels of lime, and records also show a purchase of 80' of elm. There would have been little necessity to purchase much wood for the project, as there was an ample supply on the estate which could be used. By far the largest requirement was the provision of bricks. John Yeall & Co, supplied more than 300,000, some of which were white. Mr. Whiting also supplied some white bricks, and many of the red type may have come from the local brickworks. Large quantities also came from brickworks at Ballingdon transported by river barge. The materials mentioned here were a mere portion of the immense quantities of wood, lime, stone, iron, sand and bricks which were supplied over the period of time it took to build the quay.

Once the new quay was completed, hundreds of tons of chalk came from Kent by ship, and was spread on the bed of the river in front of it. This was raked level at low tide, and after a time became compacted by the weight of ships lying on it. These chalk berths became very hard and smooth, and the flow of the tide prevented any silt accumulating in front of the quay. Every few years further chalk would be added to replace that lost by erosion, and the practice was continued until well after the last war. The use of Mistley quay by a much larger type of ship has now made this custom unnecessary.

Although no records have been found it is thought that the work probably took as long as three years.

By 1778 the quay, viewed from west to east, consisted of deal yards, coal yards, a chalk pit, a malting, a granary and two docks. The Thorne quay, with auxiliary buildings behind, led to the beach and shipyard beyond. Further to the east was the lime kiln, with brick ovens and storage areas, nearest the saltings at the extreme end. The small strangely designed quay, later called the "low quay", lay in the middle. Why it was built in the manner described is unknown, perhaps so that smaller ships could be unloaded beside it, or for small boats to slide down the slope into the river. Subsequently generations of Mistley children learned to swim from it, until it was filled in about thirty years ago.

The Thorne Quay remains one of the finest examples of the use of bricks and stone in wharf construction. Since 1778, millions of tons of cargo have been handled over it, from the thousands of the ships which have moored there. The quay remains today as a reminder of Mistley's history as a port, and to the skilful men who built it.

During the 1770s, the villagers of Mistley Thorne must have been amazed at the scale of building work taking place in their village. Farms had been renovated, houses built, and the quayside industry revolutionised. They would probably have been even more astonished when they discovered that "Squire Rigby" was planning to enlarge Mistley Hall, and employ two famous architects to rebuild their church.

Thorne Quay was built over 200 years ago.

CHAPTER 19

RIGBY AND THE ADAM BROTHERS

The four Adam brothers came to London from Scotland, and after carrying out much work in the city they became the most fashionable architects of their time. Robert and James were the best known, and became famous for the magnificent buildings they designed in Fitzroy Square, Mansfield Street, and Portland Place. The well-known Adelphi Terrace was named after them ("Adelphi" being Greek for "brothers"), Robert was the oldest and most famous of the four, and his designs for fireplaces and furniture were eagerly sought by rich Londoners who spent thousands of pounds on improvements to their properties. Many of The Adam brothers' wonderful designs have contributed to our country's heritages, and millions will have seen examples of the beautiful work they created at, for example, Osterly Park, Syon House, Luton Hoo and Harewood House.

In 1770, they were regularly engaged by Ministers of the Crown to design and improve various Government buildings, and Rigby, not to be outdone, soon commissioned them to undertake extensive alterations at the Pay Office. Never slow to make friends, he invited them to stay at Mistley Hall, and there is little doubt that his motive was to enlist their expertise, to assist him with the building work he planned in the village. The lavish hospitality offered at Mistley Hall was renowned, and Robert and James Adam were reputed to have enjoyed their stay.

Robert Adam would have been unlikely to approve of the interior decorations of the Hall, which owed much to Walpole's influence, and Rigby soon prevailed upon him to take on the reconstruction and decoration of the whole property. From this time onward Rigby engaged Robert Adam to advise him on several other projects at Mistley, the details of which are given in the remainder of this chapter.

Alterations at Mistley Hall.

Work was soon to begin on the Hall, with a new east wing added, harmonizing with the old building, and providing extensive dining and drawing rooms, with bedrooms above. A second rotunda was built to match the existing one standing on the east side of the house. Rectangular pillars known as pilasters were constructed to adorn the facade, and pediment treatment of the triangular Greek design was placed between the roof lines. Inside the Hall a number of new fireplaces were built, and a plain but beautifully carved staircase was erected from the entrance hall to the bedrooms above. Part of this staircase, and a fireplace were removed to the new Mistley Hall when the old Hall was demolished in 1845, and are now the property of the Acorn Village. Other interior decorations were carried out, which with finely designed furniture, gave the Hall an elegance admired by all who stayed there.

The Church at Mistley Thorne.

Rigby had long wished for improvements to be made to the church, so that it would stand out strikingly central in the view from the Hall down to the River Stour. Although the landscape seen from the Hall was already lovely, with the beautiful wooded area to the left of the church, and the brick cottages on the green, Rigby felt that the enlargement of the church would provide another attractive feature, and Robert Adam embarked upon a design which would achieve this purpose.

Park and Gardens of Mistley Hall.
The position of the Kentish Fences are shown by the thick lines.

Dried up pond in the middle of Tunnel Meadow. At the time of the Rigbys this was a small beautifully kept lake in the centre of the park surrounded by trees.

The northern end of the Kentish Fence or Ha Ha which ran around the wood then known as Oak Grove. The fallen tree was uprooted in the hurricane of 1987.

Above: The Church Of St. Mary at Mistley some years after the rebuilding to the design of Robert Adam.

Below: The Towers today. The east tower was purchased by Mr. Wm. Brooks, when the centre section was demolished in 1870.

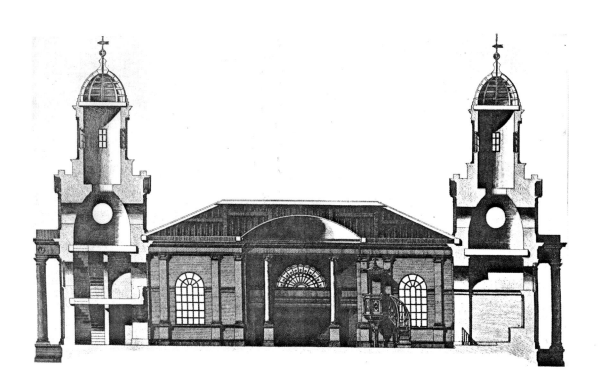

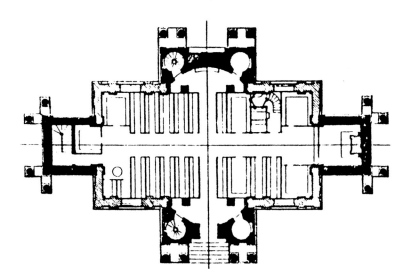

Top: Detailed drawing showing the construction of the Towers.

Bottom: Plan of the seating in the Church drawn in 1735. The dark portions show the alterations made by Adam in 1776.

(By courtesy of The Trustees of Sir John Soane's Museum)

The old brick-built church erected in 1735 was built in a plain style, and Robert Adam changed much, adding the two domed towers at either end. The eastern tower was built above the chancel, and the western one over the apse, above which had been a small bell tower. The porch leading to the centre of the nave was enlarged and completely redesigned, with a second of a similar design added to the opposite side, forming a transept. Five wide stone steps led to the south door of the porch, on either side of which were placed two lofty pillars. Four identical pillars were also erected on the north side, with a further four on the end corners of each tower. Above the entrance porch and transept were triangular pediments, resembling those of a Grecian temple, which enclosed the roof lines. Each tower supported a cupola roofed in lead, with several narrow windows of slatted wood which also had pediments. Pictures of the church show clock faces on all four sides of the towers, but it is thought that these were not actually installed. Robert Adam kept the interior of the building quite simple, though practically rebuilding it. The building thus appeared uncluttered and finely cut, with attractive decorative facings below the roof line.

The Adam brothers finished their work in 1777; it was to be the only church design they attempted. Although the church was greatly admired, Wiffin in his book on Georgian churches described it as being of Doric style, more like a house than a church, and an *"eccentricity in ecclesiastical architecture"*. Other writers described it as being of Greek or Turkish design, and one could ponder on Walpole's reaction had he seen it. Perhaps his earlier description of the old church in 1745, when he called it *"an absolute antique temple"*, may have been more fitting in 1777.

When the church was brought back into use an entry was made in the Mistley Church Register, which read:

> *"Mistley Church, after being completely finished, and ornamented*
> *at the change and expense of the Right Hon. Richard Rigby, patron*
> *thereof, was opened for divine service on the 6th day of April 1777".*

The opening was attended by the Rigby family, and Richard's friend the Earl of Sandwich, together with most of the villagers in the locality. The morning service was taken by the Rev. Richard Daniell, and his curate, Rev. Mather Thompson, who was to become Rector of Mistley in 1779. In the afternoon of this day Judith, the daughter of Jeremiah and Annie Roker, was baptised.

The inhabitants of Mistley Thorne were to worship at this extraordinary church for a further 93 years, and judging by the large congregations attending, it was loved by many.

Sadly, a few years after the Rigby estate was sold in 1844, there emerged a few influential people in the community who had a strong aversion to the church. They resented the fact that it resembled a secular building, and had been paid for by what they considered was the ill-gotten money of Richard Rigby, for in the straightlaced Victorian period the doubtful activities of Rigby were frowned upon, and some wished a complete demolition of the building. Mr. Joseph Clarke, the diocesan architect, was asked to survey it, and on 13th July 1868, he recommended that the vestry committee's wishes to demolish the church should be approved, due to the fact that the building was suffering from the worst form of dry rot. However, there is little doubt that there was much pressure applied behind the scenes, as if dry rot was present, it is unlikely to have been in the roof timbers, the rest of the building being constructed entirely of brick and stone. The vestry committee agreed that the church should be completely demolished, and a sum of £528 would be paid by the contractor for the materials recovered. The new church was to be built on a site given by the Rev. Charles Norman, whose family owned much of the estate previously owned by Rigby. It is arguable that the ancient towers church fell a victim to the then fever for Gothic revival, which in Mistley partly destroyed an interesting monument, and produced a pattern for that period. The Mistley villagers were outraged, and a deed was obtained which ordered that the towers should remain as ornamental objects. Mr. William Brooks, owner of some large maltings in Mistley, purchased the North East Tower; the North West Tower was later acquired by Mr. T. G. Kensit for £120. Although the body of the church was demolished, the Adam Towers were saved, and in order to preserve their symmetry, the existing pillars were removed, and placed at each of the corners. A public subscription was raised, in order to reimburse Mr. Brooks for the expense he had incurred in buying the first tower. Thus the towers have remained as a well-known Mistley landmark, and since 1957 have been maintained by the Ministry of Works, as guardians of the monument. It is pleasing to find that over the years Mistley residents have fought to preserve the village heritage, and the old towers have recently been made more beautiful by the floodlighting installed by the efforts of local people.

The Entrance Lodges.

The main entrance drive to the Hall led from where the Colchester, Mistley and Manningtree roads crossed, at a point now known as "Lodges Corner". Rigby had a grandiose scheme for an ornamental gate to mark the western extremity of the estate. The Adam brothers designed an entrance screen, with an arch and an elaborate wrought iron gateway, some 84' in width across the drive. Two small gates were incorporated in the plans, which were to be joined on to two tiny entrance lodges, built with white bricks, and stone dressings, and manned by a keeper at all times, who would live in one of them. However, this elaborate archway with its iron gateway was not completed, mainly, it is thought, because of cost, in 1781 two brick lodges were erected. One of these exists to this day, in the garden of the house on the crossroads, but the second one was demolished some years ago. The lodge, built by Adam is part of Mistley's heritage, but it is now partially hidden by trees and a high wooden fence.

The Swan Fountain.

The Adam design of the Swan fountain was simple, being a circular reservoir, into which water spouted from the mouth of a large model swan, set on a plinth in the centre. The swan was built at the same time as the Grapevine Cottages which stand behind it, on a site used as a yard for the storage of coal, and other cargo. A second small fountain was built behind, which joined the main basin. This small fountain is perhaps more attractive, resembling many of the delightful wall fountains to be found in Italy. It was constructed with a brick arch, below which water flowed through the mouth of a lion's head. The water fell into a shallow semicircular well below, and thence by drain into the river. The main fountain was built on three iron legs, and horses were watered from the small fountain at the back. Later, the legs were covered, and an iron fence was built, with its tiny fountain in the rear, but unfortunately no water flows to this part as the drainage system has collapsed.

It is interesting to find that the water which flowed into the fountain came from an area of many springs, adjacent to the ballast pit at the top of Mistley Hill. The water from the springs was collected in a shallow reservoir, with raised sides, in which watercress grew abundantly. From here, the water was piped through the fields and woodlands, gradually descending to the village via another small reservoir in the garden of a house at the bottom of Mistley Hill. Separating the reservoir from the roadway was a thick stone wall in which were two cavities, with iron bars across on which the villagers hooked their buckets. The overflows from the wells were set beneath the road, from which water was diverted to the swan's mouth. For years the villagers of Mistley fetched their water from these two supply points, one of which still remains today though it is no longer usable.

The fountain was given to the village in 1844, and the water which flows from the swan's mouth is piped in the same manner from the springs as it was more than 250 years ago. The springs, still giving ample supplies of water, are situated in the garden of "Shrublands", the house now belonging to Mr. William Rose. It is interesting that in the brochure of the sale in 1844 the following condition was inserted:

> *"And whereas certain springs and drains, by which the village of Mistley is supplied with water, have their rise in that portion of the park, adjoining the ballast pit, it is to be understood that the purchaser of that portion of the Park which is intended for sale, shall be bound not to do any act whereby the said springs shall be stopped, diverted from, or rendered useless to the village of Mistley, but shall on being required so to do by the majority in point of value of the inhabitants, rate payers of the said village cause such needful reparations to be made to such drains at the expense of the said inhabitants, and at reasonable times and seasons, so as to keep the said springs and drains in a state of repair for the purpose of supplying the village of Mistley with water, and further that this condition be inserted either by way of recital or otherwise, as the conveyance to be made to the purchaser of the said portion of the Park where the springs rise, and through which the said drains have their course".*

Some years ago a measurement at the source of the springs showed a quantity of 650 gallons per hour of water to be flowing through the pipework. Some of the very old pipework running through the woodlands has had to be regularly repaired, especially where tree roots have penetrated them. When the new Maltings were built in School Lane, a completely new section with manholes was built beneath them. The pipes run under the railway line, and beneath the Edme Malting works to the old reservoir. From here the water is still piped under the road to the swan, and the system is maintained by the local council, as laid down in the provisions made in the sale of 1844. The swan basin has been carefully refurbished, with tasteful alterations to the area surrounding it.

When Robert and James Adam designed this area of Mistley so long ago, they would scarcely have expected that more than a billion gallons of water would flow into the fountain, coming from the same unusual source of supply, and that it would survive as an important part of Mistley's heritage for more than 200 years.

The Grapevine Cottages.

The Adam brothers were also responsible for the four terraced cottages behind the Swan fountain. Like many of their designs, the cottages were Grecian in style, the two middle cottages being ornamented with a pediment, and having pillars on either side of their adjacent front doors.

On the left of the cottages were two tiny warehouses, and a granary, later tenanted by a Mr. Tovill, and Mr. Golding Constable. One of the cottages was rented to Mr. Tovill, who also had a coalyard on the right-hand side, with a piece of land adjoining it. Mr. Edward Norman lived in the end cottage, in which David Garrick, the actor, stayed on some of his visits to the Hall, when it was overflowing with guests at some of the more lavish occasions. Rigby's friends then stayed either at the Thorne Inn, or other houses in the village. The two middle cottages were eventually bought by the Brewers, Cobbold, who converted them into a beer house, which they called the Grapevine, after the long trailing vines which grew profusely on the south walls.

The Mistley Workshops and Pottery now stand on the site of the warehouses and granary, and the office of A.R.C. Marine is built on the site of the coalyard. The cottages are still inhabited, and are today substantially the same as they were more than 200 years ago.

The Proposed Salt Water Baths.

By far the most ambitious scheme Rigby planned for Mistley was his attempt in 1778 to turn the village into a spa. After long discussions with Rigby, Robert Adam produced a design for a magnificent building, in which hot and cold water baths, and other equipment would be placed. The scheme was to produce a reservoir from which the water would be heated by a coal-fired boiler. The reservoir was to be built in the shape of a semi-circle, with elaborate brickwork and ornamentation. A pipe was to be laid from the river to the reservoir, with a waste pipe to act as an overflow, which would have kept the supply of water at a constant depth. The design included an imposing entrance staircase of nine steps beneath a portico, leading into a large rotunda, in which were doorways to a further peristyle portico. On either side of the rotunda was a reception room, and beneath the second portico were the dressing or changing rooms, with a public cold water bath. Beneath the rotunda was a coal cellar and the boiler. Below the reception rooms, were the private cold water baths. The plans seem to show that no provision was made for hot water baths for the public. A dressing room was included in the area of the hot water baths, with two rooms set aside in which to put bath gowns.

There does not appear to have been any provision for fresh water, nor was there any way in which the water from the river could have been cleaned. It may have been felt that "pure" river water was of high medicinal value, or perhaps some doctor was advising people to bathe off the east coast - the water temperature would have numbed any pain! It was perhaps odd that Rigby should have ever considered the scheme, as a spa at the coast exposed to cold east winds, in a place described by Garrick, as being surrounded by swamps, and where it was necessary to drink brandy instead of beer, would hardly have been popular!

The outside of the building was to have been a typical Adam-style, elaborate Grecian design, with rectangular pillars, and triangular roof lines, apart from the domed roof of the rotunda. Much of the building was to have been below ground level, and the doors and windows were to have semicircular tops. There was a low curved wall on the outside of the building, between the pillars. This small building was perhaps one of the best Robert Adam ever designed. Although small in comparison with some of Adam's massive buildings, its stone facings, decoration, its strong pilasters and pediments were of the highest architectural merit.

Although much time was spent on the planning, and costly drawings were produced by Adam, the salt water baths were never built. A building of such quality and style would have cost an enormous amount of money, and this may well have been one of the reasons why it was abandoned.

Arthur Bolton, in his records of the Architecture of Robert Adam, written in 1922, gives a

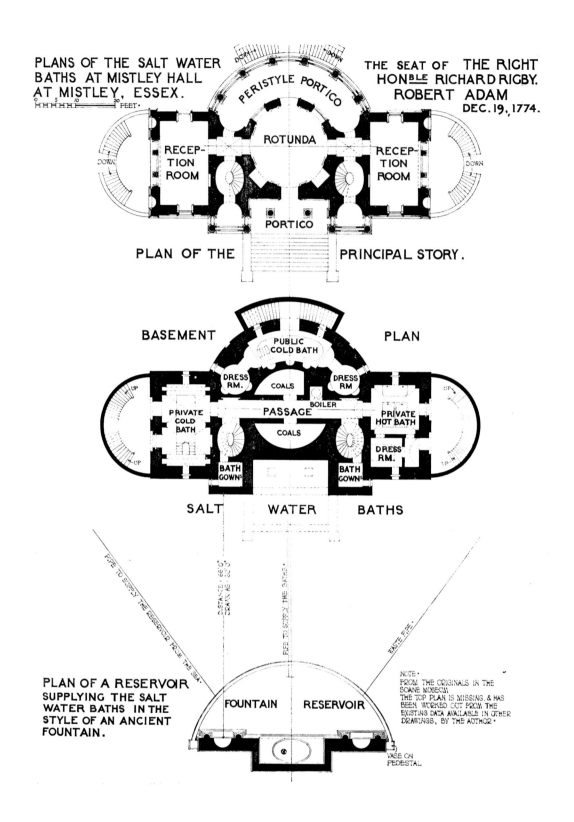

PLANS OF THE SALT WATER
BATHS AT MISTLEY HALL
AT MISTLEY, ESSEX.

THE SEAT OF THE RIGHT
HONBLE RICHARD RIGBY.
ROBERT ADAM
DEC. 19, 1774.

PERISTYLE PORTICO

ROTUNDA

RECEP-
TION
ROOM

RECEP-
TION
ROOM

DOWN

DOWN

PORTICO

PLAN OF THE   PRINCIPAL STORY.

BASEMENT   PLAN

PUBLIC
COLD BATH

DRESS
RM.   COALS   DRESS
RM

BOILER

PRIVATE
COLD
BATH   PASSAGE   PRIVATE
HOT BATH

COALS   DRESS
RM.

UP   UP

BATH
GOWNS   BATH
GOWNS

SALT   WATER   BATHS

PLAN OF A RESERVOIR
SUPPLYING THE SALT
WATER BATHS IN THE
STYLE OF AN ANCIENT
FOUNTAIN.

FOUNTAIN   RESERVOIR

NOTE.
FROM THE ORIGINALS IN THE
SOANE MUSEUM
THE TOP PLAN IS MISSING, & HAS
BEEN WORKED OUT FROM THE
EXISTING DATA AVAILABLE IN OTHER
DRAWINGS, BY THE AUTHOR.

VASE ON
PEDESTAL

Plans of Salt Water baths
(By courtesy of The Trustees of St. John Soane's Museum)

100

Detailed drawing of the side elevation.
(By courtesy of The Trustees of St. John Soane's Museum)

Rough sketch drawn by Robert Adam showing the entrance to the proposed Salt Water Baths.
(By courtesy of The Trustees of St. John Soane's Museum)

Hopping Bridge, built by the first Richard Rigby replacing the wooden structure which spanned the stream through Hopping Marsh.
Re-designed by Robert Adam in 1778.

Right: south elevation showing some of the Adam decoration.

The Swan Fountain, and the grapevine cottages behind were built to the designs of Robert Adam

Smaller fountain at the rear of the Swan basin.

vivid description of the life of Richard Rigby, and the buildings he commissioned them to design for him. He was of the opinion that the existing swan basin was to have been used as the reservoir for the salt water baths, and that the building would have been erected on the quay, in the position the Grapevine Cottages occupied. It seems somewhat unlikely that Rigby, having only just completed Thorne Quay for the purpose of increased shipping, would have placed a large building on it, and demolished four cottages which Adam had only recently erected. In addition to this, careful examination of Adam's plans shows clearly the levels of the spring and common tides, which would have determined the depth to which the reservoir was to be constructed; they show the bottom of the reservoir to be level with the lowest tide. These factors clearly rule out the swan basin as a source of supply to the baths, as it occupies a position at least 25' above this level. Had Rigby continued his plans for the baths, he might well have built them near the church in the area of park land at the western side, which would have added a further focal point of interest to the view from the Hall. At this time a new parapet on Hopping Bridge was built to Adam's design, which suggests that Rigby intended to develop in this part of the estate.

Rigby's friendship with the Adam brothers lasted for many years, and it is sad that their wonderful designs for the Salt Water Baths never came to fruition. The village is, however, fortunate to have kept examples of their architecture at the Towers, and the Swan Fountain, with the attractive cottages behind. These remarkable and much admired buildings, along with the less prominent Adam Lodge, are part of Mistley's history, which Rigby's influence brought to the village more than 200 years ago.

Many of the Adam brothers designs can be seen in the Soane Museum in London., and include most of those Rigby commissioned them to undertake.

Mistley Hall and Park from Hopping Bridge.

CHAPTER 20

MISTLEY HALL AND PARK AFTER 1770

For more than forty years the great Hall in Mistley Park, the home of Richard Rigby, and for much of the time his sister Anne, was widely known for the hospitality and friendship extended to everyone who stayed there.

Walpole, who was reported in an earlier chapter to have criticised the Hall and gardens, later praised Rigby's efforts in a letter to a friend written in 1749:

> *"You can't imagine how he has improved it. He has demolished all*
> *his paternal entrenchments of walls and square gardens, opened*
> *lawns, swelled out a bow window, erected a portico, planted groves,*
> *stifled ponds, and flounced himself with shrubs and Kentish fences.*
> *You may imagine I have a little hand in this."*

Walpole's influence was partly responsible for the transformation of the Hall and gardens, but it was Robert Adam who some thirty years later brought it to perfection. Forthcoming chapters will describe the pattern of life at Mistley Hall, as they were during the fifteen years from 1768.

The imposing Mansion House set on rising ground, was flanked by outbuildings, some of which remain at the top of Church Lane. The ancient buildings have long been known as the "Old Laundry", with the woodland of the same name nearby. Some of these buildings were in fact the offices, servants' quarters, stables, coach houses, and the laundry. Other smaller structures used for a variety of purposes, have been demolished over the years, but part of those remaining included the laundry, and servants' hall. The Hall stood on the right-hand side of these buildings, with a colonnade leading to the west wing. It faced the church and the river, surrounded by beautiful gardens and sweeping lawns.

Behind, slightly below the Hall the large Dairy House Farm was still in operation. It still stands on rising ground, with the streams and fields leading to the woods in the distance. This house was often used to accommodate visitors when large parties were held in the Hall. Adjacent to the house were offices, an excellent dairy, a laundry, brick stables, a small malt room and brewhouse. The malt room had all the necessary brewing utensils, and a large well. These amenities were shared with the Hall, and the water was drawn from powerful springs and deep wells nearby.

The interior of the Hall was richly decorated and complemented by the graceful lines of the Adam fireplaces, and fine pieces of elegant furniture. The bedrooms, however, were simply furnished. Eleven of these, with adjoining dressing rooms were reserved for visitors. The drawing room in the magnificent new wing was often used as a ballroom. On the lower floor were several exquisitely furnished anterooms, used for a variety of purposes. The walls were hung with excellent pictures and valuable oil-paintings including "Valkof at Nijmegen", by the Dutch landscape artist, Albert Cuyp, and others by David Teniers, and the French painter Nicolas Poussin, whose "Golden Calf" is displayed in the National Gallery. The imposing portraits of the 4th Duke of Bedford, by Gainsborough, and that of Richard Rigby, by Ercaadt, hung in the large entrance hall. The wonderful landscape painting of the "Woodman" by Gainsborough hung in the drawing room, which with others was purchased by the 5th Duke of Bedford in 1789, when the art collection was sold. The paintings of the Duke, and a copy of that of Richard Rigby, are now at Woburn Abbey, and Gainsborough's "Woodman" occupies pride of place in the drawing room of the Marchioness of Tavistock. The most valuable painting in the Hall was "Vertimnus and Pomona", by Rembrandt, the 17th century Dutch artist. Most of these paintings, with other fine works by less well known artists, were acquired by Rigby on his visits to the continent.

Amongst the beautiful pieces of furniture were two huge tables. These were made of mahogany, the most fashionable wood at that time. There are no records of how many could be accommodated at dinner, but it is estimated that at least fifty could be seated in the dining room. The china, silver and glassware were of the highest quality, and with the addition of flowers, would have given the table an unsurpassed elegance.

The rooms were heated almost entirely by coal fires. There were copious amounts of wood on the estate, and a regular supply of coal was available from the numerous merchants with yards on the quay. During the winter months, fires were lit in every room, and it is possible that at least one servant would have been employed just to tend them.

Rigby was seldom alone in the Hall, but when he was he spent much of his time travelling round the estate visiting his tenants. He had frequent meetings with his agent, Mr. Ambrose, to discuss affairs of the estate, and often invited him to dine at the Hall with the farmers.

As has already been said, Richard derived his greatest pleasure from entertaining his friends. Details of invitations show that he regularly arranged banquets at the Hall, where many enjoyed the hunting and shooting that the estate provided, or in summer river trips on his yacht. However, what he preferred to all else were the dinner parties he frequently gave.

The pattern of life at Mistley Hall was similar to that of most of the nobility in England in the 18th century. Breakfast was served at about 10.00 a.m. in one of the anterooms, and the meal usually consisted of home made bread and butter with eggs and kidneys. Coffee, tea and chocolate were also served. After breakfast everyone followed their own pursuits, unless hunting or shooting parties were arranged.

Dinner was very formal. It began between four and five o'clock in the afternoon, with everyone

Dairy House Farm

106

immaculately dressed, and often continued for more than five hours. During the first two hours several small courses were slowly eaten, and the host would continually press the guests to take second helpings. Nearly all the courses were based on various joints of meat and game, whether boiled or roasted; in particular there was an abundance of pheasant, partridge and woodcock, and on occasions venison from the deer park would be served. There were also vegetables from the estate. A splendid variety of fruit was available, according to the season, also grown on the estate, and puddings of many sorts were eaten with cream. During the lengthy dinner, many bottles of fine wine were consumed from the enormous stock which Rigby stored in the cellars below the Hall. After the dinner was over, crystal bowls of water would be brought so that people could rinse their hands, and in some cases their mouths. Finally the tablecloths would be removed and the polished surface of the mahogany table revealed. In the centre of this lovely piece of furniture was placed an enormous bowl of fruit, which was soon surrounded by every sort of wine and spirit.

At this time the servants were dismissed, and the ladies would adjourn to the drawing room. This was the signal for more drinking, which often developed in an alarming manner! The bottles were steadily passed to the left around the table, with Rigby, as leader, encouraging everyone to drink as the bottle reached them, and ensuring that no-one missed. Many toasts were made; they might begin by being dedicated to a political cause or one of the ladies, but were eventually proposed to the most improbable people, which caused a great deal of laughter. When the ladies had left the room a row of chamber pots was lined up on the sideboard. The maids had the thankless task of emptying them the next morning!

After another hour or so, the men joined the ladies in the drawing room, leaving the wine for another day. The ladies by this time had been served tea and coffee, and whilst this was drunk, the party divided, and hands of whist were played. At midnight, cold meat was served to anyone who was still hungry, and a bowl of punch was available for those who could drink it.

The parties at Mistley Hall usually followed this pattern, and Rigby was always at the forefront of the entertainment. His capacity for claret was phenomenal, and his ready wit kept everyone in

Dairy House Farm. The building on the right was the Brewhouse. It contained a deep well from which the water was drawn.

bouts of laughter. During the hundreds of magnificent events Rigby held at Mistley, vast quantities of wine were drunk, consignments being brought in direct from the continent to Mistley Quay. Cargoes often slipped through without payment of duty, and Rigby was in constant conflict with the customs officers, although they were evidently not averse to accepting a bribe now and again, and looking the other way!

The wine was stored in the cellars below the Hall, including one below the servants' hall. A Mr. John Lucas was in charge of the wine cellars, and in addition to being fed and clothed, he received a salary of £44-11-4d. per year. He kept a handwritten account book, showing the stock of wine stored in each cellar. The entries were carefully recorded, showing the wine purchased, and bottles drawn by the butler for use in the house. Rigby's wine cellar in the 1780s contained the following large and varied stocks of fine quality wines and spirits:

Stock of wines and spirits in the cellars at Mistley Hall, 1782.

Pacherety	36	qts. and	10	btls.
Madeira	35	" "	12	"
Sherry	32	" "	446	"
Burgandy	8	" "	60	"
Burgandy White			2	"
Champain Red	14	"		
Champain White	62	" "	217	"
Le cote	28	" "	110	"
Hock	202	" "	216	"
Red cape	15	"		
Vin de Grave	3	"		
Cyprus (30 years old)	49	"		
White Brandy	13	"		
Apricot Brandy	16	"		
Sack	54	"		
Moselle	36	"		
Rum	11	"		
Claret	1224	"		
Cyder	13	"		
Perry	21	"		
Orange Wine	9	"		
Pickardy	16	"		
Malaga	259	"		
Spirits of wine	13	"		
Saltzer water	16	"		
Vinegar	6	"		
Olives	9	"		
Port	274	"		
Cherry Brandy	24	"		
Port (pipes in wood)	2	qts.		

With 417 quarts and 3142 bottles of wine and spirits in his cellars, is it any wonder that Richard

Lodge at Mistley

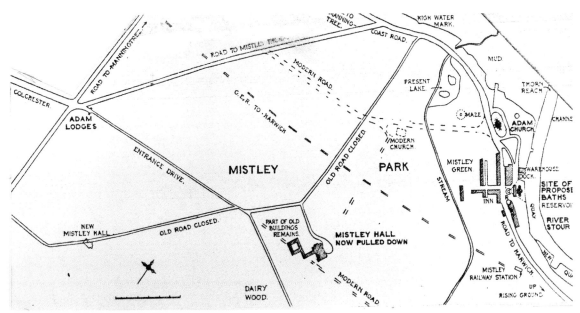

Map showing Hall and roadways in 1784. Transposed on are the railway and some of the roads as they are today. A new road from Pound corner to Lodges Corner was planned but never built (shown as modern road on map), it is now known as Green Lane

Rigby suffered from frequent attacks of gout towards the end of his life?

Apart from the huge scale of entertainment Rigby provided at the Hall, friends from all walks of life were regularly invited to use it as a halfway house between London and the continent. In order to cater for so many visitors and to look after the day to day running of the house, it was necessary to have a number of servants. The servants in the large houses in England in those days were normally at work for twelve hours, usually from six in the morning to six at night, with others on duty during the evening. They were entitled to a break of two hours during this time, laid down by an act of Parliament. When there were extra guests, it sometimes became necessary to engage temporary servants as well as those employed regularly at the Hall, most coming from the immediate neighbourhood.

Many young men and women were engaged in service in the 18th century, working long hours in the houses of the gentry. Maidservants would usually earn £14-2s. per year, as well as their keep for working six days a weeßk, and twelve hours per day, but at Mistley Hall, however, they were paid between £18/19 per year. The Hall was run by a housekeeper, and in the 1770s-80s the duty was undertaken by Mary Lucas, (the wife of John Lucas) who was paid £34-5-2d. per annum. The butler was Thomas Carrington, whose salary was far above anyone else's at £65-8-9d. per year. The organisation at the Hall was in their hands, with assistance from John Chapman and, Richard Fayers, who occupied senior positions on the serving staff, and were paid £51-3-8d. and £45-6-0d. respectively. Amongst the chambermaids were Ann Hart, Martha Simmons, Elizabeth Edwards, Alice Squirrell and Mary Ward, all of whom were paid £18 per year. The name of the chief cook is unknown, and although this duty was usually a woman's, it is thought that it may have been carried out by one of the men. Some of the men servants were James Palmer, Joseph Drew, William King, John Wheeler, John Crampin, Nathaniel Saunders, and Ben Kenningale, who were paid between £23 and £31 per year according to their duties. During the years between 1770 and 1785, Rigby had more than forty servants regularly employed inside and outside the Hall. They worked extremely hard, but were paid several pounds per year above the normal rates paid elsewhere.

The housekeeper insisted on cleanliness and tidiness throughout the Hall, and the stairways and floors were scrubbed daily from attic to cellar. This was surprising, as hygiene was not as we now know it. The kitchen in Mistley Hall was evidently kept very clean- not the accepted practice, as it is well known that the cleanliness of most 18th-century kitchens left much to be desired. The care observed at the Hall is illustrated in the amount of a linen washer's bill of 1778 which came to the large total of £55-14-8$^{1}/_{2}$d.

In 1784, in order to accommodate the large number of servants, Rigby had a new building put up for them, costing many hundreds of pounds. This still stands today, as one of the buildings known as the Old Hall, now a kennels.

There is little doubt that the servants provided an efficient and friendly service to the hundreds of guests who stayed there. They were rewarded by a good wage for their hard work, and greatly contributed to the esteem in which Rigby was held at that time. However, despite the excellent service, and the lavish meals, it must be said that one of the greatest attractions was the beauty and serenity of the surrounding countryside. The view from the Hall over the sloping lawns to the church, and the river, and the masts of the ships in the port, was admired by everyone who stayed there. On the hill the ancient windmill with revolving sails could be seen towering above the red brick cottages of the village snuggled beneath. All these things contributed to the charm of the place, and Mistley Hall and its park became known as one of the most beautiful estates in England.

The Home Park and Pleasure Gardens.

The pleasure gardens and the park land which surrounded the Hall amounted to nearly 400 acres. This was brought to perfection by the end of the 1770s. The western boundary of the park was edged by the Horsley Cross road from Lodges Corner curving southwards to Ford Farm. At the bottom of the hill at Ford Farm there is still a brook which meanders through the park to Hopping Bridge on the Manningtree road, where it enters the river. The eastern boundary enclosed the woodlands and hills, part of the present Furze Hills, as far as the ballast pit, at the top of Mistley Hill, and downwards to the south of the village. The northwest side was marked by a road which ran from the Manningtree road near Hopping Bridge, and back to Lodges Corner. At this point on the Manningtree road was a gate with a narrow driveway up to the Hall, but the main entrance began at the Lodge now known as Lodges Corner.

Much of the Home Park was criss-crossed by footpaths, which were used by the public under ancient rights. In order to provide privacy and seclusion, spinneys were planted, behind which flower gardens and shrubberies were cultivated. These were all carefully sited near the sweeping drives running through the Park, on which Rigby could drive his Post Chaise. The entire garden was planted with a variety of rare trees, some of which were not native to England. Two large tulip trees, some forty feet high, planted by his father, grew near the Hall, and in early summer, their blooms would have been a wonderful sight. Most of the trees in the park in the 1770s had been planted at least forty years before, and would have grown into fine specimens. There were hundreds of large oaks, elms and alders carefully spaced throughout the grounds, some of which exist today, but unfortunately the rare trees which Rigby planted have gone, probably because the environment was unsuitable for them.

Several shrubberies consisted of rhododendrons of various colours, and exquisite hydrangeas. These were set at selected places within the spinneys, and provided a beautiful picture in the spring. Some of the shrubberies are still scattered within the former Home Park; one can be seen today at the western end of Keepers Pond, and contains an enormous oak tree, which must be at least 250 years old. Close by are several fine alders, which would have been planted in Rigby's time when the lake was made.

The Hall was surrounded by rose gardens, the roses being mainly of the old English variety. Rigby had also purchased some fine species from the continent, which provided a glorious kaleidoscope of colour. Accounts show that in 1777 a new fence was built around the rose gardens at a cost of £21-2-10d.

Several gravel footpaths and roadways ran through the park beside the trees which had been planted to give a shaded walkway. Masses of rambler roses were trailed over them and formed arches over the paths.

A tiny pond, the remains of which can still be seen, lay on the sloping lawn below the house, in the middle of the field now known as Tunnel Meadow. Now a stagnant area and filled with rubbish, two hundred years ago it was a small well kept lake, surrounded by trees and shrubs, with an ornamental brick bridge spanning the narrow end. Set in the centre of the park it was one of the most attractive features in the gardens.

The main flower gardens lay to the south of the Hall, in the area now known as Laundry Wood. Blooms from all over the world grew here in beautifully tended beds with pathways winding between. Set beside the path, grottos were constructed with rocks, in which ferns and heathers grew in abundance.

A number of men were permanently employed in caring for the extensive gardens, and the lawns covering several acres were mown weekly. Lower down in the park was the cricket field, in much the same spot as today's now stands. In those days it was not surrounded by a fence or hedge, but merely formed part of the park lawns. An attractive thatched wooden building was used for changing. The senior experienced gardeners, named Saunders, Clarke, Hirman and Ward were employed at a wage of 8/- for a week of six days, and were also responsible for tending the huge vegetable gardens set on the western side of the park.

In 1775, Rigby met Monsieur Bernard Scale, a Huguenot, whom he had earlier known when he was in Ireland. He was a very experienced and well-known cartographer and calligrapher. Many of the landed gentry at this time had engaged him to survey and draw coloured maps of their estates. With his park land and gardens in mind, Rigby commissioned him to survey a large part of the estate. With the assistance of three men employed by the estate, Scale meticulously recorded every farm and field, showing the trees, hedges and farmhouses, down to the very gates. The Hall and gardens in the park were drawn in colour, and the individual houses in the village were sketched in great detail. A separate book, which served as a key to the drawings, records the acreages of the fields, a description of the buildings, and the tenants' names. The handwriting and drawing are wonderful examples of calligraphy, and cartography, and allowing for the survey and measurements which had to be taken in order to draw the maps, the work must have taken a long time to complete. Scale probably used a survey done in 1765 as a basis for his work, and although his drawings are dated 1778, they do not show the malting or the swan fountain which were built by this time.

The church is also drawn, showing it as it was before it was rebuilt, and it is thought that his maps of this part of the estate may have been completed much earlier. The map of the village and the port is somewhat idealised, and the river and quay show a number of sailing ships, with a tiny vessel being constructed on the slipway at the shipyard. Each of the thirty-one maps he prepared bears the magnetic direction sign, surrounded by intricate drawings of agricultural implements.

His wonderful coloured maps occupy pride of place in the County Record Office at Colchester and are some of the finest examples of 18th century cartography in this country. Whilst he was doing his work at Mistley, Scale met and married Henrietta Letch, a young lady from Dedham.

Two Frenchmen, Francois and Alexandre de la Rochefoucauld, spent most of 1784 in Suffolk. They kept a careful record of their travels, which have been the subject of a book, excellently translated by Norman Scarfe, and published by Boydell and Brewer. They visited Mistley during the summer of that year, their writings revealing their obvious delight at what they saw:

> *"If the house is beautiful, the gardens are even more so, at least they made more of an impression on me. The truth is I had already seen fine houses, but I had not seen an English garden coming anywhere near this one.*
>
> *We went first into the pleasure garden, the closest to the house. It is composed of groups of very rare trees, raised with care, and disposed with art on a carpet of turf, which is mown every week. The grass is admirably fine and smooth. The walk is a gravel path, which takes in a charming curve, every part of the garden, and is carefully arranged to pass the foot of every handsome tree.*
>
> *Leaving the first garden, which is really a large grove enclosed by a wide ditch; we crossed the road, and entered another garden, then another, and so on for more than two miles. Then we made the tour of the last, and returned along the far side of each of the gardens we*

have been through. I observed everywhere, the same care and the same neatness. The walk is wide, sometimes grass, and sometimes sand, Mr. Rigby accompanied us all the way in his open carriage. The abundance of evergreens is extraordinary, and the majority are tall and superb".

From this first hand impression, described with such obvious pleasure, there is little doubt that Rigby's park and gardens at Mistley Hall were truly magnificent.

The Deer Park.

The Deer Park adjoined the Home Park to the east. It was bordered in the north by the gravel roadway at the eastern end of Green Lane, and on the east by the Harwich Road to Mistley Heath as far as Bradfield. On the south it was edged by the road to Horsley Cross and Bradfield. The whole area was substantially that of the farm now called Dove House, at Mistley Heath. The farmhouse was then the home of the keeper, who was responsible for running the park.

The area of pasture amounted to more than 300 acres, and about 150 acres of the park was arable. On the remainder of the deer park flocks of sheep were allowed to graze. A small part was divided into fields, and in some of these cows were kept and milked at Dairy Farm.

A Gamekeeper's cottage was situated on the edge of the park near the lake called Gull Pond, which exists today south of Furze Hills. In 1770 contained fish of many species. It saw a lot of fishing by both Rigby and his guests, and trout in particular were often caught and eaten later at the Hall.

On the edge of the Deer Park boundary on the Harwich Road was the point now known as Pound Corner.

In the park were a number of small woods; one of which can be seen on the north of Ford Farm Hill, called "Beech Plantation". Another very fine wood called Oak Grove on the western side of Deer Park was, covered six acres and was full of bluebells, pheasants and woodcock. Unfortunately much of it was destroyed soon after the last war,. The "Old Mount" described in an earlier chapter, and a small spinney, "Oak Plantation", can still be seen today to the north of the television mast.

This attractive area of pasture and woodland was really an extension of the Home Park, and its fine trees and small plantations added to the splendour of the estate, already famous for its superb trees and splendid landscapes, which rivalled any in England at the time.

The Fruit and Vegetable Gardens.

The fruit and vegetable gardens consisted of nine acres, mostly enclosed by massive brick walls some twelve feet in height. In the open area, many kinds of vegetables were grown, providing the Hall with supplies all the year round. Gooseberries, raspberries, strawberries and currants were grown in different sections, while orchards of cherries, apples and other fruit, including medlars, covered a large area.

Within the walled section were five hothouses, which contained many rare fruit trees. Most of these were of the dwarf variety which Rigby had obtained from France, and by carefully controlling the temperature and humidity fruit was obtained very early in the season. Two of the five hothouses were built in two sections, and warmed by pipes through which water was provided by flues built into the hothouses, through which hot air was circulated. The walls of the garden also had flues placed within the brickwork, which heated the wall and the ground in front. Grapes and other fruit were grown against the walls, and the vines remained in perfect condition even during the winter months. With the advantage of this artificial heating an enormous number of grapes were grown very late in the year. In addition, Rigby grew cherries, melons, peaches, nectarines, and even pineapples in his hothouses.

In 1776, Rigby spent £474-15s. on extensions to the hothouses, and at the same time built a new fruit house costing £99. By 1784, he had built a further greenhouse, and extended the walled garden.

The head gardener kept a detailed record of all the produce grown, showing the dates when the vegetables were sent to the Hall, and the amount of fruit picked. Some of the entries made on 1780 give an indication of the enormous amount of fruit and vegetables which must have been grown. The gardener's records for part of the month of August included 347 bunches of grapes, 12 dozen peaches, 15 dozen nectarines, 40 apricots, 15 dozen greengages and plums, and half a bushel of medlars. Large quantities of currants, apples and cherries (red, white and black) were picked, and on one day a peck of gooseberries was delivered to the housekeeper. A bushel each of peas, runner beans and French beans were also sent, together with 15 cucumbers, 18 cauliflowers and strangely, at that time of year, 33½ dozen sprouts. Apart from the fact that sprouts in August are most unusual, the gardeners appear to have counted them individually!

In 1774, the wells in the gardens were made deeper, and a large reservoir constructed.

There were of course copious amounts of manure available for the gardens, and helped by all this, together with chalk and lime, the gardeners were able to keep the Hall supplied with fruit and vegetables throughout the year.

Rochefoucauld was shown the vegetable gardens during his visit, and his first hand account gives a delightful picture of the magnificent produce he saw. He writes:

> *"The kitchen garden stands behind this walk, and is the best I have ever seen. There are nine acres, divided into five parts, by brick walls eighteen feet high, and covered with superb fruit trees of every variety, brought from France. The hothouses are very large, and well exposed to the sun. There is a double one, arranged so that with very little imagination, here, in July, you can imagine yourself under an arbour of beautiful ripe grapes. The dwarf cherry trees, which adorn the hothouse were all red when I saw them, creating a charming effect; peaches and pineapples were of a quantity, and size, quite mouth-watering".*

It is fortunate that this confirmation of the beauty and variety of Mistley Hall gardens exists, described by a Frenchman more than two hundred years ago.

Rigby spent a fortune on Mistley Hall and its beautiful Park, and the best part of this work was done at the latter end of his life. Public footpaths which still run throughout the old Mistley Park, will, with many of its pictures, still reveal how it must have looked in the days of the Rigbys.

CHAPTER 21

THE PARTIES AT MISTLEY HALL

It would be impossible to name all the eminent and sometimes notorious, people who came to Mistley as guests of Richard Rigby after he had inherited the estate in 1747, though most of the Whig politicians with whom he served in Parliament would have visited him, and experienced his exceptional hospitality. As has already been mentioned, his first guest of note was Horace Walpole, whose advice was most useful in the construction of the beautiful gardens at the Hall. Rigby's greatest friend when he first became a Member of Parliament was Henry Fox, the 1st Lord Holland, who was also a frequent visitor in the 1740s. He used all his considerable influence to advance Rigby in his political career, but their friendship unfortunately waned fifteen years later due to political differences, and both he and his son, Charles, became enemies of Rigby.

The front of the stables and servants quarters of the Old Mistley Hall.

Charles, became enemies of Rigby.

After meeting the Duke of Bedford in 1752, Rigby was a constant visitor at Woburn and the Duke and Duchess also spent many happy days at Mistley. After the Duke died in 1771, his young grandson whom Rigby had known from his birth became the 5th Duke. They remained friends until the end of his life.

A number of politicians who had attached themselves to the Duke of Bedford were much disliked by some of the Parliamentarians at that time, including Lord Sandwich, Lord Gower and Lord Weymouth. Sandwich, known by the dubious name of "Jemmy Twicher", was the controller of the Navy from 1771 to 1782, and it was considered that his neglect of the fleets resulted in the loss of the American Colonies. He and other members of this infamous group occasionally stayed at Mistley; it was here that Lord Sandwich met his beautiful future wife, Martha Reay.

It was usual for Rigby to invite the Prime Minister of the day to stay with him, and in turn, the three Prime Ministers under whom he served, Lord Rockingham, George Grenville, and Lord North all came to Mistley. Both Foxs visited him, and the Duke of Bridgwater was often at Mistley, especially when the quay was being constructed.

It says much for Rigby's standing in the country that he counted amongst his friends the foremost members of the English nobility. Numbers of them came to the Hall: in 1770, for example, Lord Thurlow and the Marquis of Stafford were guests.

During his time in Parliament, Rigby had always loyally supported the Royal Family, and had been a constant companion of Frederick the Prince of Wales, who often came to Mistley, although the friendship later cooled. The Duke of York visited the Hall in 1765, and stayed for several days. In 1782 at the age of 20, George the Prince of Wales travelled incognito to Mistley. However, many en route appear to have been told, as crowds lined the road all the way from London. He came again in 1783, staying from Saturday until Tuesday, and was taken shooting at Walton Manor. He was very popular, and on the way back his carriage was persued through the streets of Colchester by cheering crowds. When his father went mad in 1811, he became the Prince Regent, finally succeeding to the throne in 1820.

Rigby's friendship with David Garrick, the actor, had grown over many years, and he was a frequent visitor to Mistley. Garrick, who was at the centre of the London theatre world, brought many famous actors and actresses to stay at Mistley, and Rigby, who was an ardent theatregoer, welcomed them with open arms. Rigby wrote to David Garrick on 13th June 1768:

> *"Do you imagine, my David, that any paltry consideration of office or business shall deprive me of the pleasure of our Mistley Party? I should be worth but half the Pay Office indeed if I could sacrifice the rites of Mistley to any earthly consideration; no, they begin the 15th, at Dinner - and you and your Cara Sposa are expected by her, and your faithful, humble servant.*
> *Richard Rigby."*

On October 7th 1777, Countess Spencer wrote to David Garrick from Fontainebleau:

> *"I need not say how much we were charmed with Mistley, the place, and the reception we met with there were such as you have so often, and so elegantly described."*

Although Rigby's invitations resulted in a constant stream of visitors, time was always set aside for the family especially his sister Anne, who remained devoted to her brother, and continued to have a great influence over him even after her marriage. His other sister, Martha, wife of General Hale, and their son Francis who was reputedly very fond of his Uncle, spent much time there. General Hale had become a Commissioned Officer in the Army, and although military duties kept him mostly in London, he frequently came to Mistley.

The regular family parties were quiet and informal. These usually took place in one of the anterooms next to the drawing room, and after dinner it was customary to play whist or other card games. Rigby enjoyed having the family and their friends at the Hall, and although he was a heavy drinker, he showed a quieter side of his character to them.

The Hall was especially inviting at Christmas, decorated with evergreens, holly and ivy. Carols would be sung there by parties of villagers, who would afterwards be invited into the Hall for refreshments.

For more than forty years, Mistley Hall was visited by hundreds of people from all walks of life, who were charmed by the hospitality they always received. During this time, with its beautiful gardens, excellent sporting facilities, and splendid entertainment, Mistley Hall was well known throughout the whole of England.

The social occasions were countlesss, ranging from small family gatherings to magnificent balls on a grand scale.

The noisiest gatherings were those held after the hunting and shooting. After shooting all day, and with frequent recourse to the inevitable hip flask, by late afternoon the company was very hungry, as well as more than slightly inebriated! After dinner the usual practice of passing the port ensured that everyone became drunk, and it was not unusual for one or two guests who could not hold their drink to be asleep on the floor in the corner of the room. Rigby, of whom it was always said that he "drank fair", never appeared to be affected!

The larger parties, where the ladies were present, were lavish. All the company were beautifully dressed, some of the men with wigs, powdered to retain the whiteness. The people from the village always knew when a party was being held, and gathered at the entrance to the Hall to see everyone arrive in their horse-drawn coaches. This pleased Rigby, and often, if the weather was cold, he gave the watchers punch, which was distributed by the servants.

The highlights of the Mistley scene, however, were grand balls, eagerly attended by large numbers of notable people. During the summer these took place outside, and well over two hundred people would be invited. In the winter these functions were held in the large drawing room, and fewer people would be invited.

For the summer balls there was a canopy over the lawn, supported by wooden pillars, around which were entwined all kinds of flowers and greenery; a floor being specially prepared for dancing. There were coloured oil lanterns, under which tables and chairs were placed. The musicians came from Colchester, and the sound of their music could be heard all through the night in the village. Throughout the evening splendid refreshments would be served, and the thirsty dancers would have copious amounts of wine and other delicious drinks.

Extra servants were engaged to remain on duty throughout the night, as the balls lasted until well after dawn. Breakfast was served for those resilient enough to be there until the end, and many spent the early hours asleep on the grass. It must have presented a wonderful picture to the villagers, with the great white Hall brilliantly lit, the colourful dresses of the ladies, and the couples strolling in the moonlight.

On an occasion in 1760, this romantic scene prompted the composition of a poem entitled "The Ball". It is handwritten and covers four larger than foolscap sheets of paper. The writing is most difficult to read, and the poet gives a very clear picture of a ball which was held at Mistley Hall at that time. The person who wrote it had obviously attended a ball there, and as the original was discovered in Mistley, it may well have been composed by someone close to the family.

The following verses vividly illustrate the feelings of those invited, those who watched, the ballroom, the dance, the approach of the end, and those about to go home:

> *Descriptive Fanny, fair poetic Queen*
> *Paint in thy gayest hues the enchanting scene,*
> *Which in the bowers of Mistley lately shone,*
> *And make it, if you can, once more our own.*
>
> *Draw out the various beauties of the place;*
> *Let art with nature join in fond embrace.*
> *Impatient at the evening hours attend,*
> *And think the sun unwilling to descend.*
>
> *Spectators line the roads, the chariots fly,*
> *Each gazes forward, as if all was by.*
> *Men, women, children, near the mansion stand,*
> *Allowed to see, not touch the promised land.*
>
> *The summons issues forth - to east - to west,*
> *Tis Rigby's treat - a country be thy guest.*
>
> *Pillars in rows, with flowering sucklings bound,*
> *Sustain the canopy, with garlands crowned.*
> *Pillars and ceiling gratefully make known;*
> *The hand which gave you beauties not your own.*
>
> *But hark, loud musick, now to action calls.*
> *Ready the rows, each into action falls.*
> *Eager they bound o'er the responsive turf,*
> *And all is movement, spirit, freedom, mirth.*
>
> *O', could it last; O' no, relentless fate,*
> *Denies what never ends to mortal state.*
> *The envious streaks of red, announcing morn,*
> *The sad assembly of departure warn.*
>
> *Fiery steeds, impatient of delay,*
> *Breath from their nostrils, fume and pant for day."*

Readers of this record may wish to stroll over the portion of the parkland which was the scene of these wonderful parties held more than two hundred years ago. It can be reached by walking up the present Church Lane; about three quartes of the way up would have been where the canopy was placed. Sadly, it is difficult to imagine the beauty of the old Mistley Hall and its lovely gardens. All that is left is the devastated Laundry Wood, adjacent to two ill-kept fields, with a badly surfaced lane running between.

Rigby's parties reached their peak in the 1760s and early 1770s, but even in later years, he continued to hold these social events which he enjoyed so much. They were, however, never quite the same after the death of his lifelong friend, David Garrick, in 1779.

Later, in those staid and virtuous Victorian times, when memories of the Park, and its lovely gardens were related from parent to child, there were disapproving whispers about heavy drinking at all night parties, which, it was reputed, shocked some of the villagers many years before. It will never be known, but I think it is doubtful that anyone at the time objected to Rigby's social activities. He was a colourful character who did much for the village people, and few would have denied him his right to enjoy himself, which he certainly did.

East Lodge, the lovely house on the south side of Mistley Green was the home of the Ambrose family for over 100 years.

CHAPTER 22

INDUSTRY AND RIGBY'S PORT AT MISTLEY THORNE FROM 1760

Asubstantial increase in the shipping activities undertaken at Mistley began after the building of the new Thorne Quay in the 1770s. This, together with the improved storage facilities for grain and other cargo, attracted considerable business to the already bustling port. The roadways to it were widened and surfaced in order to prevent congestion of the hundreds of horse-drawn carts and wagons coming to the ships and the grain stores.

By 1776 the quay was nearly 700' long and included a dock and a jetty into the channel. In addition there was a hard area some 200' in length where ships were loaded and unloaded, with carts driven alongside. The hard joined the shipyard, which stretched a further 250' to the east. From the end of the shipyard there was a beach of over 750',beside the channel of the river. Behind the beach and shipyard were a variety of buildings used to supplement the shipping operations.

Nearly 500 ships were registered at Mistley and the neighbouring small port of Manningtree, with a gross figure of more than 40,000 tons. Five wharfingers, sixteen shipowners, and forty-three ships' captains lived at Mistley and Manningtree, with several living in houses in the High Street, backing on to the quay.

Mr. John Ambrose, the estate steward, and his clerk, Samuel Tice, were regularly involved in legal matters on the quay, especially with the preparations of contracts for the sale of ships. Their attractive writing in the indentures and conveyances has been a pleasure to read during the research for this book.

Mistley had a resident Customs and Excise officers; for a time the Custom House was a building at the eastern end of The Green, which is now a private house. When Mr. Baxter, who also lived on The Green, was the officer in charge, he carried out his duties from the Thorne Inn. The officers were very active at Mistley and Manningtree, and searches of ships were frequently carried out by the so-called "rummaging parties".

The diverse types of cargo unloaded were stored in specific sections of the quay. There were numerous coalyards; a pit on the site where Portishead House now stands was used for storing the large quantities of chalk which were shipped in from Kent. Two sections of the quay were set aside for storing deals, one of which was on ground to the east of the church, and the second near the shipyard. Bricks were stored at the eastern end of the quay, and later a part near the beach was used, shown in old maps as the brickfield.

In the early 1800s, Mr. Edward Norman built several attractive maltings at the western end of Mistley, on land which he had leased for some time. Some of these still remain on the industrial site adjoining Manningtree opposite to the river, but have been long unused, and are now listed buildings. By 1841, seventeen maltings were fully operational at Mistley and Manningtree, paying a malt duty of more than £50,000 per annum. The Manningtree Brewery, owned by Mr. Alston, was producing 8,000 barrels of beer annually, and with Mistley and Manningtree teeming with thirsty quay workers and sailors, the public houses must have done a roaring trade.

Much of the malt made at the three maltings on the quay was shipped to London, and some to the small farm breweries in the Sudbury district. There was a small brewery at Manningtree at this time, but Alstons eventually became the major operator in the district.

With the increased trade, the population of the village grew rapidly, and in less than forty years it had doubled; by the year 1834, the population reached nearly one thousand. To all intents and purposes, Mistley had become a prosperous place for many, with trade booming in a number of small businesses. Employment, although not highly paid, was readily available, and the proportion of poor lower than in most villages at that time. There was however another side; an entry in the church register of births reads:

> *"Born, Nov. 20th 1837 - Charles Warner.*
> *Parents' names unknown - African Slave*
> *to George Howard, shipbuilder".*

Shipbuilding at the Port.

Ship repairing, and the building of very small ships, had been carried out in a small yard in front of the cliff since the 1720s. It was situated on the beach below the point where the present steeply-sloping road runs down to the quay near the railway bridge. Shipbuilding on a larger scale began in 1753, when the "Harwich" was launched. In 1760, Rigby substantially improved the facilities, constructing a lengthy slipway running down the beach to the river channel. At the top of the cliff above the shipyard was a blacksmith's shop which provided much of the ironwork for the ships. There was also a cage, presumably where the customs officers kept goods under their control, and a pound. This can still be seen today with trees and shrubs planted at the time of the Coronation in 1953.

Warehouses were erected for the storage and sewing of sails and other materials used during the construction of the ships. At the eastern end of the shipyard was a large open space set aside for the stacking of timber, which was carefully sawn into regular lengths and shaped according to its purposes by a number of highly skilled carpenters and other workers. In the early 1760s, after the improvements were completed, Rigby launched the first ship, watched by a large crowd of excited spectators.

When the yard reopened, it was managed by a Mr. Marshall, who continued to build small smacks, and other craft. In 1767, a sloop of 81 tons was launched, which was named "The Thorne" after the area, and sold to J. and G. Bridges for £100. Shortly afterwards a Mr. James Betts took over the shipyard and began to build a variety of boats of high quality, such as the sloop of 105 tons, called the Charlotte of Mistley Thorne, launched in 1772 and also sold to J. and G. Bridges. After each launching the keel of the next vessel was quickly laid and the shipyard became known for the excellence of it's workers.

Towards the end of the 18th century, when war with Napoleon was first feared, the yard was commissioned by the Admiralty to build warships. This arrangement continued for several years, which resulted in a reduction of vessels launched for purely commercial use, although some were still built; in 1790, for example, the "Industry", a vessel of 42 tons, was sold to Mr. Tolody for £710.

The construction of the warships began in about 1785. One of the first ships built was a frigate called the Terpsichore, weighing 682 tons. After she was launched, she was sailed to Harwich, where she was armed with 32 guns. In 1797, the frigate saw action with the fleet at Santa Cruz, where sadly the Captain and First Mate were killed, among other casualties. Betts also built the 32-gun "Amphian", which was for a time Nelson's flagship. A total of twelve men o'war were commissioned including the 32-gun frigate "Iphigene". During this hectic period, Betts still found time in 1802 to build a smack of 28 tons, called the "George", for which Joseph Long, one of the Mistley fishermen, paid him £308.

Soon after the turn of the century, Mr. James Howard, who already had a shipyard at Maldon, came to Mistley, and became tenant of the Mistley yard. After the battle of Trafalgar in 1805, the building of warships became less important, and Howard again began to launch craft for commercial use.

Over the years it had been customary to launch the ships, and rig them at another port, after they were afloat. Howard found it more economical to complete the rigging himself, and in 1834 he built and launched the "Countess of Wilton" fully rigged. The vessel was quickly sailed from Mistley, and immediately entered the prosperous fruit trade. The owner, Lord Wilton, was extremely pleased with the high standard of the work, and promptly commissioned Howard to build him a private yacht of 160 tons, which was laid down on the slipway vacated by the merchant ship. James Howard continued to operate the shipyard successfully to the time this story ends in 1844, and launched many fine ships. He was finally to purchase the yard in 1844.

The sails for the ships built at Mistley were for many years cut and sewn by six members of the Moore family. The four daughters of Mr. John Moore, the sailmaker, were employed in the manufacture of the sails, with three other workers engaged to assist them. A special building was set aside for the work, and the standard was reported as excellent by the many merchants who had their vessels built at Mistley.

Howard was very fortunate in having the services of a Mr. Randfield Tovill, who lived in Mistley, and was a ship designer of some note. Some of his designs, in many cases innovative, were incorporated in the ships built by Howard, and other east coast shipbuilders at that time. Every conceivable type of ship was built at this small yard, from fishing smacks to merchantmen of nearly 1000 tons (the slipways were later strengthened to allow even larger ships to be launched). Sloops, schooners, hoys, barges, and of course the men o'war, were all expertly constructed, and for many years the shipyard was a hive of activity.

Little is known of the methods of construction of the vessels, usually of carvel construction or clinker-built, although they demanded highly skilled workmanship. Even before each boat was built, there were the lengthy tasks of clearing the area and setting up the weighty bearers, which held the vessel in place while she was built. Then there was the difficult job of positioning the kelson, into which the ribbing of the hull was jointed, which required great skill and precision. The high masts had to be carefully shaped, and raised and screwed by intricate shrouds and rigging; the measurement and cutting of the canvas for the sails had to be carefully calculated. It is remarkable that such fine work could be done by hand alone, though the workers were experts in the use of the adze, and the other rather primitive tools used to shape the timbers.

It is interesting to note that the two buildings which still stand slightly to the west of the hill leading down to the present quay have always been known as Great Howards and Little Howards, thus fixing the position of the ancient shipyard.

The operations at the quay changed substantially in 1851, when the Eastern Union Railway Co. Built a branch line to Harwich from Lawford (Manningtree Station). The Act of Parliament which authorised this included a branch line to Mistley Quay, where a number of tramways were built. The barge traffic to Sudbury was devastated, but Mistley remained extremely busy, with many businesses changing hands, although the fishing industry declined as railway links were established with other ports. Mistley, however, had another asset, which enabled the village to continue its industrial tradition. The area around Mistley was rich in land suitable for growing good quality malting barley, and with the increasing consumption of beer, Edward Norman and others began a forward-looking programme of malting construction. With the River Stour nearby offering an ideal means of disposal for the water that remained after the barley had been steeped, Mistley and Manningtree were perfect places for malting. Furthermore, the grain storage and port facilities could be used for shipping malt to the large numbers of London breweries beside the Thames.

From this time, the yard stopped building ships, until some seventy years later, when Mr. Frederick Horlock opened a small yard at the eastern end of the quay in which he built a number of steel sailing barges, several of which are still sailing today.

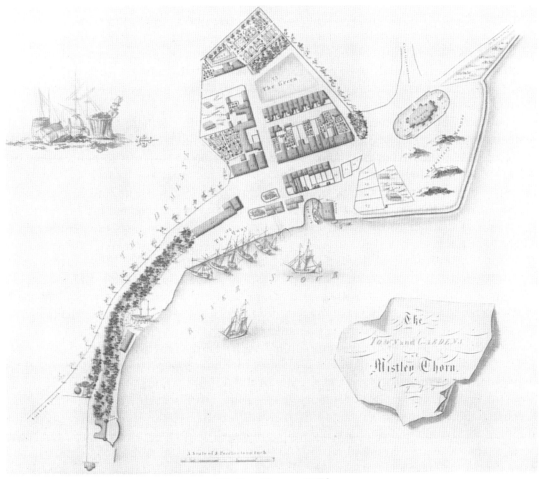

Mistley Thorn, 1778.
Bernard Scalé produced a volume of 31 maps of which this is one.
Reproduced by kind permission of Essex Record Office D/F1 E1

CHAPTER 23

SHIPPING AT MISTLEY THORNE

Ships had always sailed up the river to the wharf at Mistley Thorne, though as the channel meandered between the northern and southern banks, the passage over the last five miles from Wrabness was very difficult. The channel was quite narrow, and rather badly marked by large tree branches driven into the edges to give a rudimentary indication of the depth of the water. With the prevailing wind south-west in this part of England, tacking up to Mistley in square rigged-ships needed all the skills of experienced helmsmen and crews. Moreover, many sections of the mud flats, through which the channel ran, were covered with ribbon weed. The strands of weed were as long as five feet, and floated as the tide rose, making passage through them both slow and difficult.

About half a mile from Mistley Quay, beginning at the point called Ballast Hill, was a straight channel Miller's Reach, which led up to the quays at the Thorne. Those whose destination was Manningtree carried on up another straight part of the channel to the north, Thorne Reach. This channel at first ran to the northern shore, then turned sharply south west, narrowing and curving gently down to the small quay and adjacent beach. It split opposite the quay; the northern part, running to Cattawade, was the route taken by the barges to Sudbury.

The beauty of the extensive area of shallow water on the northern side of the channel opposite Mistley Quay, Seafield Bay, has been captured in the magnificent, if idealised, painting of "Mistley from Brantham", by Elias Martin. . Many of the houses remain, though of course they have been substantially altered over the years. The sight of Mistley Thorne, with its red brick granaries, below tree lined hills, its tiny cottages near the attractive church, and great white Hall above, must have gladdened the hearts of the thousands of mariners, who after what might have been a stormy passage, could enjoy a safe haven at last

During the unloading of the thousands of colliers bringing coal to Mistley, there was inevitably some spillage; much of this coal drifted into Miller's Reach, and lodged on the "spit" of the channel at Ballast Hill. Local fishermen collected this coal in their punts for many years. During fairly recent dredging operations in the river, the quantity of coal rendered the ballast unfit for commercial use.

After the building work in the time of the first Richard Rigby was completed, and the years passed, the amount of shipping at the port rose out of all proportion to its size. The improvements to the wharf, and the passing of the Act of Parliament allowing the River Stour to become navigable to Sudbury, had earlier made a major contribution to the tonnage handled. Apart from supplying the area around Mistley and Manningtree and shipping to London and Sudbury, the traffic handled was three times more than most ports of the same size. In the immediate locality to Mistley, hundreds of looms were at work producing materials for garments, and much of it was loaded into barges at Mistley for transhipment to London. Although a few cargoes from the Mistley farming area went to Sudbury, most of the goods sent by barge were brought by larger ships. Return cargoes came from Sudbury, were unloaded and reloaded at Mistley, and the goods were subsequently sent to London, and in some cases to Europe. Bricks had for many years been manufactured at Ballingden, near Sudbury; thousands of these were used in the building work at Mistley, and many more were shipped to other ports.

The Stour Navigation Company, which ran the barge service to Sudbury, was extremely well managed, and paid a handsome dividend of 14% to its shareholders. The traffic was very efficiently run and when working in pairs, the barges were able to transport about fifty tons of cargo to Sudbury on each trip. The water link through the beautiful Stour valley must have been one of the most attractive journeys. It is wonderful that so many examples of its landscape and horse drawn barges were captured by John Constable, in his famous paintings. This inland water route had a tremendous advantage over cartage by road. Not only were the roads rutted, and tortuous, but at least ten wagons would have been required to carry the same quantity as one barge. Throughout the Midlands and the North of the country, an increasing use was being made of the rivers and the canals which were being constructed at that time.

Five shipowners were based at Mistley, operating more than twenty vessels sailing regularly in and out of the port, the Messrs. Tovill, Norman, Page, Gray and Long, all of whom had backup premises on the quay, and handled a variety of cargoes. Whilst there was a large tonnage of agricultural produce, coal, deal, bricks and chalk formed a substantial portion of the commodities handled. Old documents also show iron, wood, material, wines, spirits and even candles and velvet. Regular shipments arrived in England carrying fruit from as far away as the Mediterranean, while some, especially lemons, came direct to Mistley. As the journeys were often prolonged, it was frequently found that the fruit did not always arrive in top condition.

The Norman family had become prominent in the port. Whilst not owning premises in the port itself, they had the tenancy of certain buildings, including a malting, on the quay. Over the years Edward Norman especially accumulated a substantial amount of money, which he used to great benefit in Mistley. He, with Jonathan and Thomas, were merchants, and were involved in selling much of the coal which arrived at Mistley. Apart from their coal and shipping interests, they also operated some fishing smacks. They eventually became wealthy merchants, owning and running a number of small businesses.

Edward at first lived in one of the houses behind the Swan Fountain, but later moved to more spacious accommodation in a magnificent Mansion House near the river. Some trading was undertaken between the members of the family; for example, Jonathan sold the smack Liberty to Thomas for £50. On one occasion, Edward had the misfortune to find that his sloop, the Two Brothers, had gone ashore on the Nore. The crew left the ship to obtain help, using a rowing boat, and on return, found that the crew from another craft had taken their best anchor and cable. Later, the ship was plundered of all her cargo, and finally she floated, and returned to Mistley. Edward sold the vessel to James Cooper and Joseph Long for £430. Perhaps he was disillusioned by his misfortune, as at the same time he disposed of his other sloop, the Deborah.

The Manningtree New Shipping Co. operated the "John" and "Sarah", "Owners Goodwill", and the "Industry", using the Iron Gate Wharf in London, and sailing every Friday. Cargoes of sugar, which had been transferred in London from the very large deep-sea vessels, were brought to Mistley in bags.

By far the greatest tonnage of cargo brought to Mistley was coal from the collieries in the north-east of England. Colliers were engaged on regular voyages from Sunderland and Newcastle, and a large tonnage was transhipped at Mistley en route to Sudbury, with the remainder placed in the merchants' coalyards on the quay. At their peak barges were carrying 12,000 tons of coal to Sudbury per year.

With scores of ships using the port, careful examinations were carried out, checking the weights and quality of the goods. These were not done only by customs men: there was also a selected number of men who were certified to carry out checking procedures in conjunction with the customs officers. These men, who had to be numerate, and able to write clearly, were known in the port as "Sworn Meters" They played an important part in the administration and and efficient running of the port and were proud to be employed on this very important duty.

Some of the grain was shipped from the port, in sacks, weighing 224 lbs. Two sacks were measured as a quarter, or eight bushels. Wheat being heavier was weighed at 252 lbs per sack, with two sacks also known as a quarter. Malt was somewhat lighter, and two sacks weighing 168 lbs each were again known as a quarter. This rather complicated method of measurement continued until the 1960s, until most grain was handled in bulk and the tonnage weight was used.

If the weights were complicated, it was nothing compared with the extreme hard work which was undertaken in filling the sacks for shipment. This operation was done by a gang of six men, who changed positions after an agreed number of sacks had been filled. One man held the sack, and on either side of him were two men, with round wooden measures with handles on each side. The two men alternately plunged the bushel into the heap of grain, drawing forward the corn with their hands and arms, lifting it and tipping it into the sack. Four bushels filled it, and such was the skill of the men that usually only a small adjustment was necessary to obtain the correct weight. The fourth man wheeled the sack to the scale on a small barrow. The fifth man weighed the sack by balance, either increasing or decreasing the grain in the sack using a small metal scoop, which he filled from a full sack of grain placed next to the scale. The sixth man wheeled the sack away, and tied the mouth with a thick coloured string made of fillis, and known as a "tier". After a row of sacks was completed, the men ceased the bushelling, and two of them grasped the mouth of the filled sack with one hand, and placed a stout stick just above the bottom of it. They gently tipped the sack backwards, so that it rested on the stick. Using the stick as a lever, the sack was lifted and placed on to the top of the sack behind. The operation was known as "topping up".

The speed and skill of the men performing these operations were phenomenal, and were matched only by the prodigious thirst it created! The sacks were loaded into carts and either slid down a wooden shoot, or winched aboard ship, where the ship loaders carried them on their backs and stowed them in the hold. It will be seen from this description that the filling of sacks, and loading them aboard ships was a very labour intensive operation. It would be true to say that this was the pattern of all the work in the port, where a great number of men were employed. The deals which formed some of the cargo had to be unloaded from the ships by the stevedores, each carrying one or two planks on their shoulders, which was protected by a leather pad stitched on to their garment. The timber was stacked in the selected area of the quay, and sold to merchants or shipped by barge to Sudbury. Coal was shovelled into wicker skips, and winched ashore by hand. Every cargo had to be manhandled, and the unloading and loading operations required a large number of strong and skilful labourers.

A disastrous accident occurred at the quay whilst the schooner, Good Intent, was being unloaded. The captain found that the mooring ropes were straining, and attempted to ease them. Unfortunately the ropes slipped, and the vessel capsized, killing a porter, and seriously injuring another.

Mistley Thorne and Manningtree were often described as being full of rough, thirsty sailors and labourers. To a certain extent this was true, and the public houses were often overcrowded, and full of smoke from the inevitable clay pipes. No reports have been found that the community at large had problems relating to drunkenness, although there were isolated cases. However, in Manningtree regular fighting and rowdiness occurred in the streets. Mistley seemed a much quieter place, and perhaps the presence of Squire Rigby, the magistrate, acted as a deterrent.

Over the years a number of river pilots were employed in bringing the hundreds of ships from Harwich to Mistley. For a time the senior post was held by Robert Eteen. Two brothers, the Warners, also piloted vessels, but it seems that they were most

"Mistley from Brantham" by Elias Martin, painted at the time of the rebuilding of the Towers Church.
(by kind permission of the National Museum of Fine Arts, Stockholm)

unpopular, and were described as idle and drunken fellows. One of them, John, was drowned on 22nd May 1786. The river was not "buoyed", and ships were guided to Mistley by the knowledge of the river and experience of the pilot. Their memory of the river channel, and depths of water, gained from many years on the river, was splendid. Each pilot had landmarks, which he lined up, to give him an indication of his position. The skill which the pilots possessed can be appreciated all the more when it is considered that the ships which they guided were under sail, and reliant almost entirely on wind speed and direction. The pilot had to board the ship at Harwich, and strange to say, no account has been found of the means they used to get there or how they knew a ship had arrived. Perhaps the shipowners made provision to transport them to Harwich in Post Chaise.

It is also remarkable that in those days more ships were trading at Mistley than Harwich, Ipswich and Colchester together. The number of ships bringing cargo to Mistley in one year under review totalled nearly 400, with a further 40 foreign ships. To show the marked difference, in the same year, 140 vessels went to Ipswich, and 147 to Colchester and Harwich. At the turn of the 18th century, the age of steam was approaching, but it had little effect on Mistley during the period covered by this story, up to 1844. The crews manning the English ships totalled nearly 1800, and some 300 arrived on the foreign vessels. The port dealt with nearly 35,000 quarters of barley (7000 tons), and handled 1180 tons of oilcake. A total of 494 horses were shipped here, and 730 loads of timber. Many smaller vessels, some carrying mail, used Mistley and Manningtree, and passengers were carried to Harwich, and Ipswich. A service was run by Mr. John Moore taking passengers to London; before joining the vessel everyone congregated at the Wherry Inn situated near the boundary with Manningtree at what is now known as Wherry Corner.

Although a very strict watch was kept by the Customs and Excise, and revenue enforcement officers, smuggling on the east coast substantially increased. Many battles were fought between the militia and large numbers of armed men who began sailing ships right up to the shore, and discharging valuable goods into carts, where they were driven through the dark countryside, to be hidden or buried. Although some ten miles or so from the sea, Mistley had its share of smuggling. In 1784, 48 bags of wool were siezed and auctioned at the Thorne Inn. Some fifteen years previously, in 1769, 100 lbs of tobacco and half a hogshead of rum were found in a cargo being unloaded and the Customs searcher was dismissed for not checking the goods against the bill of lading. Mr. G. Bridges of Mistley had been importing peas in linen bags, until the customs realised this was a novel way of smuggling linen. The practice ceased after Mr. Bridges had been warned that he would be liable for duty on the sacks. The most interesting smuggling attempt was undertaken in a five-oar galley, captained by a man named Fenn. He and four others sailed and rowed to Holland, and returned with a cargo of gin. Carts to carry the smuggled goods were arranged to meet at the bridge at Cattawade, and after waiting offshore during the day, the five rowed the galley into Harwich at night, and up the Stour on the incoming tide. Unfortunately they were not aware that there were two bridges at Cattawade, and the boat arrived at one and the carts at the other. Daylight came, and the men attempted to hide the boat, but it had gone aground. The local militia were informed, and the men were caught and arrested.

It must have been a wonderful spectacle for the villagers, who could stand on the hill high above the river and follow the passage of the great colliers, and other cargo ships bound for Mistley under full sail. Amongst the large ships would have sailed smacks, and other small craft, striving to reach the port on the tide. This attractive scene would have given little indication of the danger and hardship which the sailors might have experienced during their voyage. With little or no navigational aids, or weather information, it was left to the personal experience of the captain and mate to guide their frail craft through the sands and shoals of the east coast of England, under sometimes dreadful weather conditions. The Colchester Gazette printed an awesome account in the 18th century, which read:

> "The whole line of the coast of Yarmouth presents a scene of devastation and ruin, occasioned by the late strong gale from the eastward. Wrecks lay scattered at every step, and the melancholy conclusion is that several ships and their crews have gone down; besides these are many vessels stranded, some of which are so much damaged, as not to be worth repairing".

In 1770 thirty vessels were lost off the coast below Lowestoft, and all their crews were drowned. A further forty foundered between Southwold and Yarmouth in 1789, and 120 bodies were washed up on the beaches. Only four years later 130 men were drowned near Yarmouth, again in an easterly gale, which sank and damaged scores of ships.

The loss of life was quite dreadful, and on some occasions as many as 500 ships at a time left port, and were unexpectedly caught by gales. Wrecks could be counted by the hundred, and for many years this high price in lives was paid in order to provide England with necessities for its inhabitants.

The villagers of Mistley Thorne shared in the universal sadness of these harrowing times, and would have been ever conscious of the thousands of mariners who were daily risking their lives to bring about the prosperity which Mistley Thorne was enjoying.

CHAPTER 24

THE FISHERMEN

When Edward Rigby inherited Mistley in 1709 the small wharf at the riverside was regularly used for landing fish. Several earned their living and kept their families fed by catching fish in the river Stour. The river fishermen sold their catches locally, mostly carried round by their womenfolk, using wicker baskets. River fishing was an extremely hard and sometimes frustrating occupation in which, at times, men were barely able to scrape a living. The fishermen had, however, a wide knowledge of river lore, and the habits of fish the and wildlife they so painstakingly sought. Few of them ventured beyond Harwich, but one or two of the more enterprising went towards Walton-on-the-Naze in search of lobsters. It is recorded that some of the Mistley fishermen rowed with the tide towards Walton, where they examined their pots and returned on the next flood. There were few fishermen in Mistley at that time; more lived in Manningtree next to the quay, and this tradition continued until only a few years ago. Their art had been passed down the generations from father to son, and they formed a very tough and close-knit community.

Numerous methods of catching fish were employed in the early 1700s; whiting, mullet, flounders, bass and skate were normally caught by line or home made nets. The fish were not caught in great numbers the whole year round, but in the autumn cod and whiting were to be found at or near Harwich in large quantities. At this time a greater number of fish were to be found in the Stour than there are today. Winkles, whelks, mussels and a few oysters were gathered from the river, and eels were caught by the thousand. It is not intended here to dwell on the many ancient methods of catching fish, but then, as now, pipes were laid in selected places in the river, into which the eels would swim. The fishermen would pull out the pipes, and quickly drop the eels into waiting receptacles. Although the methods of fishing in the North Sea were many, most of the fishermen had practised the use of the long line to which hundreds of hooks were attached. Whelks were used as bait, and the fixing of them on to the hooks was a long and tedious task. The lines were laid on the sea bed, and covered enormous distances. The task of pulling the line in, and taking the fish off the hooks took hours. The fishermen were often exasperated when, after pulling in the line, they found that dogfish had eaten many of the hooked cod. Because of the distances to some of the more prolific fishing grounds, ketches began to be used, and were often at sea for more than two months. Most of the vessels had a crew of nine, but the smaller smacks often had only three. Losses continued to be severe, and the smaller smacks often disappeared without trace, making fishing the most dangerous occupation at that time. Poles, with spikes, slightly barbed, were used to prod the sand and mud, and spear the eels and flounders beneath. The fishermen wore flat slats of wood attached to the soles of their footwear, which prevented them sinking into the mud, when in search of fish. Punts were regularly used which could be rowed or sailed; these wooden, flat-bottomed craft with pointed ends and virtually no free board, were of the same type still to be seen on the river at Manningtree. The Stour has been the home of these ancient craft for generations. Apart from fishing, the punts were also used for wildfowling. The river was teeming with many kinds of bird life, and most of the fishermen mounted a large bore shotgun on the bow of the punt. Late at night, lying flat in the boat, wildfowlers paddled gently towards the many flocks of wildfowl swimming in the river, and when close enough discharged a shot into them, often killing as many as twenty at a time.

Compared with river fishing, which was itself an arduous task, deep sea fishing in smacks or cutters was one of the most hazardous jobs ever undertaken. The newer types of vessels used at the turn of the 18th century in which holes allowed water into specially constructed wells in the hold have already been described; this facility allowed the smacks to sail long distances and sadly, losses were appalling. Later in the century, salted fish were landed at Mistley from as far away as Iceland, but the two or three smacks here at that time would have confined their activities to the North Sea towards the Dogger Bank.

As the years went by, and Richard Rigby completed his improvements in the port, other smacks and cutters arrived at Mistley and Manningtree. Most of these vessels were anchored or moored at Manningtree, and in addition to catches being landed there, some were taken off at Harwich. After landing, consignments of fish were sent to Sudbury and the surrounding district, and sailing as quickly as possible, vessels carried some to London. A large proportion of fish was sold at the quayside, and from those early days, an increasing trade developed and became a feature at the quays of both Mistley and Manningtree. The fishmongers regularly travelled to the ports to meet the smacks, where a market was set up to sell small consignments, and fix the prices.

Amongst the many fishermen who eventually came to Mistley were the Longs, Normans, Legenders and Prooms. The Howards had always been present at Mistley, and later came the Lucases and the Porters who, with others, built up the fishing tradition of the place. They were typical of many earning their living from fishing in the turbulent and treacherous waters of the northern seas, where the owners of smacks regularly risked their lives in pursuit of the scattered shoals of fish off the east coast. They were also opportunists, and often turned their sailing abilities in other directions such as the salvage of the scores of craft which unfortunately foundered in the rough seas and sands off the coast.

In the early part of the 18th century, the shipping trade was rapidly increasing to all ports on the east coast. Ships often became windbound, and it is reported that as many as 2000 were anchored off Yarmouth and Lowestoft for more than a week. Scores of smacks were amongst this remarkable fleet, and when the wind became favourable they all sailed, and it was said that the sea could not be seen for ships.

Disasters continued to occur; for example, when the schooner George became stuck on the sands off Yarmouth, massive waves caused the ship to capsize, and all the crew, with captain Philip Proom, of Mistley, were drowned. Another Mistley sloop was wrecked near Blacktail Spit, with more than £300 worth of flour from the Stour Mills.

During the summer months, it was not unusual for the wives and children to go to sea, even for many days at a time. The cabins were especially furnished to accommodate the extra passengers. Thousands of tons of fish were landed at Mistley and Manningtree each year, and this trade played an important role in providing what became the staple diet of the population.

For more than 140 years successive generations of one family were involved in the deep sea fishing operations which were undertaken from the port in the 18th and 19th centuries. They were extremely experienced, handing down their smacks from father to son, through periods of great hardship. The following chapter gives an account of the Howards, who became synonymous with the fishing tradition of Mistley Thorne.

CHAPTER 25

THE HOWARDS

The Howards were a family of fishermen who were sailing their smacks from Mistley Thorne as early as the 17th century, and continued to do so during the 140 years covered by this story.

An early record shows William Howard, a fisherman, married at Mistley Heath church to Catherine Hauard in 1668, and a John Howard married Elizabeth Gossling in 1720. The story, however, commences with Jonathan and Mary Howard, whose son Samuel was born on 12th August 1750. The family by this time had built up their fishing business, and owned several smacks. They became very well known in the rapidly growing fishing trade on the east coast.

Samuel was taught to sail by his father at an early age. The business prospered, and in 1772, Samuel, who was now taking over from his father, married Susannah Barber at the Towers church. Some fifteen years later, John Howard, who was the eldest member of the family, passed away, having enjoyed nearly fifty years of fishing in his smack, based at Mistley.

Samuel and Susannah had been busy raising a family, and records show they had five sons, Samuel, Jonathan, William, James and John and three daughters. The business was rapidly expanding, and by 1805 the Howards were the proud owners of twenty smacks. The five sons were actively involved in the business, and four of them commanded their own smacks. They became well known, and their exploits made them very popular amongst the fleet, which was trading from Mistley at the time. They often went to sea in conditions of high winds, and the most inclement weather, and sometimes took risks beyond the capabilities of their small craft. Three of them married between 1802 and 1806, William to Dorothy Stevens, Jonathan to Elizabeth Orpen, and Samuel to Mary Legender, the daughter of another Mistley fisherman. For a number of years they worked extremely hard, facing great danger, and sailing long distances in the northern seas. By 1808, their brother James had also married, and was carrying on with the family tradition. There is no record of where they lived, but it is thought that some may have had homes in Manningtree, since between them they raised sixteen children, all of whom were baptised at the Towers Church. At this time, their father and mother were living in the house, which is still standing, at the end of the Thorne Inn, at the approach to The Green. This house may well have been the family home, as Samuel Howard, Jonathan's son, was living there some twenty years later, after his grandfather and grandmother had died.

The opportunism of the fishermen was illustrated when a Prussian ship bound from Holland to London, was wrecked on the Shipwash Sands, with a cargo of butter, cheese and gin. As was usual when a wreck occurred, a number of smacks set out for the ship. Upon arrival, they found that she still had all her sails set, and had several feet of water in the hold. The three Howards in their smacks called Nancy, Two Sisters and William and Mary played an important part, along with other crews, in trying to move the ship. All hope was abandoned when the water in the hold rose to eleven feet. In due course a privateer called the "Courier" arrived, with twenty men aboard. They, along with the Howards and others, unloaded more than 10,000 cheeses and many casks of butter and gin. They also collected large numbers of floating barrels of tar. Later, the mast and sails, and even part of the hull, were salvaged.

These sorts of operations were constantly undertaken, especially by the smacks, which had the advantage of having a very shallow draft.

By 1810, the Howards had become a close-knit family, and all of Samuel and Susannah's offspring had married and had their own children, all of whom lived locally. The fishing business, although booming, could not be expected to provide large incomes for everyone, and in order to supplement their normal catches, the Howards had on occasions sailed their smacks to Heligoland (well west of the German coast) where they were able to obtain lobsters. These were brought home alive in the tanks in the hold. Lobsters always fetched a very high price in those days, and were sold to hotels and large inns, with some being sent as far away as London.

On one fine spring morning, with cirrus clouds indicating the onset of high winds, Samuel (in the Two sisters), William (in the Nancy) and Jonathan (in the William and Mary) sailed their smacks to Harwich, heading for the lobster grounds. The date was 13th April 1815. Their younger brother James did not accompany them on this occasion as he and his wife Sarah had suffered great sadness, their infant daughter Elizabeth having died only a few weeks earlier. Sarah was again pregnant, and perhaps because of this, James decided to stay at home. On 14th April, the three brothers proceeded together with a light following breeze, but by the 15th, they were split up by a howling gale from the southwest, which drove them through heavy seas towards the island of Texel. Samuel was wrecked here, and the other two boats foundered. With the three brothers were four other sailors and thirteen boy apprentices, all of whom were sadly lost. Many other vessels were sunk during the gale, and the village was stunned by the news. Prayers were said in the Towers church, and such was the popularity of the family that an immediate collection raised a large sum of £379. Golding Constable and others set the money aside as a means of assisting the families. On 17th June, just two months later, Samuel Howard, the father of the family, died aged 65; it is thought that the cause of death could have been a broken heart. His widow Susannah died on the anniversary of the tragedy three years later.

The entire shipping and business community rallied to help the families and bills inviting subscriptions were printed and distributed as far afield as London. Sums of money were immediately paid to the widows, but later a charitable trust was formed, and a committee of nine gentlemen agreed to administer it. The names of the committee were Rev. Henry Thompson of Bradfield, George Elmer, Rev. John Harrison, Thomas Nunn, Robert Nunn, Edward Norman, Thomas Scrivenor, James Howard and John Moore. The three Howard brothers left three widows and fourteen children. The sailors lost were George Hatch, Jacob Cooper, Robert Brooks and Robert Stevens, leaving four widows and three young children. The tragedy seems even worse when it is known that Robert Stevens was married to Hannah Howard, and William, who drowned, was married to Robert's sister. The thirteen boys all came from the immediate locality, and the village remained in a state of sadness and mourning for many months.

The committee of the trust decided, after having made some provision for the widows and children, that the sum of £409 which remained should be used to purchase a vessel called the "Success" which would be employed in fishing, in the names of James Howard and John Moore, who would act as trustees only. These two gentlemen were, respectively, the shipbuilder and the sailmaker from the Mistley shipyard. An indenture was prepared, and the purchase of the vessel was made on 30th September 1815, from George and Press Turner of Yarmouth. James Howard and John Moore, as trustees, were to manage the vessel, and pay the profits to the charity committee, who would apply the money for the benefit of the Howard widows and children.

As the years passed the family came through their troubles, James and John having shouldered the responsibilities for running the fleet, despite its having become sadly depleted. The children grew up, and the boys followed the family tradition.

Several years later the Howards embarked on a new venture. They secured a contract on charter to take mail to Gothenburg in Sweden. For this purpose they used the "Emma", "Success" and "Emily". On many occasions, the Howards' vessels arrived before anyone else's, and were taking only sixteen days to complete the trip. These operations were only continued for a short period of time, but the Howards were living up to the family reputation of being highly skilled navigators and sailors.

The trade at Mistley and Manningtree flourished for a further thirty years, during which time improved methods of fishing were developed. In addition, an area of the Dogger Bank, christened the "Silver Pit" was found, which yielded catches of fish never dreamed of during the dangerous and laborious operations years before. With the newer types of trawls being used, large catches resulted, but there was great disappointment that the rail connection to Mistley was being constantly delayed. About this time the Manchester, Sheffield and Lincoln Railway Company was building a line to Grimsby, and amongst others, approached the Howards. It must have been a great wrench for them to consider leaving Mistley, where the family had lived for generations, but perhaps the disaster which had befallen them years before had some influence on their decision. Although many fishermen were approached, the Howards were the only owners at that time who accepted. Early in 1850, they sailed their smacks with their families and all their belongings to Grimsby, and it is felt that they never regretted it. At this time the Howard fleet was reduced to eight, and the names were as follows: British Rover, Marques, Liberty, Mary, Laurel, Success, Emma and Howard. Mistley and Manningtree were never the same without them, and after further revolutionary methods of fishing and transport of catches were introduced, many of the smaller smacks were laid up as the large companies competed for the trade.

It is possible that a few of the Howards may have remained in Mistley, or perhaps returned, as Daniel Howard, born in 1846, grandson of Jonathan, became a marine superintendent at Harwich. He was for many years a well known, highly respected resident of Mistley, living for a time in Oxford Road. Latterly he lived in a house called "Rutherglen", in Shrublands road, where he died in 1924.

The Howard family were typical of the hundreds of fishermen who in the 18th and 19th centuries sailed their small craft from Mistley Thorne to the North Sea to earn a precarious living. They experienced great hardship and constant danger from the shoals and gales for which the east coast of England is renowned. After they had left, Mistley declined as a fishing port, and never regained the proud position it had enjoyed for many years and by 1852 only five smacks were still operational. Harwich, too, was affected; its fishing fleet had departed. The story of shipping and fishing on the East Coast had been described in magnificent books written by Hervey Benham, which give a wonderful picture of east coast shipping and its mariners, many of whom were using the ports of Mistley Thorne and Manningtree in the days of the Rigbys.

CHAPTER 26

TIIE LAST YEARS OF RICHARD RIGBY

By the end of 1770, Rigby had almost finished his extensive building at Mistley, and had spent a fortune in doing so. In 1782 he retired from his position as Paymaster General, which he had held for fourteen years. For some of this time his friend Lord North, who was a favourite of George III, had been Prime Minister, and Rigby held great sway in Parliament. The period was unfortunately marred by the start of the war in the American colonies, which lasted for nearly seven years, resulting in the Treaty of Versailles in 1783, which recognised their independence. It was said that the policies of Lord North had contributed to the unhappy loss of a large part of the British Empire. The Pay Office had come in for criticism regarding the financing of the operations of the Army and Navy. Rigby, because of this and other matters, had become very unpopular during his last years at the Pay Office, and had constant battles in Parliament with those members hostile to him. He continued, however, to exert a powerful influence in the House, and fought back with the blustering arrogance for which he became renowned. He was most unhappy over the unsatisfactory way in which the troops had been led to America, and in 1779 lambasted Burgoyne, who two years earlier had surrendered his forces in the battle of Saratoga. Two of Rigby's severest critics were Charles Fox and William Pitt, both of whom were comparatively young. Fox's father was Lord Holland, who had been a friend of Rigby for years, had fallen out with him and then bad feelings arose. Pitt also had reasons for disliking Rigby, as when his father, the Earl of Chatham, died, the Aldermen of the City of London wished for him to be buried in St. Paul's Cathedral. This proposition was not approved by the King, and it is reported that Rigby, in rude and abusive language, scoffed at the idea of bestowing a compliment on the Aldermen whom he attacked for their "degenerate and detestable politics". Further pressure came late in 1782, after Lord North, the Prime Minister, had resigned, and Edmund Burke had become Paymaster General. Burke declined to make use of the country's money for his own purposes as Rigby had, and called on Rigby to repay large sums which, he alleged, had been used unlawfully. Rigby refused, and for some time seldom attended Parliament, spending most of his time at Mistley.

With his income reduced, Rigby began to sell small parts of his estate but with the rent roll having increased fivefold since he inherited Mistley, he should have had an ample income. Unfortunately, his financial affairs had got out of hand, as he had never been one to hoard money. For years Rigby had regularly lost money at Whites Club in London, and a number of creditors were pressing him to settle his considerable debts. Some parts of the estate, which were distant from Mistley, were sold, and he was able to satisfy a number of his creditors. He did not appear to be unduly concerned, and although heavily in debt, he had still not attempted to put his affairs in order. At this time he decided to make his will, and after preparation it was witnessed by John and Benjamin Lucas, and James Fenn, three of his servants. Apart from one or two legacies Rigby left his whole estate to his nephew Colonel Hale, and his two sisters, Anne and Martha.

Although Rigby's parliamentary career was by this time nearly over, he still had countless friends whom he continued to entertain both in London and at Mistley. Unfortunately, by 1782 he was suffering frequent attacks of gout, which often confined him to his rooms. He had treatment from his physicians in London, but the years of drinking claret had taken its toll. In addition to the pain and discomfort he was undergoing, he continued to be worried by reports of proceedings in the House of Commons, where Edmund Burke was demanding his impeachment. Supported by

Fox and Pitt, Burke carried out an investigation into the Pay Office book-keeping, and although these accounts had habitually been kept in a slipshod, careless manner, he alleged that during this time at the Pay Office, Rigby had used many thousands of pounds of the country's money for his own purposes. After these charges were made, Rigby lost a great deal of support in the House, especially when it became known that he had been paid more than £35,000 per year as Paymaster. Despite this somewhat undesirable state of affairs, it had not been unusual for Paymasters in the past to take advantage of their position in this way. Apart from the cash which he used personally, however, Rigby also lent money to his friends who paid interest back to him, and not to the Pay Office. Inquiries were made, and Rigby defended himself in the House, pleading that it had been custom and practice for the Minister at the Pay Office to use the money when large sums of cash were impressed to his personal account. However, although Rigby cited others who had also operated the same system at the Pay Office, Burke and his supporters were determined to embarrass Rigby as much as possible, at a time when British politics were in turmoil.

The matter finally came to a head on 28th August 1784, when Rigby came before Sir James Eyre, one of the Barons of His Majesty's Exchequer. At the hearing, Rigby acknowledged that he was indebted to His Majesty in the sum of £200,000. Rigby paid a sum of £20,000 to the Exchequer at Westminster, and it was agreed that £50,000 should be repaid on 25th March 1785, with further sums annually, with the final payment to be made in 1787. Interest was to be charged at 5% per annum on the principal sum, and Rigby paid to the Exchequer on 24th March 1785 an amount of £59,205-9-7$^{1}/_{2}$d.

By this time Rigby had retired from Parliament, while a few years earlier William Pitt had become Prime Minister. England was in a state of unrest, having lost the American colonies, and incurred financial losses of millions of pounds. The King was hated, and it was said that Pitt, with his popularity and new ideas, saved the country from civil war. Rigby was to play no further part in government, and by the end of 1785, his health was beginning to deteriorate.

Various accounts have been written concerning the last years of his life, which seemed to indicate he was ill for some time. Nevertheless, it is noticed that he appeared to be managing his estate in 1787, as on 14th August he ordered for £214-1-4d. to be paid for 300 Wether Lambs from Mr. William Clarke Woodbine of West Rainham, in Norfolk. They were driven to Mistley, over many miles of narrow winding roads, a journey which must have taken several days. Later, however, it was found that the payment was never made.

Rigby's debt to the Exchequer was obviously still causing him concern, but no records have been found of any further payments. It is thought that with his other commitments, he was unable to contribute any further sum, although it is understood that he expressed his willingness to pay interest on the principal. The writer of the Authentic Memoirs of Richard Rigby reported that much of the money for which Rigby was responsible was not retrievable without causing great distress to those who had borrowed it. Some had purchased houses and other properties, and it was not within their power to repay the loans without selling everything they owned. This was a most unsatisfactory state of affairs, as Rigby was responsible for the money he had lent. Although the non-payment had seriously embarrassed him, he refrained from requesting repayment of the loans. Most of the people concerned were his personal friends, and the principal together with the interest would have caused them serious problems. Such was the impropriety in the Pay Office in those days that even the Prime Minister, Lord North, had borrowed £30,000 from Rigby, which he eventually paid by instalments, with the last payment of £5000 made as late as 1786. Lord Cheverton had a small amount of £400, and a Mr. Charles Burbridge £7300. Although Rigby was able to recover some of the money owed, he unfortunately had several other personal debts, and in order to settle a number of pressing accounts, he borrowed a large amount of money from his relative Sir Thomas Rumbold, the Governor of Madras. Sir Thomas' daughter had married Col. Francis Hale, Rigby's nephew, and he naturally wished to assist the family at this difficult time.

These were sad days for Rigby, but he had much comfort and support from his sister Anne, together with the great help and careful attention to his affairs by his steward, John Ambrose. His sister Martha was living in London at this time, but was frequently at Mistley with her son Col. Hale, who loved the sport the estate provided.

By 1786, Rigby's poor health compelled him to seek the advice of Dr. Warren, and Sir William Fordyce, who were eminent physicians in London. They carried out every treatment possible, with bleeding being undertaken on occasions. Mr. Rogers, the apothecary, sent a bill for £17-15-3d., which reveals numerous medicines and treatments, which included senna, hartshorn, stomach mixture, pills, sulphur, manna, salts, draughts, magnesia, pearl barley and various other medicines. His servants, Ann Haste and Alice Squirrel, extracted teeth on three occasions. Without the assistance of anaesthetic, this must have been a very painful, but necessary, operation.

As time went by, Rigby engaged a Swiss servant, who waited on him day and night with great skill and kindness, but his illness became of a bilious, and eventually dropsical nature, possibly indicating a stomach disorder. Dr. Warren and Sir William Fordyce felt that the only chance to obtain some improvement was for Rigby to take the waters at Bath. They recommended that he should live there, and a house was obtained for him in the Circus there.

Whilst he was there he took Dr. James' powders and his bilious attacks diminished as he recovered his appetite. This improvement was, however, only to last for a short time; a relapse occurred, and his physicians could only declare that death was inevitable.

In the last days of his life he was unable to lie down because of the pain he was enduring, and his breathing had become very difficult. His Swiss servant remained with him at all times, and he was lovingly attended by his sister Anne, who remained with him at Bath.

Richard Rigby sadly died on 8th April 1788 at the age of 66, in a lonely room in Bath, away from his home at Mistley which he loved so much. The words below concluded the "Sketch"of the real character of the Right Honourable Richard Rigby", written nearly 200 years ago:

> *"Thus departed the Right Honourable Richard Rigby in the 66th year of his age, after having dignified every scene in which he moved, whether in public or private life - His remains, being embalmed were conveyed into Essex, and there interred in the family vault at Mistley. A general tribute of sorrow accompanied them, as they passed through the country;- it was a voluntary offering of disinterested grief, and displayed an amiable concern for the loss of Superior Worth".*

The residents of Mistley, who had gained much benefit from his devotion to the village, were sad at his passing. A further milestone had been reached in Mistley's history, and there was the usual uncertainty of what the future would hold.

Richard Rigby had, without any doubt, lived a full life, and apart from a period in Ireland, had lived in Mistley or London, where he had lavishly entertained hundreds of people. For more than forty years he had devoted much of his life and money to the improvement of the village of Mistley Thorne, and its surrounding farms. His efforts in providing industry had greatly improved the lives of the residents, who lived in houses far and away more commodious than was usual at that time. The Rigbys, both father and son, were responsible for much of Mistley as it is seen today, and will always remain an important part of Mistley's history.

A memorial tablet, with the Rigby coat of arms, was placed in the Towers church, and re-sited on the west wall of the new St. Mary's Church in 1870. It bears the following words:

"To Proclaim"

*"His excellent worth and deserts, and to perpetrate
the remembrance of the many shining virtues and amiable
qualities which adorned his mind, this marble is dedicated.*

*With the tenderest concern, and most exalted regard
to the Right Honourable Richard Rigby, a member
of Parliament, and of His Majesty's Privy Council,
and the late Paymaster General of the Forces, by
his sorrying and afflicted sisters, Anne Rigby,
and Martha Hale, and his nephew Francis Hale Rigby.
His character was frank, open, manly and sincere.
He was endowed with
brilliant parts, a strong understanding, and correct judgement.
He had a peculiar gaiety of temper,
and in his social and convivial hours, was captivating
and engaging.
By which happy talents
he gained and preserved the partial regards, and
friendships of many of the most distinguished characters
in the nation. To his relations, most generous, kind
and affectionate. To his friends, most zealously and
steadfastly attached, increasingly and assiduatively
active in conferring benefits, and kindness upon them.
No man went beyond him in doing good to all his
acquaintances in general. To the tenants upon his
estate he was abundantly liberal and indulgent. They
grew opulent by his bounty, and repaid him by their
gratitude, their esteem, and their veneration. To his
domestics he was a kind, easy, generous master. To the
indigent and distressed he was most humanly charitable,
and compassionate, and was a blessing to the whole
surrounding neighbourhood that lay within the sphere of
his existing domains. His last illness, he bore with
great calmness, and magnanimity, and was sent to his
grave amidst the deepest sincere lamentations of
multitudes who deplored the loss of their highly
honoured and justly beloved patron and benefactor.
His age was 66.
He expired on the eight of April 1788.
This faithful but inadequate tribute of affection was
written by General Bernard Hale, brother-in-law of
the deceased."*

CHAPTER 27

MISTLEY MOURNS

During Richard Rigby's last few months at the Hall, the state of his health was well known, and although it was hoped that the waters at Bath might bring relief, there were many in the village who were doubtful. The sad news of his death was therefore not unexpected.

The house he had occupied in the Circus at Bath was provided by a friend, who had done everything he could to make him comfortable. Consequently, he had few personal belongings there, and these were quickly cleared by his sister, who immediately returned to Mistley.

The funeral arrangements were placed in the capable hands of Mr. Robert Williams, a local undertaker who, as was often the custom in those days, embalmed the body. He obtained a hatchment (Rigby's armorial tablet) and arranged a suitable carriage to convey the body over the long distance to Mistley for burial, at a cost of £3-9-0. Rigby's attractive escutcheon is mounted at the top of his memorial tablet in Mistley Church, and a replica was placed on the coffin, together with family wreaths. The funeral coach was drawn by four black plumed horses, and on the long journey from Bath the cortege rested for the night in London, arriving early in the afternoon of 16th April. Rigby was very well known throughout the country, and it is reported that the route was lined with people who gathered to see the funeral coach pass. A service was held in Mistley Church, conducted by Rev. Thompson. Among many notable people who attended was the young Duke of Bedford, and other nobility, with several Members of Parliament. All the tenants from the estate, and business people from the village were present. Rigby's servants were each paid a sum of money in order that they could obtain suitable clothes for mourning, and they sadly followed the coffin into the church. The amount given for mourning was between five and ten guineas for each servant. After the service the coffin was taken to the old churchyard at Mistley Heath, and interred beside those of his father and mother in the family vault, beneath the Church porch. The Rev. Thompson was paid five guineas for conducting the service, and a further sum of one guinea for opening and closing the vault.

Richard, like his father before him, had been a very popular figure at Mistley Thorne for a period of more than forty years, and the village remained in a state of mourning for several weeks. Many of the villagers wore black, and most of the children went to school wearing black armbands.

Richard Rigby, although a more flamboyant character than his father, had had a real love of the village. He had readily helped the needy in the village, the, and was held in high esteem by the whole community. He had assisted the village people in many ways, had always encouraged sport in the village, and although he had ceased playing cricket many years before his death, he had allowed a team of local players to have regular fixtures in the park. The village children had loved the parties hc hcld in the grounds of the Hall during the summer, his tenants had enjoyed close friendships with him, and his servants were very fond of him.

Most of the inhabitants at Mistley Thorne, and the tenants of the farms knew his nephew, Colonel Hale, and hoped that there would be no changes in the running of the estate. There was, happily, little scope for change, as Colonel Hale soon became heavily involved in dealing with the serious financial problems he had inherited in connection with Rigby's job as Paymaster General.

The estate accounts, however, meticulously kept by Ambrose, were causing no trouble, and he and Col. Hale were for the time being, able to run everything satisfactorily.

Mistley Thorne gradually returned to normal, with work available for most of its inhabitants, the population by now having risen to 240 males and 302 females, living in 103 houses. It would now be left to Col. Hale, with the assistance of John Ambrose, to manage Mistley and endeavour to settle the considerable debts which Richard Rigby had incurred for many years before.

CHAPTER 28

COL. FRANCIS HALE RIGBY

After Rigby had died, and the will had been proved in the Court of Canterbury, Col. Hale had extended his name by the addition of Rigby, in accordance with the terms of Rigby's father's will made in 1730. Although he now shared the estate with his mother Martha, and his aunt, Anne Rigby, both in their sixties, it was left to him to administer it, with the loyal assistance of John Ambrose.

Of Richard's two illegitimate daughters, one, Jenny Pickard, was left an annuity of £100 per year, to be paid from the profits of the estate while the other Sarah Lucas, was left £5000, and her mother, £1000. Richard's daughter Sarah was treated as a member of the family, and it was at Anne Rigby's house that she met, and later married, the Rev. Newman of Little Bromley. When Anne died, she left her entire estate to Rev. Newman, in order that Sarah would always be provided for.

After Richard Rigby's funeral, by arrangement with John Ambrose the porch at the old Mistley Heath Church was renovated, and the area of the ruins made tidy. The grass in the churchyard was cut by the labourers on the estate, and almost every grave was marked with a stone. The entrances to the ancient vaults were clearly marked by flat stones with the names of those who were buried there. This part of the old Mistley Heath Churchyard, with the vaults housing the remains of the Rigbys and others, is part of Mistley's heritage, and it is to be regretted that the whole area had been sadly neglected.

Col. Hale Rigby was only 31 when his uncle Richard died, but as he had been a frequent visitor to Mistley from his early childhood, he had a good knowledge of the estate. His father, General Bernard Hale, had brought him up in the military tradition, and was proud that his son had served with some distinction in the army. The family resided in London at St. James' Place, but over the years they had all spent time at Mistley Hall. General Hale and Richard Rigby had become firm friends, and throughout the last years of his life he had given every support in the political battles Richard had fought. The family had become very close, and were often joined by Sir Thomas Rumbold and his wife, whose daughter had married Col. Hale Rigby in 1786. The whole family loved Mistley, and the villagers held them in high esteem.

Col. Rigby's wife, Frances, gave birth to a daughter in 1786, who took her mother's name of Frances. She would eventually inherit the estate, and in 1808 she was married to Horace William Beckford, who had some business with traders on the quay. A road at the eastern end of Mistley bears his name, but no record has been found that he and his wife ever lived in Mistley at that time.

Because of his army duties, Col. Hale Rigby and his family were required to spend much of their time in London. With the Hall mostly unused, much of it was then let to Lord Galway. Accounts show payments of £70 and £190 for use of the furniture in the Hall. This venture was later much regretted when it was discovered that Lord Galway was a "lunatic". Staff were specially engaged to look after him, but his eccentric behaviour caused much annoyance in the village. He was to stay at the Hall for about three years, and it required protracted legal proceedings in order to secure his departure. He owed a great deal of money to the tradesmen in the village, and everyone was glad to see the back of him.

Col. Rigby, whilst being delighted to become involved in the administration of the estate, soon found that the accounts needed careful examination. After only a short time he became very concerned indeed when he discovered the serious state of his uncle's finances. He had long discussions with Daniel Macnamara, who was his uncle's executor, and although he was able to settle local accounts with money from the estate, accounts were constantly arriving from large numbers of creditors. Col. Rigby personally paid all the servants' wages, and their mourning payments. The bill from Robert Williams of £405-1-0 was paid for the funeral expenses, which had included the embalming of the body. Other local tradesmen's accounts were from Mr. Robert Watkinson, the grocer, £13-6-4d, Mr. John Box, the saddler, £15-14-10. Other local tradesmen's accounts were from Joseph Page, a breeches maker, £3-15-0; Robert Gooding - joiner, £1-15-7; John Everitt - cooper, £1-14-11; John Malby - coachmaker, £11-10-6, Robert Reynolds - horse farrier, £7-16-0; and Charles Cox, for fruit trees, £1-12-0. Daniel Macnamara was also receiving money from debtors, and cash already held by the estate, but the list of creditors was growing. Col. Rigby was not to know, at this time, the extent of the complicated legal investigations which were to take place over the years ahead. With the vast amount of money owing, the preservation of the estate must have been constantly in his thoughts. He would, however, have been spared much concern, had he known that the care taken by his great-uncle in the preparation of his will in 1730, would preserve Mistley for the Rigbys.

CHAPTER 29

THE FINANCIAL NIGHTMARE

Although his years at the Pay Office brought Rigby great riches, he saved none of it. He had always been fond of gambling, and regularly attended clubs, where he invariably lost large sums of money. His visits to racecourses all over the country had also been the source of losses of thousands of pounds. The extensive building operations and entertainment at Mistley had cost a fortune, and unfortunately Rigby did not follow the careful management practised by his father in handling his financial affairs.

The clerks, who were responsible for keeping Rigby's account at the Pay Office, must have been remarkably poor accountants, as he was compelled to engage a Mr. Lawrence to investigate them. He spent weeks endeavouring to put them in order, and was not very successful, as on most ledgers Lawrence was unable to declare proper balances. He was, however, paid £21 for his efforts.

Apart from the vast amount of money which Rigby owed to the Exchequer, he had a number of other creditors relating to the estate. It appears that apart from the first payment, he had paid nothing further and with the interest at 5%, the debt was rapidly increasing. By 1788 this had again risen to more than £200,000, and although some of the creditors returned money which they had borrowed, much was never recovered. Some of the income returned was used by Hale Rigby to repay the Exchequer, and in order to assist, a sale was arranged in 1789 of some of Rigby's effects. Strangely, the Archbishop of Canterbury bought his black gelding for £51. The Duke of Bedford bought many of his paintings at a sale arranged by Christies, including Valkof at Nymagen, by Albert Cupt. This painting still hangs in Woburn Abbey. The sale realised many thousands of pounds, all of which was used to settle the debts. The years passed, but by 1795, the debt to the Exchequer had only been reduced to £151,783-3-6.

Soon after Rigby's death, Col. Hale Rigby made every attempt to settle the accounts, but it soon became apparent that there was no possible way, with the income available from the estate, that the creditors could be satisfied.

Because of this unsatisfactory state of affairs the case was heard in the Court of Chancery, and on 5th March 1790 a decree was made. In 1793, an order was made that an enquiry should be instituted by a Mr. Graves, one of the Masters of the High Court of Chancery. Mr. Graves embarked on what was to be one of the most difficult tasks he had ever undertaken. Not only were the accounts he examined misleading, many of the loans made had different rates of interest, with conditions attached which were not clearly understood. The investigation revealed income due to Rigby from Antigua, Jamaica and Granada in respect of coffee, cocoa and sugar. He also owned parts of estates in these countries, and had one share in a ship called Walpole.

In order to settle part of the debt to the Exchequer, Rigby had, as previously noted, borrowed £112,000 from Sir Thomas Rumbold. By the time Mr. Graves had completed his enquiry, both Sir Thomas and his wife had died, and the executors, Ewan Law and the Rev. Sheepshanks, were claiming about £55,000.

In addition to the enquiries into Rigby's income and assets, together with money owed to him, Mr. Graves had to satisfy the speciality creditors. Notices were placed in the London

Gazette, and several more creditors emerged. Mr. Graves received much help in his investigations from Daniel Macnamara, the executor of Rigby's will. Col. Hale Rigby, and especially John Ambrose, spent months endeavouring to unravel the complicated transactions which Rigby had arranged when he had lent money to his friends. Apart from the creditors, Anne Rigby, Martha Hale and Col. Hale Rigby were residuary legatees. Jenny Pickard had not received her annuity, and neither had his other daughter, Sarah, or her mother. Mr. Graves had to take these into consideration, as in addition to the creditors these legacies were a charge against the estate. Daniel Macnamara had successfully secured £62,378-4-9, in his capacity as executor, and this sum was paid into the account which Mr. Graves was compiling. More than £27,000 of it was immediately paid to the Exchequer in order to defray the interest which was being charged on the principal.

The length of time which the enquiry was taking was causing some concern, as by the year 1795, the debt to the executors of Sir Thomas Rumbold had been increased by interest which now amounted to £19,065-7-3d, bringing the total up to £69,112-13-0^1/2d. The legacies which had not been paid to Sarah Lucas, or her mother, were also increased by interest, totalling £1203-5-8^1/2d., and £240-13-1^1/2d. respectively.

Mr. Graves submitted his report to the Court of Chancery on 14th April 1795, and it was found that the total debt to be settled then amounted to £281,859-15-1^1/2d. Included in this sum were amounts due to the residuary legatees. Sarah Lucas and her mother were now, with interest, entitled to nearly £7500, and Col. Hale Rigby and Daniel Macnamara, who had each been left £2000, were now entitled to interest amounting to £481-6-3^1/2d. The total amount owing to these legatees amounted to £12,406-11-5^1/2d., which was eventually paid. Mr. Graves stated in his report to the Court of Chancery that there were insufficient assets available to settle the very large amount which was owing. Soon after presenting his report, Mr. Graves died, and Mr. Campbell, another Master of the Chancery Court, took over his responsibilities. After the court had examined the report, the terms of the decree issued in 1793 were invoked, and there remained no other alternative but to sell the estates in order to settle the demands of the creditors, of which the Exchequer was by far the largest.

For some time a legal battle took place, in which the terms of Rigby's father's will, made in 1730, were examined. After long deliberation, the court agreed that the complicated wording which Rigby senior had inserted in his will precluded the entire estate being sold. The will had irrevocably provided that after his son had died the estate would descend to others, and went so far as providing that any future legatee should change his name to Rigby, which Col. Hale did in 1788. It was therefore agreed by the Chancery Court that no part of the estate which had been left in the will of 1730 could be disposed of, and only that part of the estate which had been purchased by Richard Rigby since his inheritance in 1747 could be sold. Under these reservations, the village of Mistley Thorne and the farms which Edward Rigby had inherited in 1709 would remain in the hands of Col. Hale Rigby, his mother Martha and his aunt Anne. John Ambrose had been appointed Steward of the Estate in Richard's will at a salary of £150 per annum, and he continued in this position, much to the relief of Col. Hale Rigby, who did not reside in Mistley regularly.

Rigby had, over the years, acquired a vast amount of property in the Tendring Hundred, and also had estates in Bedfordshire and Warwickshire, with other land in Suffolk. The rent roll of the Estate was more than £5000 per annum, which was more than five times that of his father's in 1730. Mr. John Ambrose was requested by Mr. Campbell to prepare a document giving details of the property which could be sold, showing the rents and profits applicable.

After he had completed the extensive document, he was asked to swear an affidavit that the accounts were correct, and this was placed in the Chancery Masters' book on 7th July 1797.

The elder Sarah Lucas had eventually married Isaac Fisher of Wherstead, but after only a few years of marriage he sadly died. Sarah was not to enjoy her legacy for long, as she also passed away in 1797. Remarkably on 14th June her body was brought to Mistley, and the entry in the church register shows her name to be Sarah Lucas, widow, from Harwich. Her body was interred in the vault alongside Richard at Mistley Heath. Although there is no evidence (Richard Rigby's will has never been discovered), it is thought that in it he had expressed a wish that this unusual arrangement should take place. Perhaps it was an indication of the deep affection Richard had continued to feel for her.

It is interesting to note the vast amount of agricultural property which Richard Rigby had purchased in the Tendring Hundred in only a few years. The Court of Chancery ordered that these should be sold in order to defray his debts. Those inherited by Rigby in 1747, to remain unsold, are marked with an asterisk. The properties are listed below.

Walton Hall Farm	- 326	acres.
Walton Hall Wood	- 45	"
Hubbards Farm, Walton	- 27	"
Snow's and Devereux's, Kirby	- 144	"
Gallup's and Stebben's Farms, Kirby and Thorpe	- 127	"
Hare Wood	- 34	"
Maidenhead, alias Whitehead's Farm, Thorpe	- 35	"
Rectory of Walton - with the Great Tithes of Walton	- 800	"
The Manors of Kirby, Thorpe and Walton		
Landermere Hall Farm (exclusive of the wharf)	- 212	"
*Trinity Farm	- 79	"
*Mistley and Lawford Mills (one water and one wind)	- 11	"
Marsh and Saltings, Walton	- 805	"
The Tower, used as a shooting seat		
Saltings belonging to Hubbards Farm	- 24	"
Thorpe Park Farm	- 464	"
Markhouse lands and cottage	- 36	"
Dale Hall and Causeway End Farms	- 472	"
Manor of Dale Hall, Lawford		
Turners Farm and Leech's lands	- 145	"
Bradfield Hall Farm	- 383	"
Bockins and Martin's Farm, Mistley	- 69	"
Marjerum's Hall Farm	- 78	"
Bradfield Lodge Farm	- 161	"
Slipes Farm	- 75	"
Gule's and Ferries Farm	- 108	"
Spinnels Farm, Wix	- 121	"
Hempstalls Farm, Wix	- 188	"
Wix Lodge Farm	- 228	"
*The Manor of Mistley		
*The Manor of Newhall, Tendring		

*The Advowsons and rights of the Church at Mistley		
*The Rectory of Bradfield with the Great Tithes		
*Tofts and pieces of wasteland in Mistley, with wharf		
*The Salt House, Manningtree		
*The Manor of Newhall Farm	- 279	"
Foggett's Wood, Wix	- 25	"
Horsley Cross Wood	-84	"
Manningtree House divided into two tenements		
Cottage and garden in Manningtree		
*The Manor of Sheddinghal, also Shedding Hall		
*Manor of Sheddinghal Farm	- 334	"
*Manor of Dickley Hall		
Netherhall Farm, Bradfield	- 240	"
Whites Cottage and Land	- 8	"
Crossmans Farm	- 97	"
Cockfield pasture	- 6	"
Barton's and Everett's Farm	- 28	"
Wick's Dairy Farm	- 216	"
The Great Tithes of Wix	- 818	"
Stone's Wood, Wix	- 41	"
Marjerum's Wood, Horsley Cross	- 33	"
Gamekeepers House of the Tendring Manor		
*Manor of Dickley Hall Farm	- 282	"
*Farm in tenure of George Martin	- 136	"
*Several Closes called Swan Lands and Bowling Lands	- 88	"
*Chapell Fields and Chapell Lands	- 7	"
*Several woods and wood ground and soyle in Mistley, Manningtree and Bradfield	- 276	"
*Stacies Farm	- 334	"

The farms and lands to be sold totalled nearly 7000 acres, and were spread between Mistley and the coast at Walton-on-the-Naze. The Mistley estate amounted to about 1800 acres, which were to remain in the hands of the legatees.

More than nine years had passed since the death of Richard Rigby, and although the legacies had by now been settled, it was several years before the final sale of the properties was arranged. Jenny Pickard was receiving her annuity, and that of Sarah Lucas and her mother had increased considerably, having had a large sum added on account of interest.

By 1798 both Martha and Anne had died, leaving Col. Hale Rigby the sole owner of the Mistley property. Anne Rigby was buried in the family vault at Mistley Heath, having lived for most of her life in Lawford Place. She had been a much-loved resident of the parishes, and details of the sale of her household effects, which makes interesting reading, are held in the records office at Colchester. She had spent her whole life helping her brother Richard, especially during later years when he came under great pressure in Parliament. Her friendship with his daughter, Sarah Lucas brought her much happiness.

With the financial problems all but over, the estate was much reduced, and consisted mainly of the property which Richard had inherited in 1747. It is believed that the sale of the large portion of the estate would have realised sufficient money to settle the debts, and satisfy the Exchequer, who was the largest creditor.

The following interesting account is taken from the "Authentic Memoirs of Richard Rigby" written by General Bernard Hale, who attempted to show that this debt was paid. This may have been the intention at the time the General was writing (soon after Rigby's death), but it was certainly not the case.

> *"In the fluctuating and desperate politics of that day, when the fate of a Ministry turns upon a voice, he became the marked object of either party - and your vote, or your money was the implied language of each as it prevailed. To what, but this, shall we ascribe the extents which were issued against him on the part of the Crown, and what rancorous spirit which pursued him nearly to his grave. To collect his balances on Ministerial demand was impractical. The money was widely scattered, to relieve the necessities of several of the fairest characters in the Kingdom, whose estates were at that time so depreciated in value, that to compel the payment of their mortgages would have been in fact to dis-possess them of their patrimony. In this dilemma, he stated to Parliament his readiness to pay his balances by quick instalments, and in the interim to allow 5% interest for the same. The Country, as it were with one voice applauded his conduct, and a compromise took place upon it, by which Mr. Rigby paid £10,000 for the interest of a specified balance, although his predecessors had never been called for a similar amount".*

There is little doubt that Rigby had lent to his friends large sums of money which he had obtained from the Pay Office revenues, but acted in an honourable manner by refraining from calling in the debts. By acting in this manner, he placed himself in a very difficult position, as he was responsible for the lands, and had no other alternative than to settle them himself. It was always accepted that the bookkeeping at the Pay Office was unsatisfactory, and with the millions passing through Rigby's hands, on account of the American War, it is most unlikely that the amount set against him was accurate.

It seems that the financial problems which arose after Rigby's death took more than twelve years to solve. By this time, many of his critics had left Parliament or died, and few would have known exactly the course the proceedings were taking, or if they were being resolved. Careful examination of the detailed accounts prepared by the Master of the Chancery Court show that much of the criticism of Rigby by numerous writers many years ago was often exaggerated.

In 1802, the affairs of the estate were concluded, and John Ambrose, who had played a prominent part in Rigby's affairs for more than thirteen years handed over his position of steward of the estate to his son John, who had given him valuable assistance during these difficult times. For many years he had carried out his duties with great skill and understanding; John died in 1805 at the age of 71. He is buried with his wife Frances in a grave marked by a large box stone and surround in the Towers Churchyard.

CHAPTER 30

COLONEL FRANCIS HALE RIGBY - LORD OF THE MANOR

With the financial problems almost behind him, Col. Rigby finally came to live at Mistley. Lord Galway having departed from the Hall, where had lived for three years. The running of the estate had been in the sound hands of the Ambroses, but Col. Hale Rigby was determined to play a greater part in the management of the estate.

One of his first actions was to sell the Bedfordshire and Warwickshire estates, which, although showing a profit, would have needed costly maintenance and repairs in the years ahead. He also disposed of the property in the West Indies, and the Suffolk estate was sold as well. The estate remained almost the same as it had been when his great-uncle had inherited it, although many more buildings and dwelling houses had been built upon it. There were now more than one hundred properties and farms, and with the industrial premises and dwelling houses, the collection of rents, sanctioning repairs, the administration of the estate had become very time-consuming. In order to simplify the running of the industrial part of the estate, an agreement was made with two businessmen named Bridges and Elmer, to lease the whole port for twenty-one years. The complicated agreement had been drawn up by John Ambrose, and was signed on 18th July 1811. It was agreed that the tenants who occupied premises on the quay would continue to do so at equitable rents. Mr. Edward Norman would be permitted to load malt at the quay, and all the properties would be kept in good repair. Permission would have to be obtained before any repairs were carried out, or new premises erected. Ships would be supplied with ballast, from points within two miles distant, at 6/-s. per ton, and application would be made in good time, in order that the place of digging could be indicated and supervised.

It was also arranged that Bridges and Elmer would immediately construct, at their own expense, a new malt office (malting) and granary. This would be at the eastern end on Thorne Quay, between the lime kiln and the Swan. The position selected was on a site where a malting now stands, opposite to offices occupied by Messrs. Edme. Traces of the foundations can still be seen, and the present malting was built on the same site as the smaller one some seventy years later. The building was to be constructed no less than 32' from the edge of the quay, and its dimensions would be 90' by 20', with a kiln 12' by 12'. The granary would be 70' in length and 20' in breadth, and would consist of two floors. The building would be constructed using bricks of the finest quality. It was further agreed that the malting and granary would revert to Col. Hale Rigby at the end of the lease, at a price equal to half its value at the time. The rent to be charged for the lease of the port was fixed at £1400 per year.

It seems, however, that the lease did not run its full time, as records show further agreements with Col. Hale Rigby made in 1819, with individual tenants occupying the property.

A company called Finch and Stammers hired a coalyard for £18 per annum, and further premises were let to Stephen Harris and William Strutt for £11. John Moore worked in his sail warehouse for £5-5-0, and Abraham Constable was tenant of a granary and coalyard for £53. Edward and Francis Norman had part of a granary for £40, and the lime kiln and iron shed were let to George Elmer for £38. Other records show coalyards, chalk pit, deal yard and malting office; by 1808, the tenancy of the shipyard had changed from James Betts to James Howard.

The farms were continuing to run satisfactorily, although records show that the rotation of crops was not always being practised. One farmer grew four years of oats and wheat, and three years of potatoes and wheat. Others grew four years of potatoes, and four years of oats and peas. It is not known what effect this annual sowing had, but in 1819 it seems that the Mistley farms may not have practised the recommended points of good husbandry.

Although it is not absolutely certain, the selling of the greater proportion of the large estate in 1802 may not have settled all debts, as upon examination of the valuation at that time, less than £100,000 may have been obtained from the property sold. Some years later Col. Hale Rigby mortgaged several parts of the estate. One indenture related to specified lots on the quay and in the village amounted to £75,000, with the Trustees of the Globe Insurance Office, and a similar transaction for £20,493-0-6d. of 3% Consuls. These demands on the estate would remain unsettled for many years, and it is felt that the arrangements may have been made as a further result of the debts incurred by Richard Rigby many years before.

The industry in the village was still increasing, and the population had risen to more than 800. The shipping from overseas, brought goods for the barges to Sudbury, some times more than the barges could handle. The passage to Cattawade from Mistley, and to a lesser degree from Manningtree, was often very difficult, as the barges had to be "poled" up to the channel on an incoming or outgoing tide. On windy days this was a very tricky operation, and many barges went aground on the mudflats. It was always a relief when the horses took control on the bank to the south of the tiny bridge at Cattawade.

At this time Daniel Alston, the Brewer, rented premises on the quay, and his Brewery at Manningtree was working to full capacity. Duty of one year's brewing operation amounted to more than £100,000 and the small maltings were paying a malt duty of £50,000. With the beer at less than 2d. per pint, this duty must have represented a considerable amount of liquor.

Not long after the turn of the 18th century, a large number of public houses and off licences had been built, and the "Pilot", at the bottom of the steep hill down to the quay, did a roaring trade. On the western end of this brick-built inn was painted an advertisement for "Fine Ales and London Porter". This inn was eventually closed, and became a dwelling house inhabited by one of the horsemen employed by the Railway on the quay. His name was Abraham (Abe) Fox, and the building was known as Fox's House long after he had died. In the 1950s the owners of the malting complex on the quay gave it to one of their workmen. He promptly pulled it down, cleaned all the bricks and slates, transported, and re-erected it on a piece of land in Cants Lane, off Beckford Road in Mistley. The laborious operation of demolishing, transporting and re-erecting the entire house, which is part of Mistley's history, was an inspired undertaking; it is sad that it is not now known as Fox's House. Mr. Hugh Spencer, an employee of Free, Rodwell and Co., performed this remarkable operation, and his widow still lives in the house in which thousands of pints of beer had been consumed by the thirsty dockworkers!

Col. Hale Rigby was very anxious that provision was made for the consumption of beer, and to enhance the social activities in the village, other beer houses were built near the Thorne Inn. Eventually, there were sixteen hostelries in Mistley and Manningtree, and at least five of these were situated around the Swan Fountain.

With the increased population, many more of the villagers were attending church, and Rev. Watson, who was the incumbent in 1806, did much good work in the village, where hardship still existed in some of the larger families.

Col. Hale Rigby maintained a friendly attitude to the local farming fraternity, but had very little experience in farming, and most certainly never measured up to his uncle in popularity. It is apparent that during his ownership of the Mistley estate, and the great Mistley Hall, the years of lavish social events and visits by notable people came to an end. Nevertheless the business of the village prospered, and the tenants enjoyed stability, with opportunities of work for most of the inhabitants. Farm labourers' wages had risen to 9/- per week, which was an increase of 3/- per week over a period of 100 years. The estate farms were most profitable, especially as John Ambrose was himself a farmer, and made sure that the tenants ran their farms properly.

At the end of the 18th century, Great Britain was involved in the long and disastrous war in Northern Europe, following the expedition of the Duke of York and Abercrombie. Col. Hale Rigby supervised the vessels arriving at the quay bearing the soldiers wounded in the battle, from where they were immediately transferred to the barracks at Colchester. Later, a great number of the regiments arrived at Mistley, and also at the ports of the Hythe and Wivenhoe. Some of the soldiers were in a deplorable state, ill-equipped, and in some cases without shoes or stockings. More than 1200 men arrived in the ports either badly wounded or suffering from ague.

The end of the century saw a great increase in the building of warships, many at Mistley. A temporary respite from the French and Spanish was gained by Nelson's glorious victory at Trafalgar, but it was 1815 before the war was finally won by Wellington at Waterloo.

There is no doubt that the adversity which the country had to undergo at this time swung many of its people towards religion. There was an increase in Anglican congregations, while many turned to Methodism. Manningtree residents were rewarded by the building of the Wesleyan Chapel in 1807, and a strong movement led to the erection of an Independents Chapel in 1818. Col. Hale strongly supported the church, and diligently used the income from the Advowson to the full in keeping the buildings in a good state of repair.

When he was resident at Mistley, Col. Hale regularly entertained his friends at the Hall, most of these being officers from the army, and local people. He became a close friend of General Slater Rebow of Wivenhoe Park, both being members of the King's Head Club at Colchester, which was attended primarily by army officers from the Colchester Garrison. During the war with the French, much concern was being expressed that their force might attempt to land on the Essex coast, and Col. Hale Rigby assisted in obtaining volunteers to support the regular army. A force of nearly 30,000 men was raised, many of whom were from the parishes around Mistley. A small force was raised from the servants at Mistley Hall, which was formed into a platoon, receiving full training by members of the regular army. They were fully equipped with army uniforms together with the necessary armoury. Fortunately they were never called into action, but Col. Hale Rigby was very proud of his volunteers.

As the years passed the shipping industry continued to expand, with imports and exports still increasing, and although only a small port, hundreds of ships were still registered there. After 1800, the fishing fleet had continued to grow, and vast tonnages of fish were regularly landed at both Mistley and Manningtree. Sadly, however, the high price in loss of life of the fishermen continued unabated.

It must be said that although the era presided over by Col. Hale Rigby continued to be profitable to many in the village, it never recaptured the exhilarating and exciting times which Mistley Thorne had enjoyed under his uncle Richard.

CHAPTER 31

A VISIT TO MISTLEY HALL

Just after the turn of the 19th century, two young ladies stayed at Mistley Hall on their way to Harwich for a visit to the Continent. The following letter, written by one of them, gives a wonderful description of Mistley Thorne and its port, and the hospitality which they received from Col. Hale Rigby and his wife. She writes:

"We were fortunate to be invited to stay for two nights with Col. Rigby and his wife at their seat at Mistley Hall, which conveniently broke the journey for us, as the passage to Harwich is but ten miles distant.

When we arrived after a tiring journey, it was quite dark, and we were glad to be shown to our rooms, which were spacious, but simply furnished. The attractive Hall was built by Col. Rigby's great-uncle nearly 100 years ago. Later, we were entertained to an excellent dinner, served in a beautifully furnished rotunda. I slept well, and awoke to the sound of horses neighing, and the chorus from many birds, which sounded delightful. Eagerly, I drew the curtains, and revealed a view, the like of which I have never seen. Before me was a garden of unsurpassed beauty, with a green velvet lawn sweeping towards a line of tall trees, beside a wide expanse of water. In the distance, seemingly on the very river bank, stands a magnificent white edifice, with twin cupolas resembling a veritable temple. We were to learn later that it was a church, which had been specially designed by Mr. Adam for Col. Rigby's uncle. Behind a neat row of leafy trees were tiny cottages, over which could be seen the tall masts of sailing ships, and bathed in sunlight, three tiny smacks were barely moving in the gentle breeze. After breakfast Elizabeth and I strolled in the spacious gardens, where the scent of the roses, still lightly covered with morning dew, will forever be remembered.

The Hall is magnificent, built of white bricks, surrounded entirely by a sunken fence, over which are placed ornamental bridges of brick and stone. In the distance shrubberies and fine trees stretch over undulating lawns, and onward to a dense forest of closely growing trees. Near the house is a fine tulip tree, in full flower, and most certainly over 60' in height. We longed to explore, but Col. Rigby had promised to escort us around the estate in his post chaise.

A uniformed coachman brought the chaise to the forecourt, and Col. Rigby suggested that Elizabeth should drive, but after viewing the sprightly horse, she declined gracefully.

We set off at a slow canter, and over a tiny bridge to the long drive, where Col. Rigby pointed out the kitchen gardens, seemingly enclosed by immense brick walls. We soon arrived at the entrance gate, with twin lodge houses on either side, also designed by Mr. Adam. The tree-lined road descended gently to the river, close to a small town with fine houses, called Manningtree. We paused to enjoy the view, and then trotted over a small bridge to the village of Mistley Thorne. The approach to the village is dominated by the unusually designed church, where behind it is a large pit containing heaps of chalk. Adjacent to the pit were piles of timber, neatly stacked, and nearby were large wooden and brick compartments holding massive heaps of coal. A fine brick granary stood beside an inlet into the quay, which served as a dock, in which were two ships. From one of these men were unloading deals, walking with them on their shoulders, up precariously placed gangways.

Beside the granary is a fine malting, with steam belching from the tops of two lofty kilns. We drove amongst the many workmen and mariners, and some of them winked at us, and guffawed loudly at some closely concealed joke. A further tiny malt house stands on the approach to a shipyard on the beach, where a large vessel was being constructed.

The quay was swarming with men of strong physique, and with numerous horses and carts, it was difficult to perceive the nature of the operations which were being carried out. Col. Rigby drove quickly through the melee, and at the very end of the quay was a building of a peculiar design. We were told that it was a kiln, which produced lime from rock, for the mortar for laying bricks. It was obviously a very hot and dusty operation, and we were glad to reach the higher levels up a steep track to the road above.

After having experienced the beauty and tranquillity of the Hall, I felt it strange to find that close by was the hustle and bustle of industry, so closely integrated in the village.

The chaise was driven down a hill above the port, where we stopped at an inn, called the Thorne. In front is an attractive fountain, with water flowing from the mouth of a model swan seated on a pedestal. We adjourned to the hostelry for coffee, and were ushered into a panelled room, marked Captains Only. We were the only occupants, and were almost overwhelmed by the smell of beer and stale tobacco from countless pipes, to say nothing of the stables in the courtyard. The coffee, brought by a genial host, was, however, excellent, and served with minute home made biscuits, which we found to be sweet and delectable.

After enjoying the coffee, we rejoined the chaise, and again ascended the hill, which had trees on either side. At the summit, Col. Rigby reined in the horse, and we alighted to enjoy another breathtaking view down the river towards Harwich. Several sailing ships, which were slowly approaching the port, added to the picturesque scene. Near the top of the hill was a substantial white cottage, which Col. Rigby told us was the home of the miller. The remains of his mill nearby having sadly served its time, had been demolished some years before.

We continued on the road between two pits, screened by trees, in which men were busily loading small tumbrils. It was explained that these were ballast pits, from which sand and shingle was taken to repair the roads, and place in ships for weight, when they were leaving port empty.

Col. Rigby was eager to drive us to Mistley Heath, which was also part of the estate. After only a short time we arrived at the ruins of the old Mistley Church, and were surprised to find that a fine flint-covered porch had survived. We were told that the porch was the entrance to the family vault, which had been constructed nearly 90 years ago. I found the churchyard, with its many gravestones, to be a place of great tranquillity. On from the ruined church, we came to a green, with tiny cottages, and a blacksmith's shop, which we understood to be Mistley Heath. In the distance we could see a neat farm, and amongst the tree-covered park land, a small herd of deer was grazing. We took a track over the fields for nearly a mile, and returned to the Hall down a leafy roadway, which we were told was called Green Lane.

The Mistley Hall estate is truly beautiful, and throughout our journey, the men touched their forelocks, and doffed their caps, and the ladies smiled and curtsied prettily, as the chaise went past. The whole time we were at Mistley the sun shone brightly, and we were delighted to receive a further invitation from Mrs. Rigby to stay at their beautiful residence later on in the year."

Numerous friends of the Rigby family stayed at Mistley Hall over a period covering more than seventy years. Some conflicting accounts have been written, but without exception everyone has agreed that Mistley Thorne was a place of great character and beauty.

CHAPTER 32

FROM THE RIGBYS TO THE RIVERS

The period of the management of the affairs of Mistley between the years 1800 and 1836 covers the time after the debts of the late Richard Rigby had been settled, and a major portion of the estate had been sold.

Col. Hale Rigby held the position of Lord of the Manor for most of this time, in which he carried on much as before, with farms and industrial businesses continuing to flourish. The industry and the shipping operations were attracting extra workers, and some new houses were built during this period, most of which were on land adjacent to Manningtree, not forming part of the Rigby Estate. There had been a further increase in population of 200 by the end of this period, with most of the men being employed in the maltings and breweries. Mr. Alston, the prominent brewer at Manningtree, occupied the largest brewery, and in addition to the tiny brewhouse at Dairy House Farm, a further small one had been constructed at the Thorne Inn. The Page family were engaged in maltings on the quay, as was Edward Norman, who had made a great deal of money in his shipping and coal businesses. During this period, Edward built a complex of eight maltings on land which he leased in west Mistley, and two of these delightful ancient buildings still remain. Records show that on special occasions one of the maltings was used for entertaining at least three hundred people to lunch. Many years later in 1870, at the consecration of the new Mistley Church, 350 members of the congregation presided over by the Bishop, sat down to lunch in the malting, which was then owned by a Mr. Brooks. Maltings were also constructed at Manningtree, near the river, and as both malting and brewing were labour intensive industries, numerous jobs became available.

Col. Rigby's daughter, Frances, had received private education in London, but spent a great deal of her young days at Mistley. Parties were arranged for her at the Hall, where she entertained her numerous friends. She was married in 1808 to Horace Beckford, whose uncle, George Pitt, was the 2nd Baron Rivers of Sudeley Castle in Gloucestershire. Horace and Frances had a house in London where she was preparing to live, but they were frequent visitors to Mistley, which they loved, and made friends with the local farming community. Frances usually entertained in London, where she played a prominent part in the dazzling social scene of that great city. In 1809 Horace and Frances had a daughter, Fanny, and over the next few years, two sons, George and Horace, and another daughter, Harriet Elizabeth.

Col. Hale Rigby made his will on 18th July 1823, in which he left the estate to his wife, Frances, and following her death to his daughter Frances, then Mrs. Beckford. Sadly, soon after this time, he became ill, probably suffering from a stroke, as he appeared to be confined to an invalid chair until the end of his life. He had appointed his close friends the Duke of Dorset and Robert Harper to be his trustees before his death on 21st August 1827.

Some three years later John Ambrose retired and his son, John Thomas Ambrose was appointed as Steward in his place, at a salary of £150 per annum. Thus there became a further change of management, but from all accounts the trustees carried out their responsibilities in a very satisfactory manner, and the estate continued to prosper, although the expenses upon it were very great. Repairs were costly, and the interest on the mortgages was a constant drain on the revenues. In December 1827, the trustees leased the entire port to Horace Beckford for £1121-18-0 per annum for a period of twenty-five years. He became responsible for all the tenants, and possibly made some profit in the transaction. For a further nine years the estate remained in the hands of Col. Rigby's widow, Frances, under the control of the trustees. Horace Beckford, whose wife would eventually inherit the estate, assisted them for a short time, although he continued to live in London.

A number of meetings were held at this time, and the trustees realised that the rents from the estate, and expenses needed for running it, together with other mortgage repayments would leave little margin of profit. Rents were increased where possible, but expenses continued to rise, and the trustees expressed some concern for the future of the estate. Finally it was agreed to carry on, and for some years little profit was made from the once great estate.

In 1828 Horace Beckford, following the death of his uncle, George Pitt, the 2nd Baron Rivers, inherited the title. He immediately assumed the name of Pitt Rivers, and became the 3rd Baron Rivers of Sudeley Castle. His wife, as reported in a previous chapter, daughter of the late Col. Hale Rigby, became Frances, Lady Rivers.

Their son, Horace, was to remain a bachelor, but George married Miss Susan Georgina Leverson Gower, the eldest daughter of the Earl of Granville. A lavish wedding was held in London, attended by great members of the nobility, and the couple settled in a house in St. James' Square.

It seems that all the families appeared to enjoy the town life in London, and soon after Col. Rigby's death the Hall was leased to the Right Honourable Manning Sutton, the Speaker of the House of Commons. He and his wife continued to live there for several years, and their daughter was christened at the Towers Church in 1829.

Mistley, with the careful administration of John Ambrose, carried on without the advantage of a Lord of the Manor until 1831 when a great tragedy occurred in the family.

Horace Beckford, now Lord Rivers, was a regular visitor to the many gambling clubs in London, and Crockfords was easily the most popular establishment in the City, widely patronised by the nobility. It was once said of the Master of this great feasting and gambling house that: "He filled the hungry and thirsty with good things, and the rich he sent empty away".

Horace, having spent a convivial night at Crockfords, was sadly discovered drowned in the Serpentine the next morning. There was no evidence to show how he ended up in the water, but after a party at Crockfords, he may have been tempted to swim across for a wager. The mystery of his death was never solved, and it was even more strange that he had travelled to the club by his coach, but afterwards did not return to the vehicle. The mystery became even deeper when the Colchester press reported Lord Rivers' sad demise. It stated in a comprehensive account that he had stayed at Mistley some days beforehand and had collected a large amount of money in estate rent from John Ambrose. Evidently he was not seen after leaving Mistley until some days later when his body was discovered. The report also stated that Lord Rivers was very short-sighted, and on the estate had been seen with a glass to his eye (presumably a monocle). It was presumed that he had stumbled into the Serpentine because of his poor sight. It is strange that two different accounts were given over his tragic death, but presumably the family gave the Colchester report which makes no mention of Crockfords.

In due course Lord Rivers' eldest son claimed the title, and became George Pitt Rivers, the 4th Baron Rivers of Sudeley Castle. He and his wife, Susan, continued to live in London, but he took over much of the responsibility of the estate, together with the trustees.

Lord Rivers and his wife had four sons, whom they named George, Horace Pitt, Granville and Beckford Pitt. His mother, Frances, widow of the late 3rd Baron, became known as the Dowager Lady Rivers, and following the death of her mother, Frances Hale Rigby, in 1836, became the sole owner of the estate at Mistley. Her son, George, the 4th Lord Rivers, continued to accept the responsibility of the estate for her, although legally the administration was in the hands of John Ambrose under the direction of the trustees.

Two simple memorial tablets were placed in the Towers Church and eventually moved to the new Mistley Church in 1870. They record the deaths of Col. Francis Hale Rigby on 21st August 1828 age 70, and his wife Frances on 27th September 1836, age 73.

The year 1836 was to be a very unhappy one for the family, as Lady Rivers' daughter Fanny, who had recently married Frederick Cox, died in the February of that year, aged only 27. A memorial tablet, recording her death, also hangs in Mistley Church.

The trustees of the estate had changed by this time, the Duke of Dorset having died and Robert Harper having retired. The new trustees were the late Fanny's husband, Frederick Cox, and Mr. Gurdon Rebow.

Lord Rivers and his family were still living in St. James' Square and after some time Mr. Manning Sutton gave up the lease of the Hall and returned to London. Mistley Hall now stood empty, and the ownership of the estate by the Rigbys had ceased after a period of nearly 130 years, in which time Mistley had changed from an obscure village with a tiny population to an industrial centre with a model port, to which ships sailed from all over the world. For the next few years it would be left to the Rivers family to overcome the difficulties which were bound to arise, and decide on the future of the Mistley estate, and that of many of the villagers who lived there.

CHAPTER 33

LORD RIVERS AT MISTLEY

Soon after the death of the late Col. Rigby's wife in 1836, Lord Rivers and his family came to Mistley and resided at the Hall. He was very fond of the place, and although, somewhat money-conscious, always made an effort to assist the villagers on occasions of hardship. His mother, the Dowager Lady Rivers, often stayed at the Hall with them after the tiring journey from London. She, particularly, was very much loved by the Mistley people, and insisted that she was informed of any problems which occurred in the village. John Ambrose regularly discussed matters of the estate with her, and she became friendly with many of the families and their children. She frequently gave money to some of the poorer people, especially the elderly, and became very interested in village affairs. She was always in the congregation at the Towers Church, where a special family pew was reserved.

The population of the village had again risen, and by 1836 it stood at nearly 900, which represented an increase of 350 in just over thirty years.

The family loved Mistley, but unhappily Lord Rivers four sons all suffered illness during the first winter, which was extremely wet and cold. They were to stay at Mistley for only a few years, during which time, they were constantly ailing. Their health deteriorated to such an extent that eminent physicians were consulted, and Lord Rivers was advised to move from Mistley, as it was considered to be too cold and damp in the winter months. The physicians suggested that the family should move to Wiltshire, where the weather was more temperate. The family reluctantly departed from Mistley Hall in 1839, and made their home at Rushmore Lodge, near Salisbury. This was to be their main residence, but sadly the children's health did not improve, and a large house was acquired at Brighton, which became a second residence for many years.

Lord Rivers frequently made the long journey to Mistley, and often stayed in London at the University Club to break his journey. He also stayed at Ushers Hall, and had apartments at Windsor Castle, where he was privileged to take his turn in waiting at the Palace.

Although not living in Mistley, and having many other duties, Lord Rivers diligently attended to his mother's interests in conjunction with the trustees, and the Steward John Ambrose.

During this time covering a period of nearly four years, he wrote many letters to John Ambrose on important matters relating to the estate. These have survived, and much of the information in them has been used in this record of Mistley's history. In many of the letters he gave unhappy news of the illnesses of his "poor boys". They all appeared to have had weak dispositions, and were rarely well, especially during the winter months. Presumably they had colds and chest troubles, and Lord Rivers' letters written during the summer were still mentioning their illnesses. The air at Brighton appeared to help, but tragically in the years ahead they all died at a young age. Eventually when Lord Rivers died the title fell to his brother Horace, but he had no children and the title finally became extinct.

After Lord Rivers had left Mistley in 1839, the Hall was leased to Sir William Anson, Viscount Canterbury, who lived there with his family until 1845.

During the time that Lord Rivers was away from Mistley, he still concerned himself with all aspects of life in the village, and on one occasion, in a letter to John Ambrose, expressed his worry on the subject of a Barbara Lawrence, the old dairy maid. It appeared that she had, some years before, lent £80 to the wheelwright named Kerridge, who lived at Horsley Cross. He was to have paid her interest at 5%, but had not done so. Lord Rivers asked Ambrose to speak to Kerridge, who was a tenant on the estate, to request repayment of the loan, reminding him that on the last occasion he had been successful in getting £20 returned. He was also seeking information about an old letter carrier, more than 80 years of age, who was still taking letters between Mistley and Bradfield. Lady Rivers wished to know, "Is she in great distress?"; she wanted to send her some money.

Amongst his many qualifications, Lord Rivers was a very experienced farmer. He took great interest in the estate farms, and was constantly meeting the tenants, to whom he regularly gave sound advice. This advice was not always accepted, and often looked upon by some of the farmers as interference. However, the relationship with the tenants remained good, especially as John Ambrose was a friend of everyone.

Lord Rivers had, for a number of years, endeavoured to find improved methods of farming, and frequently read the literature which was being published at that time. One of his letters to John Ambrose asked for information about a farmer named Wilkins, who lived at Wix. Ambrose wrote back giving an account of Wilkins, and his farming abilities. Lord Rivers replied, thanking him for his account, and wrote:

> *"I was led to ask about him from reading a published letter from him, in the Gardeners' Chronicle, and Agricultural Gazette, on 26th June, in which he spoke of himself as a practical farmer of forty years standing, and offers to challenge the "whole of England" with his present wheat crop, sewn at less than three pecks to the acre, which he considered "two thirds too much", and says that one peck of wheat and not more than two of barley or oats is all the seed that true agricultural science can advise for an acre of land. I suspect there was something bordering on what you describe as "humbug", although I am the strongest advocate of thin sowing upon some lands, and under some circumstances."*

From the scores of letters which John Ambrose received from Lord Rivers, it seems that his memory was often somewhat suspect. He was constantly querying bills sent for work on the estate, and in 1842 he could not approve one sent by a Mr. Curtis. He wrote to Ambrose:

> *"Curtis's bill is like many others - on that I cannot swear I do not owe, but hardly think I owe, as it was my wish to pay up every bill before I left Mistley. I have no receipt for inspection of the plantations."*

A later letter reported:

> *"I can give you no satisfactory information upon the subject of Mason's large and unexpected demand on the estate. While I resided there, I must have paid him several bills, as he did the necessary glazier's work for me to the best of my recollection. I*

feel certain I neither owe him nor any other person in the County of Essex a farthing, except the bill which Masters received the money, and others applied it. The new pump in the paddock, I think, was ordered by myself. I have, however, no proof of it. It is really irresponsible of Mason to have long neglected to make known his claim, without any means of proving how far it may be a just one. Why didn't your father know, it should show in the accounts."

Presumably, the accounts were eventually paid, as no further mention is made in later letters.

On another occasion Lord Rivers, on holiday in Europe, addressed a letter to Ambrose from the "Chateau d'Herrenspeins, Par Worms, Hirse Damstadt", and in the postscript was quite worried about a bill from a man named Durrant. The following letter was written to Ambrose, which most certainly revealed Lord Rivers attitude to some of his employees. There is little doubt that Durrant was not one of his favourites, but there is no record to show that he was dismissed.

Berkeley Square,
April 19th, 1842

My Dear Sir,
I received your letter yesterday morning, before leaving Rushmore, and upon the subject of it I agree with you most fully. It was one of the things while I was living at Mistley, that I used to talk to your father about most anxiously, and when any trifling objection was argued against employing a permanent carpenter and man under him, the former to have 18/- a week, the latter at 12/-, to do all the carpenters work upon the estate, I used to say, "then every job however trifling, for which an estimate can be obtained, must be done by contract, and such jobs as cannot be estimated, and which must be consequently charged as day work, should be accounted for, and paid for every Saturday evening". To this, I could not at the time, nor can I see now any objection, or difficulty. It would have enabled the jobs estimated to have been continued, and even valued previously to their being done by some respectable and understanding tradesman, such as Salmon, or others, and he would certainly have obtained the power of contracting to a certain extent, and more than we now can, the only charges that need be uncertain ones - a week's instead of a quarter's charge for day work must be more easily questioned, and sifted into if there are any reasonable grounds for doubting the fairness of it. Bit I am still of the opinion that 30/- a week, employed as I have suggested upon a really hard-working industrious and desirable outlay - for speaking of Durrant's accounts, twice it had depended upon you to overlook

these, having accumulated to (at the rate of) £150 a year for the management of the plantations, Thus my method of providing for the general and necessary repairs of the estate could cause a saving of the difference between 30/- a week and £150 per year, namely £72 per year, and his would effect also an exchange of an uncertain and incontrollable man for a certain one.

Durrant himself I never had by any means a good opinion of, and I am for some reasons sorry that I did not express myself sufficiently strongly, and get him dismissed from the estate. I can now, however, no longer hesitate to say that this will be my wish, and my reasons for entertaining such a wish. I am sure you will allow me only just and good ones - without being (as far as I know) directly dishonest, indeed I do not at all suspect him of being so, he is indirectly so, if I may so express myself, by not working hard and efficiently during the many "half days", and "three-quarter days", that may constitute the chief charges in his most unsatisfactory accounts. He is a very slow stupid man, and I know he drinks. My advice therefore either would be to get rid of Durrant altogether, which I think the most advisable course to take, or to have the whole of his work estimated, however trifling it may be, and any that cannot be accounted for, and paid for every Saturday evening. Will you let me know what you think of all this, as soon as convenient to you. I am returning his accounts. I am indeed most sorry to have received the poor report of your father. The compatible part of his case is that his constitution is so <u>strong</u> a one that it may, and I hope will get him over this and even worse attacks to which I fear he will now from time to time be subject.

Yours truly,
George Pitt Rivers

Lord Rivers addressed many similar letters to John Ambrose over a period covering four years, during which time his father did, in fact, suffer a deterioration in his health. His Lordship's relationship with some of the workmen and tenants deteriorated over the years, as further chapters will show, and he would be engaged in further difficulties which were again to arise in the financial matters of the estate.

CHAPTER 34

THE SAD DECISION

In 1843, Lord Rivers had the first of a great many meetings with John Ambrose and the trustees to discuss the financial problems that had arisen, which could possibly lead to the disposal of the Mistley estate. He had, first of all, acquainted his mother with the unhappy state of affairs, and she reluctantly agreed that the matter should be carefully considered, and to explore any possible alternatives which may be revealed by discussion. She hoped that a sale could be avoided, but it was difficult to see what alternative existed, as the rent roll was barely enough to keep the estate going, and pay her large annuity.

Apart from the heavy interest demands set against the estate, there were other encumbrances which had to be taken into account. The list below was prepared, from which it will be seen the estate owed various people a sum totalling £113,313, and if a sale was arranged, at least £5000 should be added to take account of the expenses incurred in the sale.

The Estate Encumbrances

	£
In settlement of loans	18,500
Globe Insurance Co.	75,000
Redeeming Annuities	5,500
Secured on loan	5,000
Wm. Nunn - on bond	2,000
J. Miller - on bond	1,000
W. Bastard - on bond	2,000
M. Drummand - on bond	1,000
Expenses of a sale - about	5,000

TOTAL   £118,313

It seems that if the estate was sold, a total of £118,313 would have to be realised from the proceeds, plus a further £10,000 which, if invested, would bring in interest of about £500 each year to satisfy the annuity of Lady Rivers. Research into the financial responsibilities at this time appears to show that the annuity to Lady Rivers had risen to £1000, and not £500 as provided for in Col. Hale Rigby's will. No explanation can be found concerning this, and if it was in fact the case, it would appear that the sale of the estate would have had to realise £138,313 in order to break even, and settle all encumbrances.

During the long discussions, John Ambrose prepared a detailed report on the prospect of operating the estate. He felt that there was scope for increasing the income, by raising the tenants rents, as most were operating flourishing businesses, Lord Rivers was pleased with the report, but the trustees were not convinced that enough income could be generated in this way.

After much consideration it was finally decided to look into the possible methods of the disposal of the estate, and a London auctioneer, Mr. Hoggart, valued it at £140,000, on the basis of selling it in individual lots. Gurdon Rebow, one of the trustees, also had a valuation done, which forecast £131,000, and Lord Rivers was most upset when a third estimate amounted to only £127,000. Much time was spent considering the method of disposal, if any, should be adopted. In 1844 John Ambrose's father, who was unwell at the time, wrote a long letter to Lord Rivers and the trustees, giving his opinion, and his son also wrote, saying it was with great regret that he found the estate might be finally sold. Lord Rivers replied, saying that he also regretted it, but it was prudent to dispose of it. He had painful feelings, but he knew that no-one belonging to his family would ever live at Mistley. Although the estate would be theirs, and the tenure by their descendents as long as his mother lived, at her death the estate must be sold, and it would be an act of madness not to sell it now. Despite the fact that they would not have had a sale forced upon them, the needs of his mother had to be considered. In further letters Ambrose proposed that only part of the estate should be sold. Lord Rivers and the trustees considered this suggestion very carefully, and their reply showed how very concerned they were over Ambrose's position as steward of the estate. It was naturally a very sad time for him and his father, and Lord Rivers was committed to them for the long and valuable service which the family had given to the estate.

In August 1844, Lord Rivers wrote:

> *"It is very satisfactory to me to find that so many persons interested in various ways in which the sale of Mistley are in favour of being effected by a sub-division of the estate, as this is the only course, finally agreed upon to be adopted. My opinion may, perhaps, not be worth having, but it remains unaltered. In the first instance we ought to have attempted a sale in its entirety, and in the event of our failing to do so, on such terms, as were thought right, say (£140,000), which Mr. Hoggart brings the reserve price to amount to, then resort to the plan of a sub-division. He says that nobody would give you the worth of the estate sold as an entirety. This is a matter of opinion, not a matter of fact, and if by any chance he could have been proved wrong in this opinion, it would have served us an infinity of double risk, and expense. The mode we are adopting is one to procure business for the lawyers, and auctioneers, the result of a lengthened sale, which they invariably like. This is strongly as ever my opinion, although I may have consented to subscribe to the opinion, and views, of others".*

It was, therefore, finally settled that the estate should be sold by auction, in individual lots, as soon as possible.

A further problem had arisen affecting the sale of the estate; that of the proposed railway. In 1844, a line had been completed between London and Ipswich, and the Eastern Union Railway Co. had placed a bill before Parliament to request powers to construct a line between Lawford and Harwich. This bill was entitled, "The Eastern Union Railway and Harwich Pier Act". The line was planned to run almost to Horsley Cross, and onward through Wix and Wrabness

This letter was written to John Ambrose, by Lord Rivers on this subject:

> *"I am really alarmed at the proposed line of railway coming through Margerum's Wood. Mistley is, to a certain extent, dependent on the shooting it affords for being a desirable residence. It is the only sport it does afford, and this must be lastingly affected by its best and largest wood being cut in half, and for the prospect during the progress of the work absolutely destroyed. I am writing to you what I sincerely think about it, and not making an extravagant sum of money in compensation. I think the line could not have been chosen worse for the sale of Mistley, except by passing thro' my part of Home Park. I conclude it is to be a branch line from Mistley to Harwich".*

Lord River's fears were in fact realised, as in 1845 a further Parliamentary Bill altered the direction of the line to Harwich, and in 1852, it was built through Home Park, where it still runs today. By this time the Mistley estate had been sold, and many others lost their homes, especially in the Manningtree area.

With the sale being arranged Mr. Hoggart, the auctioneer, and estate agent, came to Mistley to value the amount of compensation which the railway company ought to give in order to obtain withdrawal of Lord Rivers dissent to the proposed line. The matter was resolved satisfactorily, and later the second bill gave power to construct the line from Lawford (Manningtree Station) to Harwich Pier, with two branch lines to Mistley Quay.

The decision to sell had now been taken, and it was left to the trustees and auctioneer to make the necessary arrangements. The sale of the land and property would seriously affect the lives of many, provide others with an opportunity to increase their businesses, and substantially alter life in the village of Mistley Thorne.

CHAPTER 35

THE FINAL ARRANGEMENTS

Although the estate was to be sold, and Sir William Anson was to remain at Mistley Hall until the sale was concluded, Lord Rivers and his mother were anxious that some of the paintings, furniture and china which were in the Hall should be set aside for their own use.

Extensive work had to be done by the trustees in conjunction with the auctioneer, in order to produce the necessary details of the hundreds of lots which would be sold. In addition to the agricultural estate were the port and all its ancillary buildings, with the village and a number of houses and shops.

Their first undertaking was to place a bill before Parliament which was entitled, "An Act to authorise the sale of the fee simple of the estate of Francis Hale Rigby, of Mistley, in the County of Essex, deceased, as devised by his will, and for laying out the money to arise by such sale". The contents of the bill occupied eighteen pages, saying that there were no funds or property which would enable the owner of the estate to repay the mortgage and other encumbrances. The mortgages were set against specified portions of the estate, which, because of the terms of Richard Rigby's will in 1730, could not be sold. The bill also gave details of the names of the trustees, and the family of Col. Hale Rigby, their marriages and their children. His will had followed that of Edward and Richard Rigby, and the estate was left in the hands of the trustees, to be passed down the line of successors. A further trustee was appointed, which made three in all, and the bill requested consent for them to dispose of the estate either by auction in lots or by an individual sale. The name of the new trustee was William Loftus Lowndes, who was a Barrister at Law, at Lincolns Inn in London.

The bill was duly presented, but unfortunately delays occurred, and Lord Rivers expressed concern in a letter to John Ambrose, over the expense which was being incurred. The bill was eventually given assent, and the final arrangements were begun.

In 1844, Lord Rivers wrote a long letter to Ambrose, and in it, expressed his thanks for the loyalty of his family, and the service they had given him for so many years. He further stated that he saw no reason why he and his parents should not be secure in their house on the Green. The Ambroses did, indeed, continue to occupy East Lodge, and they were given the area of Mistley Green for their own use forever.

At this time the village people were obviously disturbed by rumours, and many were worried about their businesses. It was alleged that the trustees were arranging to demolish the Hall, and build a row of villas with the materials recovered. It was announced immediately that the rumour was unfounded, but strangely there may have been some truth in it, as when the Hall was eventually demolished after the sale, a large house was built at Great Oakley using the bricks and other materials recovered. Great numbers of the bricks and other materials were used in the construction of the new Mistley Hall, now part of Acorn Village. Part of the Adam Staircase is still in this Hall, together with one of the fireplaces, and the top of one of the rotundas.

A letter was written to John Ambrose by Lord Rivers, concerning the old church and churchyard at Mistley Heath. He wrote:

"I have received a letter this morning from my mother, strongly expressing her desire, as well as that of Mr. Cox (trustee), that the old church and churchyard at Mistley Heath should not be included in the sale of the estate. It is a point upon which they entertain the strongest feelings, and I consequently take the earliest opportunity of making you aware of it, according to their wishes, as time approaches for the sale".

Lady Rivers had regularly sent money to Mr. Ambrose for repairs to the tiny porch, as she wished the area containing the family vault to be kept in a tidy condition. The churchyard was accordingly excluded from the sale, and it was arranged that the Rector and Churchwardens of Mistley would become responsible for its upkeep. As has been previously explained, the porch had been allowed to decay through the neglect of those responsible for its upkeep.

There had been some differences of opinion between Lord Rivers, the trustees and the auctioneers as to the method to be adopted in the disposal of the estate, but it was finally decided to sell it in individual lots. The sales, which would be by auction, would be performed by Hoggart and Norton at their Auction Mart., in Old Broad Street, Royal Exchange, London.

Several sales would be necessary, and well-illustrated particulars and plans were prepared. These particulars could be seen in most of the inns in the district, including Ipswich and Colchester. It is certain that most of the Mistley villagers examined those at the Thorne Inn, and carefully noted the reserve prices of the individual lots. It had been expected that after the sale particulars had been examined, a number of lots would be acquired by private purchase. There were, however, only four lots which were purchased in this way.

It was arranged to hold the main sale of "The Town and Port of Mistley" on 9th August 1844. This would include the entire quay premises, together with a number of dwelling houses nearby, comprising 45 lots.

The second sale was arranged for 13th September 1844, which included all the farms on the estate, and the remainder of the cottages, including those on the Green, totalling 30 lots. Further sales were planned for the wines, furniture, pictures, oak trees and many other individual items.

With the sale imminent, Lord Rivers and his mother were anxious to retain as much of the furniture and ornaments as possible, which were still at the Hall, where they had remained from the time it was occupied by Richard Rigby. Lord Rivers was constantly in touch with Ambrose, and requested him to make arrangements to dispatch many articles from the Hall. Some of the furniture was sent in wagons by road direct to Rushmore Lodge, and other items were sent to Colchester, and loaded into trucks for Shoreditch, and then by road to Lady Rivers, who lived in the City. On most occasions, as was Lord Rivers' custom, the cost charged by the carrier was queried, and he also impressed on Ambrose the need for careful packing. On each case a full description of the contents had to be inscribed. He required the clock over the stable door, and asked for the length of chains on which the weights were attached. All the Dresden China was to be sent, and the ornamental inkstands - not the ebony ones. James Large, the carrier, arranged for one wagon to go to Shoreditch for £12. This wagon contained bedsteads and bedding, and Lord Rivers enquired about the picture of the Duke of Bedford, which was hanging in the dining room. He also asked Ambrose to send the painting of Richard Rigby to Woburn Abbey for the Duke. This painting, and the one of the 4th Duke are still at Woburn, and the copies of these paintings were kindly given by the curator. Lord Rivers wanted six old chairs sent, which had been purchased by an old woman named Gould for a Mrs. Fullerton. It seems that a great deal of the furniture from the Hall was retained by the family, and one consignment consisted of a double bed, one single bed, the ornamental china, three servants' beds, a terra cotta vase, the small bedroom tables, two chests of drawers and a very old bedstead. Most of the items they required were sent, but as Sir William Anson was still in residence at the Hall, permission had to be obtained from him, as in addition to renting the Hall, he had the use of the furniture.

The build up to the sales was a difficult time for the residents of Mistley Thorne. Many tenants became very disturbed after they had learned the reserved prices of the property they occupied, and were endeavouring to raise as much capital as they could, living in hope that they might be able to secure their property below the reserve prices. Great secrecy was being exercised, as some tenants had arranged for others to bid for them. There were , unfortunately, a number of businessmen in the Colchester and Sudbury areas who were casting covetous eyes on some of the properties, to the dismay of the villagers. In addition rumours were circulating that the route of the the railway was being altered to pass through the centre of the village. For many months the village was in turmoil, and everyone was concerned over their businesses, employment and even the security of the houses in which they lived.

It was, indeed, a sad time for the village people, who had for years enjoyed the security of the Rigby era at Mistley Thorne.

CHAPTER 36

A PROBLEM FOR THE VILLAGERS

Much worry and concern of the villagers were expressed in numerous letters which they addressed to John Ambrose and Lord Rivers, as the time for the sale of Mistley grew closer. The particularly pathetic one shown below was written by Mr. George White, the village shoemaker. The property in which he lived was the fourth house, which still stands on the north side of Mistley street, to the west of the Swan Fountain. The letter reads:

> *My Lord*
>
> *I humbly beg your pardon for taking the liberty on a subject of this nature, but the bread of my family is quite dependent on your kindness respecting the premises I now occupy, and the reserve price being so much, that I have no means of procuring the premises. The most myself, with my friends, can raise is £300 for them. My Lord, if you can refer to Mr. Ambrose, and he can give you a full description of the premises, and myself and my family before me have been tenants for nearly two centuries past, and I fear it will put me and my family to great trouble. I earnestly and most humbly beg you will consider both me and my family, and shall ever remain my Lord,*
>
> *Your most humble and obedient servant,*
> *Geo. White.*

Lord Rivers did not consider that he could make an exception in his case, and George White had to wait until the sale to see if his bid of £300 would be successful.

James Howard, who occupied a large portion of the quay and beach, with buildings behind, was extremely worried, because the area had been split into five lots, with the reserve price totalling £2000. The slipway from which the ships were launched was on one lot, and on the adjoining four lots were the back up services necessary for the shipbuilding. There was obviously a possibility that others may purchase lots which were part of his shipyard, and thus divide and destroy his undertaking. He expressed his annoyance that the shipyard, which was being operated successfully, was not offered for sale in one complete lot.

Several householders were concerned that if they were unable to buy their homes, they may be compelled to leave them, and possibly seek houses in another village. The tenant farmers did not show too much concern, as it was expected that the agricultural estate would be purchased as an investment, and they would be able to remain as tenants of the farms they occupied, though perhaps paying more rent. There was little chance that the farmers would have sufficient capital with which to purchase the property they rented, but sales of this sort were taking place all over the country, and the tenants were usually allowed to remain on their farms.

As the day of the sale approached the worries of the villagers grew, but the family which gave Lord Rivers the most trouble was, without doubt, the Tovills.

For months, this family had been referred to in the many letters from Lord Rivers to John Ambrose, and even before the sale, Charles Tovill had difficulty in making a profit from the business on the wharf he occupied.

There were several families of Tovills in the village at this time, all of who were earning their living as tenants of property on the quay. George Randfield Tovill was a ship designer, and his brother Richard dealt in coal, shipping and fish. Samuel Tovill and his son were involved in coal and operating a wharf. Charles, who was Richard's son, occupied a wharf some 130' in length in front of the dwelling houses known as Grape Vine Cottages. In 1819, Charles married Mary Howard, the daughter of Samuel Howard, whose sons had perished at sea some four years earlier.

From Oxford Square, on 31st July 1843, Lord Rivers wrote a long letter to Ambrose concerning Tovill's rent, which had been reduced by the trustees by £100, due to the poor state of his business. Lord Rivers was very annoyed that the rent had been reduced, but reluctantly agreed, stating it was an unacceptable drain on the estate. This rather mean and uncompromising side of his character was illustrated in many of the letters which he addressed to Ambrose at this time. Continuous correspondence took place between them relating to Tovill's problems, during which Lord Rivers rarely expressed any compassion over the troubles which he was experiencing. It was, of course, not Lord Rivers' responsibility for the agreement of rents charged, as the estate was being administered by the trustees on behalf of his mother. It is apparent from reading the considerable correspondence between Ambrose and Lord Rivers that he assumed a great deal of responsibility, which bordered on interference with the duties of the trustees. In his correspondence he showed little concern for the tenants on the estate, but his mother, Lady Rivers, was quite the opposite, and it appears that she was always sympathetic towards Tovill's wife, Mary, whom she knew personally.

Lord Rivers wrote again to Ambrose in November 1843, saying that the:

> *"question of the wharf was so embarrassing a one that he could scarcely answer upon it is Tovill's inability to consider renting it provided from the actual state of Tovill's private finances, and the difficulties in which he had placed himself?*

Still feeling that the rent charge at 500 was too low, he also wished to know:
> *"Is the wharf in so depressed a state, that under proper management it was not truly worth £600 per year rent"*. *He still felt the rent charged at £500 was too low. He went on to say that Tovill was an experienced businessman, and if he was insistent in remaining as a tenant of the wharf, it would in due course be an advantage to him.*

He concluded his letter by saying:
> *"Our Mistley accounts are, I am sorry to say, too heavily squeezed for me to be able to run the smallest risk, and if we had a little more margin, I should be all for saying so, and for allowing Tovill to relinquish his occupation at Christmas - more particularly so, as the sale of Mistley will be affected upon the actual state of the rental, not upon the profitable swelling of the rental. If the wharf is let at £500 per year, at that rent it will be sold, and it is first a question in my mind, whether it might not be desirable not to reduce the rent of £500, but hold it, at*

consequently more rent profitable to ourselves, during the period of the sale of the estate. I name any idea that hastily comes to me, without feeling at all sure that it is the one that claims my attention, but when you have had some further conversation with Gurdon (trustee), upon all these points perhaps you will let me hear from you again."

In the meantime Tovill was still having great difficulty in profitably running his wharf, as by now there were a number of tenants in competition with him. He was extremely worried over the question of a sale, as his wharf had a reserve price of £1000. It is hard to understand the method of valuation of property in those days, when a capital value of £1000 commanded a rent of £600. Strangely, the rents of adjoining wharfs were not valued to the same extent as that of Tovill's, and it seems very clear that Lord Rivers had used his influence in pitching the valuation rather high. Although there is no evidence of a dislike of Tovill by Lord Rivers, his very actions appear to indicate that this was the case.

Lady Rivers remained in touch with Mary Tovill, and often sent her money for her young daughter, who was unwell. In February 1844, she sent £50 to help to defray the cost of the rent, and the heavy losses which Tovill had sustained. Finally he was compelled to borrow money to survive, and Lord Rivers was amazed to find that Tovill's debt ran into thousands of pounds. Soon after this time, Mrs. Tovill and her daughter left Mistley, and went to live in London. No explanation has appeared for her unusual departure, but it was felt she had gone in order to try to earn some money to help to pay the considerable debts which her husband had incurred. She was a very good needlewoman, and whilst in London did attempt to make small dresses and other clothes, which she sold by taking them round to the houses of the gentry living there.

Upon hearing of her plight, Lady Rivers, who also lived in London, obtained her address and travelled to see her. She found her living in an attic flat in Soho. She was very distressed, especially when she found that her daughter Mary was very ill. Lord Rivers also went to see her, and both gave her money to help her, advising her to return home to Mistley. Some months later, the following letter was sent to Mr. Ambrose from Lord Rivers at Rushmore Lodge:

"I have today had a somewhat curious and painful visit from Mrs. Tovill. I saw an empty carriage, with post horses driving through the woods in the direction of the house, which made me stop and question the postboy. His answer was, the lady is walking behind. Upon going home, a letter was given me, signed by Mrs. Tovill, and asking me to see her, and I did so. A second letter was put in my hand, which I enclose for you. I have refused to advance the money for the loan, of which she had petitioned me. A similar petition was made about six months ago, by another person to some extent, and even may I say to a great extent. I have not the means for £500 without security, whose only claim is to be in distress. Mrs. Tovill comes under this heading, and as he appears to be in the hands of Mr. Norman, and being liberally paid for his services, and has some expectations from an old Aunt. Mrs. Tovill cried so much, and I

may say so hysterically that I could scarcely bring the visit to an end, it having lasted more than one and a half hours. She told me that you had encouraged her in coming to see me, and said if she would do so, that you could "back" any letters which her husband would write to me. I read her some mention of her husband in one of your letters to me, which although briefly written, did not tend to convince me that her visit today for such an object, was with your approval, and encouragement".

It is very likely that John Ambrose did give some comfort to the Tovills, but there is no doubt that Lord Rivers was not prepared to help in any way whatsoever.

Mary Tovill continued to live in London for some time, and it was later confirmed that she was in fact making dresses and fancy goods. Sadly, her daughter died, and she eventually returned to Mistley, where her husband was able at least to secure some property. Their troubles were partly overcome by their friendship with Edward Norman who used Tovill's experience as a trader by giving him employment. The Tovills were, however, to remain poor, because of the debts they had incurred, and as late as 1847, Lady Rivers sent them £10. At this time, in letters to John Ambrose, Lord Rivers was enclosing gifts from Lady Rivers to the local people, especially to the Tovills. She was a lady of great compassion, and was much respected in the village. There is, however, little evidence of kindness given to the village people by her son, Lord Rivers, who whilst he loved Mistley, concerned himself in extracting every penny from the tenants of property they rented. In the one hundred or so letters which Lord Rivers wrote to John Ambrose, from which part of this story has been compiled, it has been found that in many of them he denied owing money to local tradesmen, and argued about rents owing to the estate. He made great play over the financial problems of the family, and emphasised that the sale had to take place to safeguard his mother's interests, and especially the annuity she received. It is very sad that the Rigbys, whose efforts to develop Mistley had benefited most of the village people, should have been succeeded by a person of such a miserly nature. A paragraph from a letter written to Ambrose on 13th August 1844 shows him to be a perfect hypocrite.

From Rushmore Lodge - Salisbury:

"I have a note from you, bearing the date 22nd May 1844, in which you speak of a sum of about £55,000, coming to my mother on Mr. Charles Rumbold's death. Do you know more accurately the amount? and can you ascertain Browe's account too?
Yours respectfully,
George Pitt Rivers."

(The 'enclosed from poor White' refers to the letter at the beginning of chapter 36)

Charles Rumbold, from whom Lady Rivers was to inherit £55,000, was her uncle, and this considerable amount of money represented quite a fortune in those days. It is obvious that Lady Rivers had no financial worries, but there is little doubt that the Tovills and many other people in the village were extremely concerned over the forthcoming sale, and the effect it would have on them.

CHAPTER 37

THE GREAT SALE OF MISTLEY

s soon as the assent of Parliament was given, Mr. Hoggart, the auctioneer, set in motion the procedure for the disposal of the property. Meetings with the trustees and Lord Rivers were, however, still taking place right up to the end of July, with the date of the sale less than a fortnight away. A letter, written by Lord Rivers to John Ambrose, again illustrates his wish to see Mistley sold as a complete estate.

He wrote from Windsor Castle on 28th July 1844:

> *"I am very glad to find that it suits both yourself and Gurdon, that our meeting should take place with Mr. Hoggart tomorrow week in Suffolk House, at half past two. Many points will have to be considered, and finally settled. With reference to the applications you have received, or may receive from persons desirous of purchasing Mistley as a place of residence, and as one entirety, Mr. Hoggart recommends that you should name no sum as being that which we should take for it, but rather leave them to offer one. He is still very much in favour of at once at the auction, putting up the estate in lots. He says that people will have sufficient time before the sale of purchasing the whole by private contract, if so disposed, and any question of its being thus sold at the auction would inspire the sale of it afterwards, if sub-divided. I am not of his opinion, but he ought to be the best judge."*

Despite the uncertainty over the method of disposal, the preparations for the sale had to continue, and reserve prices allocated to each lot number. This became a lengthy and difficult operation, which was undertaken in close liaison with John Ambrose, who had to supply the intricate details of acreages, field names of the farms, and the occupiers of the numerous premises. The concise details in the beautifully printed particulars of the sale must have taken weeks to compile, but Ambrose, no doubt, had the advantage of the wonderful record of the estate drawn by Scale, some seventy years previously, which would have given him much of the information he required.

It had been decided that it would be necessary to have several auctions, in case some of the lots at the main auction remained unsold. The particulars had been widely circulated throughout the country in various newspapers, and prospective buyers did enter into talks of contracts of individual lots, at the reserve prices. It was expected that the disposal of the estate would take nearly a year to complete, as the Hall, furniture and grounds could not be disposed of until Sir William Anson left; his lease of the Hall ran until March 1845. Immediately the estate was advertised, a number of inquiries were received to buy the estate in its entirety. Unfortunately nothing came of this, as the reserve price of £140,000 could not be reached. One inquiry came from Lord Wellesley, and at one time it looked as though he would buy it, but he withdrew before negotiations could be finalised. Elaborate colour maps were prepared listing all the lots by number, together with the exact measurements, and showing the buildings on them. Lady Rivers had included the sale of the Advowsons of the Bradfield and Mistley Churches, which brought in a considerable sum of money in tithes annually.

The First Sale.

The first sale took place in London at 12.00 noon on 9th August 1844, attended by a large crowd of people. The auctioneer announced the details, which included forty dwelling houses, the Thorne tavern, wharfs and quays, capital warehouses, shipbuilding yards, business premises, and valuable building land.

He began with lot no. 1, which was a piece of land running to the Harwich road in the south, and to the low water mark in the north, which included the beach. It was described as forming part of a hanging wood, possessing brick earth of the finest quality, and having a frontage to the river of 313'. It was admirably adapted for the shipbuilder's yard, where vessels of 1000 tons might be launched. The lot totalled more than 4 acres. It had a reserve price of £400, but was sold to a Mr. Downes of Sudbury for £500. The reason will never be known, but soon after the purchase, Mr. Downes sold it to Mr. Charles Tovill. Perhaps he had bought it for Mr. Tovill; Tovill evidently found the money somewhere, and it is suspected that perhaps his friend Edward Norman may have assisted him. In due course the railway to Harwich bisected the plot, and the branch line to the quay also ran through it. Sometime later a clay pit was worked on it, and bricks were stored in an area beside the river. A quay, which was soon built, became known as Bramble Wharf, and the property was eventually acquired by Taylor and Butler, long-standing timber merchants at Manningtree who changed the name to Baltic Wharf.

Lot 2 was similar to lot 1, stretching to the Harwich road in the south, and again without a tenant. Its reserve price was £300, but a Mrs. Allen, who made bricks at Ballingdon near Sudbury, bought it for £450. Lots 3,4,5,6 and 7 consisted of the shipyard occupied by Mr. James Howard and his sailmaker, Mr. John Moore. The whole area was nearly 700' in length, and had several buildings on it. Lot no.3 was bought by Mr. James Cutting for £439, of which £59 was for timber on the site. The reserve price had been £250. Lot no.4 was unsold at the auction, but later a Mr. Leonard Cook bought it for £340, having probably secured it on his behalf by arrangement. Lot no.5 was sold to Mr. John Stuck Barnes, a rich Colchester businessman. James Howard was able to retain the main part of his shipyard by purchasing lot no.6, but Mr. William Wymark bought lot nos.7 and 8 for £600 and £710 respectively. It seems that James Howard was confined to only one small portion for his shipbuilding operation, and for a short time operated it in conjunction with others nearby. Sometime later a malting and granary were erected, and a rail tramway was placed through the site. Sadly, in 1852, shipbuilding ceased on this part of Mistley quay, after more than 100 years, during which time many fine ships had been launched. Lots 9 and 10 running 228' along the riverside had several buildings on them, including a malt office, or malting. These lots had the Thorne Quay in front, and were tenanted by several businessmen. One of them, Mr. Edward Norman, purchased the whole site for £2360. Lot 11 was unsold, but later a Mr. Baxter bought it for £600, over which he had to give right of way to Mr. Norman to his malting. Eventually the malting was demolished, and a shop with a dwelling was built on the site. These stood on the opposite side of the road to the Thorne Inn, and were finally pulled down by Messes. Brooks, when they built their provender mill just after the war. Lot no.12, over which Lord Rivers had been so concerned, remained unsold. It measured 113', alongside Thorne Quay, with a width of only 36' it had no buildings on it, and the reserve price was set at £1000. This was a ridiculous price for such a small area, and it was suspected that Lord Rivers had set the price unreasonably high in order that Tovill would not be able to buy it. There was, however, great loyalty between the businessmen and the tenants, and no one made a bid for it. Lot 13 was occupied by George Tovill and Golding Constable, and contained several capital warehouses, granaries and other buildings. This is the site of the present Mistley Workshops and Pottery, and it is hard to understand the glowing description given at the sale, as the same buildings still occupy the site. The lot was brought by Mr. Allen of Ballingdon for £600, against a reserve price of £500. This property was the quay and premises which had to provide the contribution to the Rigby Charity, already described in a previous chapter. Opposite to lot no.13 was no.19, which was the attractive brick built granary which had been erected in 1727, and was now occupied by Mr. Benjamin Long. Mr. Robert Page, who was the tenant of the spacious new malting built on lot no.20, bought it together with lot no.19. Lot 21 occupied by George Tovill, and lot no.22 unoccupied, constituted land behind the Towers Church. These were bought by a Mr. Hawkins for £800. The remaining three lots in the area of the port were nos.23, 24 and 25. These were not sold, and placed with other lots in the third sale held later on in the year. The Mistley Thorne Inn was sold to Mr. D. C. Alston, the Manningtree brewer, for £2000. His family brewery supplied the public house with beer brewed at Manningtree until long after the turn of the century, but few spoke well of it. When the brewery at Manningtree finally closed, the Thorne was sold to Daniel and Sons Breweries of West Bergholt, in whose possession it remained until after the last war. Mr. Alston also bought two of the cottages behind the Swan Fountain, one of which he eventually turned into a public house. The two centre houses were bought by Mr. Cobbold of Ipswich, who also turned them into a public house, called the Grapevine. The name can still be seen on the back of the two cottages facing the river.

It was announced at the sale that Lord Rivers had given the Swan Fountain, and the surrounding area in front of the Thorne, for the use of the village. This area has recently been made attractive, with a new brick roadway and surround; the fountain has been renovated by the Parish Council. At the end of the sale it was found that seven industrial lots, and five houses, had been unsold, but these were eventually disposed of at the third sale later on.

Some of the 45 lots offered had more than one occupant, and of these 24 industrial tenants, and 20 housing tenants, found that they had new landlords after the sale. It is expected that some would have been allowed to continue as tenants, but it is unlikely that these were limited in numbers. Mr. Edward Norman, Mr. Robert Page, and Mr. D. C. Alston were the principal buyers, but several lots went to traders outside the district, who proceeded to run the businesses themselves. Nine of the houses contained shops, and Mr. Baxter bought his ironmonger's property. Mr. J. Disney lost his blacksmith's forge, but managed to buy his tailor's shop. Mr. Hurring lost his baker's shop, and George White, who wrote the pathetic letter to Lord Rivers, managed to buy his shoemaker's property at the third sale. Strangely, he also bought a house in the same row, backing on to the quay, which he immediately resold. Soon after, he also sold the original property he had secured, but as the lot consisted of two dwellings, he, no doubt, remained in his house and shop. The barber's shop was also part of two lots, and the house bought by a sea captain named Crisp.

It is not known how many businesses had to be closed, or how many of the original tenants were allowed to remain by the new purchasers of the properties. It was, however, apparent that the whole village was devastated, and the loss of tenancies resulted in hardship to many families. The entire Tovill family, who had been prominent traders, were practically wiped out as operators in the port. Samuel and his son lost their houses, a coal yard and office, and George and Charles were only able to secure two lots, one of which was an unworked wooded area alongside the beach. They were also unable to buy their houses, and until the time of the sale the family had been tenants of nine properties. They had used coalyards, granaries, maltings, wharfs and storage areas, and it is clear that the Port of Mistley had changed hands overnight. In the years ahead, with the coming of the railway, there were to be fewer small businesses, and the pattern of trade would change dramatically, with the building of extensive maltings and granaries. It is certain that if Lord Rivers had had his way, and the Port of Mistley had been sold in its entirety, a different situation would have occured. No doubt most of the tenants would have remained secure in their holdings, but probably only for a few more years.

In hindsight, if the sale of the port and land around it had been delayed until the plans of the Eastern Union Railway Co. had been finalised, the property would have been far more valuable. Lord Rivers, however, appeared to be content, as in the following letter sent to John Ambrose, ten days after the sale, from his home at Rushmore Lodge, he wrote:

"In the first place, you must in future direct to me at Rushmore Lodge, Shaftesbury.

I have been, on the whole, satisfied with the first sale of poor Mistley, and am only now anxious that the whole affair should be concluded, and the subject of ti dismissed from my mind. It cannot but be a painful one to me, and one which at times overcomes me, by the many reflections, and recollections of bygone and very happy days, which it, in spite of myself, gives rise to.

If I ever know as much, I hope I can know the same kind of happiness, as I have known in that dear place, and am led to feel it, and be more aware of it, now that I shall probably never see it again.

I have answered the enclosed from poor White, by expressing most sincerely the regret I have felt in receiving it, but by of course pointing out to him the improbability of his request being granted, which I have told him is in fact to the effect, that I would use my influence to put the reserve prices set upon the previous lots lowered accordingly to the means of those desiring to purchasing them. Did Tovill purchase any lot - or none? I have heard from Hoggart that the next sale is postponed until the 13th. Are you aware whether the clock over the stable archway can be safely removed. If it could, I would like it when I remove other articles from the house.
Yours very truly,

George Pitt Rivers."

The Second Sale

The second sale was widely advertised in the same way as that of the port and town, and should have taken place in August. It was, however, delayed until 13th September, as negotiations were going on with several prospective buyers who wished to purchase the whole agricultural estate. In due course it was found that no-one would pay the price required, and the sale was again held in London, arranged by Hoggart and Norton, at their auction mart.

The attendance was not so large as at the previous sale, and the auctioneer began the proceedings by giving the particulars of the thirty lots on offer which could be purchased in individual lots, or in their entirety. The auction had proceeded for only a short time before it was realised that the Mistley estate was to fall into the hands of only a few people. Although the names of some of the purchasers are known, no records have been discovered showing the names of some of the small lots which were sold. A Mr. Henry Page purchased New Hall Farm, and Mr. John Mann and John Stuck Barnes secured land at the end of the quay, which ran up to the Harwich Road and formed part of Cliff farm. The area of the ballast pit was bought by builders and changed hands several times, eventually being divided into residential plots. As the years passed a number of dwellings were erected, and in 1848 a highway was constructed through the centre of the ballast pit named "California Road". It was in this year that gold was discovered in California, and although it is not certain, the name may have been given to commorate the famous Gold strike. The road remains bearing the same name today. Only a few years later the tall dwelling on the Harwich Road was constructed, and named "Alma House", which coincided with the bloody battle which took place in the Crimea in 1854.

One of the problems which the auctioneers experienced at the time of the sale was the lack of knowledge of the exact route of the railway line to Harwich, which the Eastern Union Railway Co. were planning. Prospective buyers were naturally worried that having purchased land, they might find that a railroad would split it in two. Consequently prices were depressed, and a number of lots remained unsold.

Edward Norman, who had purchased a considerable amount of property in the first sale, secured land running up to his maltings next to Manningtree. He was, at this time, certainly the most prominent businessman in Mistley, and already had farms in Bradfield, and alongside the river in the east of Mistley. He was also involved in shipping, and selling coal, but his main business was undertaken in the large complex of maltings which he had constructed on land owned by Rigby adjoining Manningtree, together with a smaller one on the quay. The land on which the maltings were built was on a 99-year lease, of which 60 years were still to run. Edward had a very good friend in London, named Thomas Glover Kensit, and no doubt through this friendship he often visited Mistley, becoming very fond of the place. He came from a very wealthy family, and was clerk to the Skinners Company. Most of the farms, and some of the land offered were purchased by him, including the Advowsons of the churches at Mistley and Bradfield. After the sale was concluded, it became apparent that Thomas Glover Kensit, from Skinners Hall in London, had become the principal landowner in the village, and he accordingly assumed the title of Lord of the Manor, the new squire of Mistley. Mistley Hall and stables had not been offered for sale, although much of the park around it had been acquired by Mr. Kensit.

Lord Rivers wrote to Ambrose from Rushmore Lodge soon after the sale, saying:

"I am upon the whole satisfied with the second day's sale at Mistley. Some lots I felt certain would be bought in, and I hope they will be such as will readily find purchasers by private contract, and the sums which these lots have realised, have exceeded the reserve prices set upon them by £2,720. We have now sold by auction property estimated as being worth £69,740 for £72,090. I have just written to Mr. Hoggart to request him to send me a correct account of all the lots sold by private contract, and also to let me know when he proposes to sell the house, furniture and fixtures, timber etc.

Perhaps you will be good enough to explain to him that all the articles of furniture etc., in the house will not be sold, in consequence of my requiring some of them to be sent to me here - I will beg you to send me any, and all newspapers, that may make mention of the sale of the estate, as I should be curious to read them. I will also beg you to bear in mind, that the present year 44 must end my subscriptions to various charities, and societies in the County. I have innumerable calls on me here that I think it but fair to answer the claims of property by a transfer of my subscriptions in Essex to this County.

Yours very truly,

George Pitt Rivers."

The Third Sale.

A further small sale took place at the Cups Hotel, Colchester, on 4th February 1845, at which some lots which had remained unsold at the time of the first and second auctions, were offered. All the ten lots offered at the sale were quickly sold, one of which was the wharf on which Charles Tovill was a tenant. The reserve price had now been reduced to £600 instead of £1000, and was immediately bought by Edward Norman. The other lots were at the eastern end of the estate, and included the magnificent walled kitchen gardens, and the land to the south known as Cups Field. The area called Barnfield, on which the National School had been built, was purchased by the wealthy Mr. Page, who already owned farms and the large malting on Mistley Quay. He also purchased the kitchen gardens and land close by.

The Fourth Sale.

The sale of the furniture in the Hall was held at the Cups Hotel on 11th March 1845, again organised by Hoggart and Norton. Lord Rivers had taken the greater part of the furniture, and Sir William Anson had come to the end of his tenancy, and had left the Hall. Some paintings and stocks of wine were also sold, but unfortunately no records have been found. It is known, however, that some paintings went to the Duke of Bedford at Woburn. Local people also made purchases, mostly of small items, some probably as keepsakes.

Lord Rivers wrote to Ambrose on 8th April 1845:

"I have a letter today from Mr. Hoggart, giving me a statement of the result of the sale of the furniture, of which I had not previously received, also a statement of the sum at present obtained upon the sale as a whole.

Namely   £123,745-11-6

There is still one lot on land bought in estimated at £1,000-0-0
The materials of the building are estimated at £3,555-0-0
Timber estimated at £7,000,0-0
Making a total, supposing the estimated item is received of
the unsold property £135,248-11-6

This calculation, I understood from his letter to be correct. I shall beg either from him or you to receive an account each day of the sale - I shall be here (19, Lower Belgrave Square) until Thursday next, on which day I return to Rushmore. What is the meaning of the advertisement in the Times of 100 oaks standing on Dove House Farm, as I expected that the whole of the timber would have been sold at once at a valuation. Will you produce for me some explanation of this? The first wagon load
of goods arrived quite safely at Rushmore, and my wagon arrived in London tomorrow for the second one.
Yours very truly,
George Pitt Rivers."

It seems from Lord Rivers' estimates that it had been decided to demolish Mistley Hall, as the £3555 for materials probably refers to this building. No doubt the builders of the house at Oakley, and Mr. Page who built the new Mistley Hall, purchased these materials. Lord Rivers had evidently not been informed that a sale of oak trees had been arranged to be held at the Cups Hotel in 16th April 1845. The details showed 120 oak trees adapted for shipbuilding, growing on Dove House and Dairy House Farms. The trees were sold in 14 lots, and 25% of the purchase price had to be deposited immediately. All trees were to be cleared by 1st June, and strict instructions were given to avoid damage. Any trees left after 1st June would be retained by the vendor. Fourteen trees stood in the lovely Oak Grove, totalling 621'. Six very large trees measuring 507' stood in Kennel piece. The total measurement of the oaks amounted to more than 6000', and it is remarkable that this amount of timber could be felled by hand and transported by horse in less than six weeks.

Sadly, this sale brought to an end the influence of the Rigby family, which during the previous 136 years had transformed Mistley from an obscure hamlet to a thriving village community. It is, however, pleasing to find in the years ahead, that the Kensits, with the Normans, who had acquired the greater proportion of the estate, would continue to play a major part in promoting industry, and caring for the village people.

CHAPTER 38

DETAILS OF THE SALES

Duuring the research for this book, the original particulars of the first sale were discovered. They are enclosed in a large hardbound cover, on the front of which is printed Mistley Estate, Town Property. The set of particulars are Mr. John Ambrose's personal record of the sale and were evidently retained by a Manningtree solicitor. It was given to a local businessman who was interested in local history many years ago. The record was discovered in a most unlikely place - in a large black metal box in a cellar under a brewery at Burton on Trent. Amongst the particulars is the Act of Parliament authorising the sale of the property. Also included is a large linen-backed plan, showing each lot in the sale. On it are shown the lot numbers in various colours, and on the back of each page of the 45 lots for sale is written the reserve price, the person who bought it, and the amount paid. A copy of these particulars and the map are shown in the following pages.

The particulars of the second sale which consisted primarily of the agricultural estate were also found, and maps showing selected parts of the farmlands, with details of field names and woods are also shown in the pages ahead. Many of these fields and woodlands can still be identified, and a number of them have the same names today. The houses on the green were sold at this time, but no information has been discovered regarding the purchaser. It was, however, thought to have been Mr. Kensit.

The printing of the original documents and the accompanying maps is of the highest quality, and survives today in a first class condition after nearly 150 years.

The bills of sale and associated maps are reproduced in appendix one and two.

CHAPTER 39

IN CONCLUSION

Following their purchase of the greater part of Mistley, the friendship between Edward Norman and Thomas Glover Kensit ripened, and their interests merged. Whilst Edward had always lived in Mistley, Thomas Kensit was a Londoner, and his important position in the Skinners Company precluded him from living in the village. He was, however, able to carry out his duties as Squire of Mistley, with every assistance from Edward Norman.

Edward had built himself a fine mansion house near his maltings, which he called Mistley Place, and later a further dwelling was built, which still exists near the Police Station, called Mistley Lodge. The Abbey, near the Thorne Inn was also erected, and the Page family had built the new Mistley Hall on the site of Rigby's walled kitchen garden. The Hall is now the principal building on the Acorn Village.

The heir to the extensive estate of farmland and industry owned by Edward Norman, was his nephew Charles, who was aged only sixteen, at the time of the sale. He had received an excellent education, and had become a parson at Portishead in Somerset.

The long friendship between the Kensit and Norman families was cemented when Kensit's daughter Janet married Rev. Charles Norman. They eventually came to Mistley, and for a time dwelt in the house next to the Towers Church, which they named Portishead House, in memory of Charles Norman's first living in Somerset.

Sadly, Edward Norman died in 1862; he was a well-respected resident of Mistley, where he had spent his whole life. He had built the Mistley Norman School in 1856, on a site near the Ballast Pit, and had commenced erecting a large mausoleum in the Towers churchyard. This imposing tomb can still be seen, and after it was completed his body was exhumed, and interred within it. In his will, Edward had made generous cash provision for his "loyal clerk", William Brooks, and also gave him all his farm and malting utensils. The Brooks family eventually obtained some of the farms ad other property, and carried on the malting tradition of Mistley well into the 1950s.

Rev. Charles Frederick Norman inherited the estate, and was soon to be appointed Canon. Later he went to live in his uncle's residence at Mistley Place, and although not Rector of Mistley church, strongly supported it, and made provision for the land in New Road, on which the present church of St. Mary was built in 1870.

Canon Norman and his wife Janet had eight children, and adopted the name of Kensit Norman. Janet eventually inherited the estates from her father, Thomas Glover Kensit, and thus most of the old Rigby farms descended into the hands of the Norman family. Canon Norman became Lord of the Manor, and as Squire of Mistley was respected by all the inhabitants. His son Edward died in 1902, and Charles passed away in 1913. As a mark of respect, Mistley Institute was erected in his memory by public subscription of the villagers.

The Norman family influence in Mistley extended for more than 100 years, during which time they continued to encourage industry, as had the Rigbys in the years before.

The sale of the Rigby estate in 1844 had coincided with the construction of the railway line from Lawford to Harwich, and not Margerums wood, as previously planned. A tramway was built leading from the main line to Mistley Quay, and this became operational in 1854. The arrival of the railway was to have a profound effect on the pattern of trade at Mistley.

Shipbuilding ceased in Howard's Yard, as the tramway along the quay ran straight through it. The fishing operations, which had already been decimated when the Howards left for Grimsby, were further depleted with Harwich taking over, using larger trawlers and the new rail facility. The transhipments into barge for Sudbury began to fall away, and more goods were sent to London by rail, which reduced the shipping using Mistley.

In the meantime, many businessmen had arrived in the village, and land prices had doubled. Mr. John Barnes from Colchester had sold the area on which Mistley Station is built, after a long high court action in which he was successful against the Eastern Union Railway Co., over the price which they wished to pay him for it.

Some years later it became apparent that the main industry in Mistley and Manningtree was to be malting and brewing. The Eastern Union Railway Company had purchased part of the quay, and by 1875 there were docks, piers and wharfs stretching from Rigby Quay in the west to Northumberland Wharf in the east. Smaller tonnages of coal were handled, but with the arrival of a Mr. Robert Free from London, together with Messrs. Rodwell and Heanage, seven modern maltings of magnificent design were built before the turn of the century. A further large malting was erected on the quay by Mr. Page, and soon sold to Brooks, who were also quickly expanding their considerable agricultural trade. There were four massive maltings on Mistley Quay, with a further four on the high ground above. At the peak, there were twenty maltings in Mistley and Manningtree; one, by far the largest, was built next to the Ballast Pit, together with more than one hundred houses.

The village once again became a thriving community, with nearly 400 men employed in the grain and malting industry, and a considerable trade in timber. The principal companies, three of which operated the whole of Mistley Quay, were Free, Rodwell & Co. Ltd.; Brooks (Mistley) Ltd.; and Taylor and Butler Ltd., with the Edme Malt Extract Works near the station. Grain was now coming from all over the world, with barley from Smyrna, Canada and California in small hessian bags transhipped in London, and brought to Mistley by sailing barge. This was to be the pattern until the second war. Latterly, the trade again changed dramatically, with massive new maltings replacing the old ones, an increase in a changing trade at Edme, and a thriving commercial port with a deeply dredged channel from Harwich.

When Richard Rigby had been so farsighted as to realise the potential of Mistley Thorne and its small wharf, he would have been pleased to find, after more than 200 years, modern industry (sadly with fewer men employed) still playing an important part in the village. During these years, many thousands of men had found employment on the farms and in the ever expanding industry. Ships from all over the world have sailed here, from the square rigged colliers, hoys, ketches, schooners, men o'war and tiny smacks. Later came the russet sailed barges, and now modern cargo ships of nearly 3000 tons capacity. When Lord Rivers was compelled to sell Mistley, he had hoped that the estate could remain in the hands of a landed gentleman. This was not to be, and the open sales held in 1844 allowed small businesses to develop, expand and prosper.

History will record with gratitude that Mistley's heritage, much of which can be seen in the village today, was the result of the years when the Rigby family lived here. It is regrettable that their remains lie unrecorded in a disused churchyard at Mistley Heath.

The malting in the background was the first of seven built by Robert Free. The barge was carrying Californian barley transhipped overside in London.

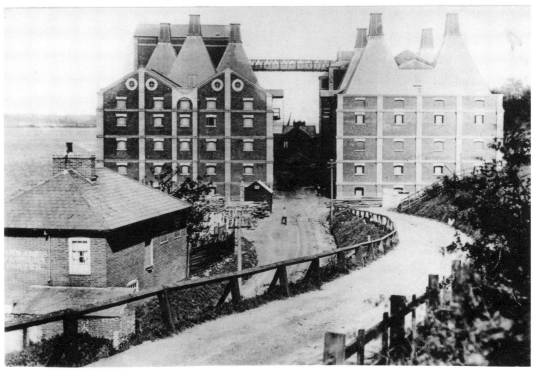

Two imposing maltings built fifty years after the Rigby sale. The building on the left was the Pilot public house.

Edward Norman's Mansion House was a public school for many years, and sadly demolished after the war.

Appendix one

The First Sale

The Home Park

The position of the old Mistley Hall can be clearly identified at the top of the present Church Lane. It will be noticed that at this time, there were plans to build a new road between the Pound and Lodges corners. The road patterns were almost the same as they are today, with the exception of one leading to Mistley Thorne from Lodges corner, which then ran to the Manningtree riverside road, joining it just to the west of Hopping Bridge.

Map of Home Farm
Section

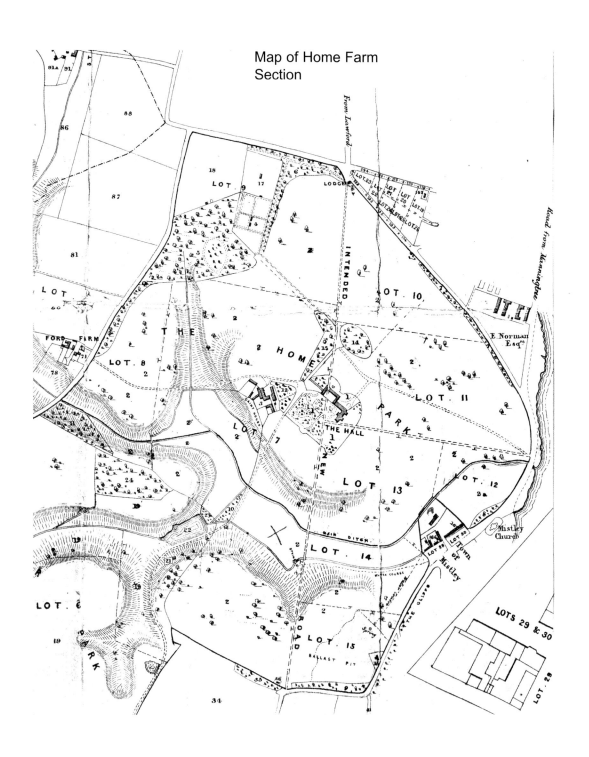

Key to the Home Park section:

The Woods
No. 5. Alder Car Plantation.
  " 6. Garden Plantation.
  " 6a. Lodge and Garden.
  " 7. Plantation.
  " 8. Church Plantation.
  " 9. Ballast Pit Plantation.
  " 10. Plantation.
  " 11. Beech Plantation.
  " 12. New Plantation"
  " 13. Clock Plantation"
  " 14. The Round Clump.
  " 14. The Old Grove.
  " 35. Plantation.

Some of the fields
No.2a. Church Meadow.
  " 18. Cups Field.
  " 19. The Deer Park.
  " 8. Stable Meadow.
  " 87. Mistley Field.
  " 88. Great Gravel Pit.

Sundry
No.1. Hall, garden, lawn and woods.
  " 2. Ballast Pit.
  " 3. Dairy House Farm, laundry and brewhouse.
  " 4. The Hall Kitchen Garden.
  " 15. Cottage in three tenements.
  " 16. School House (Pound House).
  " 17. The paddocks, stables and sheds.
  " 21. Keepers Cottage and garden.
  " 22. Keepers Pond.
  " 166. Dwelling house and schoolroom.
  " 167. Twelve brick built residences on green.
A. East Lodge

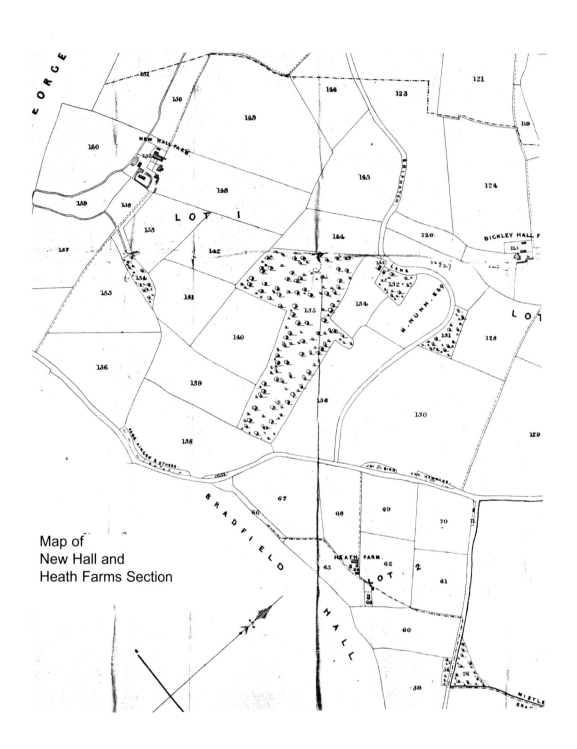

Map of
New Hall and
Heath Farms Section

New Hall and Heath Farms

New Hall farm still remains, but Heath Farm has been incorporated into Bradfield Hall. Skiphatch Lane is still in existence, and also uses the drive leading to Dickley Hall Farm.
The roadways shown are practically the same today.

Key to New Hall and Heath farms section:

The woods
No. 26. Oak Plantation.
" 58. Plantation.
" 131. The Spinney Wood.
" 132. Warners Grove.
" 135. Margerums Wood.
" 154. Alder Car Wood.

The fields
No. 59. Quick field.
" 127. Pigthle.
" 136. Wood field.
" 139. Margerums Barn field.
" 141. Lower Horsley Cross field.
" 142. Upper Horsley Cross field.
" 145. Gt. Skiphatch field.
" 146. First Highwoods field (formerly a wood).
" 147. Further Highwoods field (formerly a wood).
" 148. Mynets field.
" 156. Frantics field.
" 157. Pains field.

Sundry
No. 63. House and garden.
" 64. Homestead.
" 133. Keepers Cottage and garden.
" 152. New Hall Homestead.

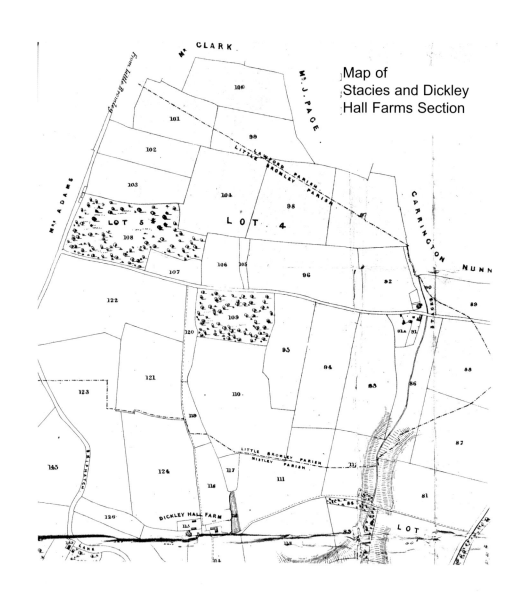

Map of
Stacies and Dickley
Hall Farms Section

Dickley Hall and Stacies Farms

These farms are still in existence. Great Chequer wood is almost demolished, and Little Chequer wood has gone completely.

The names of the plantation and fields numbered 83 and 84 identify the position of the brick kilns which were worked at Dickley Hall in the 18th century.

Key to the Dickley Hall and Stacies farms sections:

The woods
No.   84. Brick kiln plantation.
 "   108. Gt. Chequer wood.
 "   109. Lt. Chequer wood.

The fields
No.   83. Brick kiln plantation.
 "   92. Potash field.
 "   97. Gt. Thorn field.
 "   99. Lt. Cocks (formerly woodland).
 "   100. Gt. Cocks (formerly woodland).
 "   101. Thatchers (formerly woodland).
 "   102. Chequers field (formerly woodland).
 "   110. Haythorns.
 "   111. Forelands.
 "   113. Yellow field.
 "   114. Kitchen field.

Sundry
No.115. Homestead.
 " 116. Pond.

Dove House and White's Farms

These farms are still in existence, and the site of the old church ruins and churchyard still remain. The portion of land owned by Mr. Robert Goss, covered by scores of cherry trees, was always known as the Cherry Orchard. His family lived for generations in a small attractive wooden cottage alongside the Bradfield road at Mistley Heath. The Cherry farm continued until long after the second world war, but was sold after the last Robert Goss died. A popular Mistley resident, Mr. Goss, a tall upright figure, was regularly seen walking across the fields from the Heath to the village, where he was a regular visitor to the Lord Denman Inn.

Key to Dove House and White's farms section:

The woods
No.   25. The Old Mount Plantation.
"   26. The Oak Plantation.

The fields
No.   19. The Deer Park.
"   27. Heath piece.
"   28. Park piece.
"   29. Workhouse field.
"   32. Church field.
"   34. The paddock.

Sundry
No.   20. Homestead and pond.
"   31. Barn meadow (formerly site of old rectory).
"   55. Barn and yard.
"   56. House and garden.

No. 25, the Old Mount Plantation, was the site of the old Mistley Hall, and no. 29 was almost certainly the position of the Mistley workhouse, now the Mistley Heath allotments.

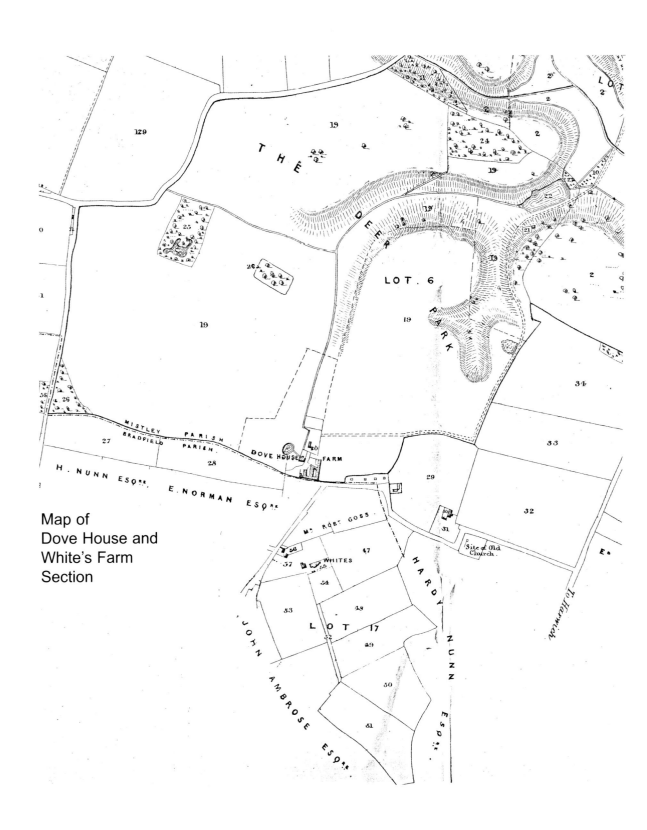

Map of
Dove House and
White's Farm
Section

Appendix Two

Details of the second sale

Capital and very valuable Estates
situate at
Manningtree and Mistley.
In the County of Essex on the borders of Suffolk,
comprising numerous farms
in a high state of cultivation
with excellent farm houses and buildings
offering investments of the first character.
Various plots of building ground adapted
for the erection of villa residences.
The advowsons of Mistley and Bradfield.
Freehold rent charge.
Dwelling houses and cottages in the Town of Mistley,
and other properties.
The whole containing about
2130 Acres,
these estates are conveniently situated
for the shipping of corn from the Port
Of Mistley to the London Markets,
and the poor rates are remarkably low.

The following land and farms, comprising the whole agricultural estate were offered for sale:

New Hall Farm	364 acres	£454 rent per annum		
The Heath Farm	88 "	£ 94 " " "		
Dickley Hall Farm	349 "	£465 " " "		
Stacies Farm	290 "	£362 " " "		
Ford Farm	80 "	£126 " " "		
Dove House Farm	467 "	£674 " " "		
Dairy House Farm	78 "	£ 78 " " "		
Home Park	25 "	£ 35 " " "		
Mistley Park	62 "	£156 " " "		
Part of Home Park	29 "	£ 40 " " "		
Meadow with grazing lands with lawns	45 "	£ 62 " " "		
Gardens and shrubberies				
Water Meadow	14 "	£ 19 " " "		
Meadow land	33 "	£ 49 " " "		
Arable and meadow land	60 "	£- " " "		
White's Farm	57 "	£105 " " "		
Miscellaneous Land				
Meadow and water meadow land	18 "	£ 26 " " "		

Ballast Pit	20 "	£ -	" " "
Meadow land and church - Bradfield	5 "	£ 11	" " "
Various plots of building land			
Great Chequer Wood	22 "	£ -	" " "

Rectory of Mistley and Vicarage of Bradfield.
Advowson - Tithes commuted at   £834-2-0 per annum
From which is deducted;

Annual payment to the curacy of Manningtree;	£40-0-0	
Curacies of the two parishes	£120-0-0	
Poor and other rates	£86-14-0	£246-14-0

Net income   £587-8-0 per annum

Parsonage house, gardens and glebe lands - 33 acres
Payable in lieu of Great Tithes of Bradfield: £450-19-0

Repairs to chancel	£5-0-0	
Poor rate	£70-0-0	
£5-12-0 per cent. increase in above communication charge	£25-4-0	£100-4-0

Net income   £350-15-0 per annum

Three dwelling houses on entrance to green
Tenants - Mr. Howard
Mr. Chandler
Mr. Etern
Also the school room.

12 substantial cottage residences on the north
side of the green.   Rent £96 per annum

The purchasers of this lot have for the purpose
of recreation, the use of the ground in front,
and will be restricted from any rights of
ownership, the same having been awarded to
John Ambrose, Esq., under the same shall
never be built upon, or made use of in any
offensive manner.

PLAN

OF THE

TOWN AND PORT

OF

MISTLEY.

For Sale by

MESS.RS HOGGART & NORTON.

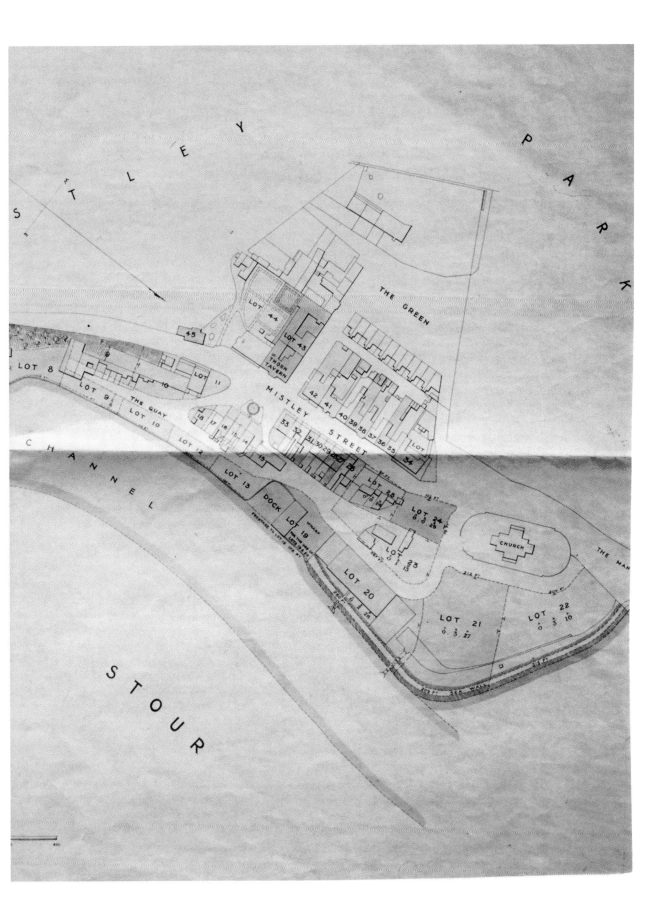

ESSEX.

PARTICULARS

OF

A HIGHLY IMPORTANT AND VALUABLE

FREEHOLD PROPERTY,

SITUATE

Close to Manningtree, and about Nine Miles from Colchester,

IN THE

COUNTY OF ESSEX,

COMPRISING

THE TOWN AND PORT OF MISTLEY,

CONSISTING OF ABOUT

FORTY DWELLING HOUSES,

THE THORN TAVERN,

WHARFS and QUAYS upon the STOUR,

CAPITAL WAREHOUSES,

Ship Builders' Yards and Business Premises,

VALUABLE BUILDING GROUND, &c.

Which will be Sold by Auction,

BY MESSRS.

HOGGART & NORTON,

AT THE AUCTION MART,

On FRIDAY, the 9th of AUGUST, 1844, at Twelve o'Clock,

IN FORTY-FIVE LOTS.

May be viewed by permission of the respective Tenants; and Particulars had at the Thorn Tavern, Mistley; and at the principal Inns at Colchester and Manningtree; also of Messrs. AMBROSE and SON, Solicitors, Manningtree; of Messrs. FLADGATE, YOUNG, and JACKSONS, Solicitors, Essex Street, Strand; of Mr. GILBERT, Land Surveyor, Colchester; at the Auction Mart; and of Messrs. HOGGART & NORTON, 62, Old Broad Street, Royal Exchange

THOS. HARRILD (late B. CLARKE), Printer, Silver St., Falcon Sq., London.

(2)

Particulars.

THE FOLLOWING VERY IMPORTANT AND DESIRABLE

FREEHOLD ESTATES,

CONSISTING OF

The Town and Port of Mistley,

IN THE

COUNTY OF ESSEX,

WITH EXTENSIVE

WHARFS AND QUAYS FRONTING THE RIVER STOUR,

IMPORTANT SITE FOR THE ERECTION OF VILLAS,

VALUABLE BRICK EARTH,

DWELLING HOUSES AND PROPERTIES,

SUBDIVIDED AS FOLLOWS:—

LOT 1.

A VALUABLE FREEHOLD ESTATE,

Forming a Portion of the Hanging Wood,

SITUATE

CLOSE TO THE TOWN OF MISTLEY, ON THE HARWICH ROAD,

In a beautiful Situation for Building.

POSSESSING BRICK EARTH OF THE FINEST QUALITY,

And extending to the Navigable River Stour, with a Frontage thereto of 313 Feet, capable at high water of receiving Ships of considerable burthen,

AND ADMIRABLY ADAPTED FOR A SHIP BUILDERS' YARD,

Where Vessels of 1000 Tons might be Launched.

AND CONTAINING ALTOGETHER

Four Acres, One Rood, and Nine Perches.

Lying as follows :

	A.	R.	P.
Wood Land	3	0	16
Saltings and Beach to Low Water Mark	1	0	33
A....	4	1	9

IN HAND.

The Fence on the East side of this Lot, also an equal moiety of the Fence against Lot 2, to be made by the Purchaser of this Lot.

197

LOT 2

A FREEHOLD ESTATE,

Adjoining, and of a similar description to, Lot 1,

HAVING A FRONTAGE TO THE RIVER STOUR OF 313 FEET,

AND CONTAINING

Three Acres, One Rood, and Twenty Perches,

Lying as follows:

	A.	R.	P.
Wood Land	2	3	0
Beach to Low Water Mark	0	2	29
	3	1	29
Deduct portion of New Road	0	0	9
	A....3	1	20

IN HAND.

The Purchaser of this Lot to Fence against a moiety of Lot 1.

LOT 3.

A FREEHOLD ESTATE,

Adjoining Lot 2,

FORMING THE WOODLAND CLIFF, WITH PART OF THE SHIP YARD AND BEACH,

The Wood is in hand, and the remainder is in the Occupation of Mr. James Howard,

WITH A FRONTAGE TO THE RIVER OF 150 FEET,

CONTAINING

One Acre, One Rood, and Seven Perches,

Lying as follows:

	A.	R.	P.
Wood Land	1	0	16
Beach	0	1	5
	1	1	21
Deduct portion of New Road	0	0	14
	A.....1	1	7

The Purchaser of this Lot to Fence against Lot 2.

LOT 4.

A FREEHOLD ESTATE,

Adjoining Lot 3,

COMPRISING PART OF THE SHIP YARD AND BEACH

Having a Frontage to the River of 148 Feet,

WITH THE WOODLAND CLIFF IN THE REAR,

AND CONTAINING

Three Roods and Thirty-one Perches,

Lying as follows :

	A.	R.	P.
Wood Land and part of Ship-yard	0	2	31
Beach	0	0	36
	0	3	27
Deduct portion of New Road	0	0	13
	A.... 0	3	14

As shewn on Plan,

The Cage, Pound, and the Blacksmith's Shop, are in the Occupation of Mr. James Howard, and part of the Blacksmith's Shop on the Cliff is in the Occupation of Mr. Baxter, and the remainder is in hand.

The Purchaser of this Lot to Fence against Lot 3.

(4)

LOT 5.

A FREEHOLD ESTATE,

Adjoining Lot 4,

CONSISTING OF A PORTION OF THE SHIP BUILDING YARD,

Having a Frontage to the River of 130 Feet,

AND CONTAINING

One Rood and Thirty-three Perches,

Lying as follows :

	A.	R.	P.
Cliff and Ship Yard	0	1	4
Beach	0	0	29
Total	0	1	33

As shewn on Plan.

In the Occupation of Mr. James Howard.

All the Buildings belonging to the Vendors within the Boundary of this Lot (as shewn on Plan) will be included in the Purchase.

The Purchaser of this Lot to Fence against Lot 4 as far as the New Road.

N.B. The purchasers of Lots 1, 2, 3, 4, 5, and 5*, are to have a right of way over the intended Road as shewn on the Plan within the red dotted lines, the said Road to be made in conformity therewith, at the joint expense of the Purchasers of these Lots, and the purchasers of Lots 2, and 3, are to allow a right of way through their several lots to Lots 1, 4, and 5 ; any timber coming within the line of Road will belong to the Purchasers. Lots 4, 5, 6, 7, and 8, are also sold subject to rights of way through their respective Lots. No division Fences are to be erected so as to interrupt the rights of way herein mentioned.

LOT 5*.

A PLOT OF FREEHOLD BUILDING GROUND,

In the Rear of Lot 5,

And having a Frontage to the Harwich Road of 111 Feet, and 51 Feet in Depth on the East side.

As shewn on Plan.

IN HAND.

The Purchaser of this Lot to Fence against the remainder of Lot 4.

LOT 6.

A FREEHOLD ESTATE,

Adjoining Lot 5.

COMPRISING PART OF THE SHIP BUILDING YARD, CLIFF, AND BEACH,

With a Frontage to the River of 130 Feet,

Together with such part of the Buildings, Boat House, Sail, Pitch and Tar Warehouses, as are now standing thereon, within the Boundaries of this Lot,

The whole containing together

Two Roods and Two Perches, including Beach,

As shewn on Plan.

In the Occupation of Mr. James Howard.

The Purchaser of this Lot to Fence against Lot 5.

LOT 7.

A FREEHOLD ESTATE,

Adjoining Lot 6.

COMPRISING THE REMAINDER OF THE SHIP YARD, CLIFF, AND BEACH,

Having a Frontage to the River of 130 Feet,

AND CONTAINING

One Rood and Twenty-nine Perches.

As shewn on Plan.

The Ship Warehouse, and Sail House over, in the Occupation of Mr. John Moore ; and the remainder is in the Occupation of Mr. James Howard.

The Purchaser of this Lot to Fence against Lot 6.

LOT 8.

A FREEHOLD ESTATE,

Adjoining Lot 7.

CONSISTING OF A VALUABLE WHARF TO THE RIVER, OF 112 FEET FRONTAGE.

WITH THE CLIFF IN THE REAR INCLUDED,

Together with such Buildings as are within the Boundary of this Lot,

Part of which are Occupied by Messrs. Tovill and Long.

The Purchaser of this Lot to Fence against Lot 7.

LOT 9.

A FREEHOLD WHARF,

Adjoining Lot 8.

With a Frontage of 114 Feet to the River,

EXTENDING IN DEPTH 36 FEET TO THE INTENDED NEW ROAD,

AND A FURTHER DEPTH IN THE REAR,

Together with all the Buildings and Erections thereon within the Boundaries of this Lot,

As shewn on Plan.

In the several Occupations of Messrs. Norman, Tovill, Long, Wymark, and Howard.

The Purchaser of this Lot to Fence against Lot 8.

LOT 10

A FREEHOLD WHARF,

Adjoining Lot 9.

With a Frontage of 114 Feet to the River,

EXTENDING IN DEPTH 36 FEET TO THE INTENDED NEW ROAD,

AND A FURTHER DEPTH IN THE REAR OF ABOUT 80 FEET,

Together with all the Sheds, Granaries, and Buildings thereon, within the Boundaries of this Lot,

As shewn on Plan.

In the several Occupations of Messrs. Norman, Brooks, and Baxter.

The Purchaser is to Fence against the upper portion of Lot 9.

LOT 11.

A VALUABLE FREEHOLD PROPERTY,

Adjoining Lot 10,

As shewn on Plan,

COMPRISING

A Capital Detached Warehouse, and Iron Yard, spacious Shop in three Divisions,

COAL HOUSE &c.,

WITH A COMFORTABLE DWELLING HOUSE,

CONTAINING

Three Bed Rooms, Two Servants' Rooms, Two Parlours, Kitchen, Scullery, Cellar, and Offices, with Garden.

In the Occupation of Mr. Baxter

LOT 12.

A FREEHOLD WHARF,

Adjoining Lot 11,

Having a Frontage of 100 Feet to the River, and extending in an average Depth 36 Feet,

As shewn on Plan.

In the Occupation of Mr. Tovill.

LOT 13.

A FREEHOLD WHARF,

Adjoining Lot 12,

Having a Frontage to the River of 100 Feet and extending in an average Depth 35 Feet,

TOGETHER WITH

A valuable Parcel of Ground in the rear,

UPON WHICH ARE ERECTED SEVERAL CAPITAL WAREHOUSES, GRANARIES, AND BUILDINGS,

Such of them as are within the Boundaries of this Lot will be included in the Purchase, as shewn on Plan.

In the Occupation of Messrs. Tovill and Constable.

LOT 14.

A FREEHOLD DWELLING HOUSE,

Adjoining Lot 13,

AND CONTAINING

Three Bed Rooms, Dressing Room, Attic, Two Parlours, Counting House, Kitchen, Washhouse, and Cellar with Garden in the front.

In the Occupation of Mr. George Tovill,

LOT 15.

TWO FREEHOLD DWELLING HOUSES,

Adjoining Lot 14,

EACH CONTAINING

Parlour, Two Bed Rooms, Attic, Kitchen, Pantry, Small Yard, Office on Quay, and Small Garden in Front.

In the Occupation of Thomas James and Widow Thompson.

The Quay Office on this Lot, and occupied by Mr. George Tovill, is to be pulled down to make room for the Road.

LOT 16.

A FREEHOLD DWELLING HOUSE,

Adjoining Lot 15, as shewn on Plan

AND CONTAINING

Parlour, Counting House, Two Bed Rooms, Attic, Kitchen, Pantry, Coal Shed, Yard, and small Garden in Front.

In the Occupation of Mr. Edward Norman.

(8)

LOT 17.

A PIECE OF FREEHOLD GROUND,

Adjoining Lot 16,

And now used as a Coal Yard,

TOGETHER WITH

A SMALL ALLOTMENT TOWARDS THE STREET,

In the Occupation of Mr. George Tovill.

LOT 18.

A PIECE OF FREEHOLD GROUND,

Adjoining Lot 17,

Having a Double Frontage to the Road,

As shewn in Plan,
In the Occupation of Mr. George Tovill.

LOT 19.

A VERY VALUABLE FREEHOLD PROPERTY,

Adjoining Lot 13,

COMPRISING

A Stack of Brick Built Corn Warehouses of Four Floors,

With Arch to admit Barges to Load and Unload,

THE EXCLUSIVE DOCK,

With a Frontage to the River of 172 Feet, and an Allotment on the West Side of 20 Feet Wide, together with the Wharf (as shewn on Plan) which is for the joint use of Lots 19 and 20,

The Water Way in Front belongs to this Lot.

In the Occupation of Mr. Benjamin Long

LOT 20.

A VERY VALUABLE FREEHOLD ESTATE,

Adjoining Lot 19,

COMPRISING

THOSE SPACIOUS AND SUBSTANTIAL WELL-BUILT MALTING KILNS,

WITH COAL YARD AND PREMISES,

HAVING A FRONTAGE TO THE RIVER OF TWO HUNDRED AND EIGHTY FEET,

With the use of the adjoining Wharf as stated in Lot 19,

WITH AN ALLOTMENT ON THE NORTH SIDE, JETTY, AND SLUICE,

THE WHOLE CONTAINING TOGETHER

Two Roods and Twenty-six Perches,

In the Occupation of Mr. Robert Page.

The Purchaser of this Lot to Fence against Lot 21

203

LOT 21.

A VALUABLE FREEHOLD PROPERTY,

Adjoining Lot 20,

And in the rear of the Church to which it has a Frontage of 212 Feet to the intended New Road, and a Frontage to River of 209 Feet,

ADMIRABLY ADAPTED FOR A WHARF AND BUILDING PURPOSES,

CONTAINING ALTOGETHER

Three Roods and Twenty-seven Perches.

In the Occupation of Mr. George Tovill.

The Purchaser of this Lot to Fence against a moiety of Lot 22.

LOT 22.

A FREEHOLD ESTATE ADJOINING,

Possessing similar advantages to Lot 21,

AND CONTAINING

Three Roods and Ten Perches,

Having a Frontage in the Rear to the intended New Road of 304 Feet, and a Frontage to the River of 315 Feet,

The Purchaser of this Lot to Fence against a moiety of Lot 21.

IN HAND.

Note—The Purchasers of Lots 20, 21, and 22, are to enter into mutual covenants for the preservation of the Wall abutting upon the Stour. The Sluice in Lot 20, is subject to the uses of Lots 21 and 22.

LOT 23.

A VALUABLE PLOT OF FREEHOLD BUILDING GROUND,

WITH THE BUILDINGS THEREON,

A DOUBLE COTTAGE AND WASHHOUSE OPPOSITE TO LOT 20,

A Frontage to the Road of 367 Feet,

AND CONTAINING ONE ROOD AND THIRTEEN PERCHES,

In the several Occupations of Messrs. Page, King, and Wright.

The Purchaser of this Lot to Fence against Lots 24 and 25.

LOT 24.

A FREEHOLD ESTATE,

COMPRISING

A PLOT OF BUILDING GROUND,

SITUATE

At the Entrance to the Town, near the Church,

Having a Frontage of 102 Feet to the Street, and a Frontage of 75 Feet abutting on the Church,

IN HAND.

The Purchaser of this Lot to make the Division Fence against Lot 25.

LOT 25.

A PLOT OF FREEHOLD BUILDING GROUND,

ADJOINING

Now Occupied as a Garden by Mr. Tanner,

With the COAL SHEDS, YARDS, and part of a STABLE, Occupied by Mr. Wymark,

COAL SHED and YARD, Occupied by Mr. Harris,

And part of COAL YARD and GARDEN, Occupied by Mr. Samuel Tovill, Jun.

Having a Frontage of 97 Feet to the Street.

As shewn on Plan.

The Purchaser of this Lot to Fence against Lot 24.

LOT 26.

A FREEHOLD DWELLING HOUSE,

Adjoining Lot 25,

CONTAINING

Two Parlours, Two Bed Rooms, Two Attics, Kitchen, Back Kitchen, Washhouse, Yard, and Garden,

With a Right of Way to Pump in Lot 28,

In the Occupation of Mr. Samuel Tovill, jun.

The Purchaser of this Lot to Fence against Lot 25.

LOT 27.

A FREEHOLD DWELLING HOUSE,

Adjoining Lot 26,

CONTAINING

Two Parlours, Two Bed Rooms, Two Attics, Kitchen, Scullery, and Yard,

With Right of Way to Pump in Lot 28,

In the Occupation of Captain Thompson.

LOT 28.

A FREEHOLD DWELLING HOUSE,

Adjoining Lot 27,

CONTAINING

Two Parlours, Two Bed Rooms, One Attic, Kitchen, Coal House, and Scullery,

Subject to the rights to Pump.

In the Occupation of Captain Malden.

N.B. The Tenant Claims Wood House.

LOT 29.

A FREEHOLD DWELLING HOUSE,

Adjoining Lot 28.

CONSISTING OF

Two Parlours, Two Bed Rooms, One Attic, Kitchen, Scullery, and Yard,

With right of way to Pump in Lot 28.

In the Occupation of Captain Eade.

LOT 30.

A FREEHOLD DWELLING HOUSE,

Adjoining Lot 29.

CONSISTING OF

Two Sitting Rooms, Two Bed Rooms, One Attic, Kitchen, Scullery, and Yard,

With right of way to Pump in Lot 28.

In the Occupation of Captain Morley.

LOT 31.

A FREEHOLD DWELLING HOUSE,

Adjoining Lot 30,

CONTAINING

Parlour, Bed Room, Kitchen, Washhouse, Pigsties, and Yard. In the Occupation of John James,

ALSO,

A Barber's Shop and Sitting Room,

In the Occupation of A. Hempson,

With Right of Way to Pump in Lot 28.

LOT 32.

TWO FREEHOLD DWELLING HOUSES,

Adjoining Lot 31,

One Occupied by Mr. George White, and containing

Sitting Room, Shoemaker's Shop, Keeping Room, Two Bed Rooms, One Attic, Washhouse, Workshop, and Warehouse, and Yard with Pump of Water,

The other occupied by Mr. James Wright, containing

Two Sitting Rooms, Two Bed Rooms, One Attic, Kitchen, and Coal Shed

LOT 33.

A FREEHOLD DWELLING HOUSE,

Adjoining Lot 32,

CONTAINING

Two Parlours, and Office, Three Bed Rooms, Two Attics, Kitchen, Cellar, Laundry, Stable, Yard, and Small Garden,

In the Occupation of Mr. Samuel Tovill, Sen.

LOT 34.

A VALUABLE FREEHOLD ESTATE,

COMPRISING

AN EXCELLENT DWELLING HOUSE,

Near the Church, at the Entrance to the Town of Mistley,

AND CONTAINING

Entrance Hall, Dining and Drawing Rooms, Breakfast Parlour, Anti Room, Five Best Bed Rooms and Dressing Room, Two Attics, Front and Back Staircases, Two Kitchens, Butler's Pantry, Store Room, Washhouse, Wine and Beer Cellars,

TWO-STALL STABLE, COACHHOUSE, COAL AND KNIFE HOUSES, YARD AND GARDEN, AND PUMP,

With a Plot of Ground added thereto on the North side of the House.

In the Occupation of Mr. Tanner.

LOT 35.

A FREEHOLD DWELLING HOUSE,

Adjoining Lot 34,

IN EXCELLENT ORDER,

Containing Two Parlours, Three Bed Rooms. Two Attics, Kitchen, Scullery, and Cellar, Chaise-house, Stable, and Garden,

In the Occupation of Miss Nunn.

LOT 36.

A FREEHOLD DWELLING HOUSE,

Adjoining Lot 35,

Containing Two Parlours, Four Bed Rooms, Two Attics, Kitchen, Washhouse, Cellar, Store Room, Stable, Wood and Coal Houses, Yard, and Garden,

In the Occupation of Mr. W. Brooks.

N.B. The Tenant claims the Partition in Garden.

LOT 37.

A FREEHOLD DWELLING HOUSE,

Adjoining Lot 36,

And containing Parlour and Office, Two Bed Rooms, Two Attics, Kitchen, Washhouse, and Cellar, with Stable and Garden.

In the Occupation of Mr. Mark Davis.

LOT 38.

A FREEHOLD DWELLING HOUSE, AND BAKER'S SHOP,

Adjoining Lot 37,

And containing Two Sitting Rooms, Two Bed Rooms, Two Attics, Washhouse, Garden, Biscuit Room, and Oven.

In the Occupation of Mr. Hurring.

The Tenant claims the Wash and Coal House.

LOT 39.

A FREEHOLD DWELLING HOUSE,

Adjoining Lot 38,

And containing Sitting Room, Two Bed Rooms, Attic, Kitchen, Washhouse, and Cellar, with Chaise House, and Garden,

In the Occupation of Captain Scott.

LOT 40.

A FREEHOLD DWELLING HOUSE AND TAILOR'S SHOP,

Adjoining Lot 39,

CONTAINING

Two Parlours and Shop, Two Best Bed Rooms, Two Attics, Kitchen, Workshop, Wash and Coal Houses, Piggery, and Garden,

With a Right of Way to Well in rear of Premises,

In the Occupation of Mr. John Disney.

N.B. The Tenant claims the Piggeries and Coal House.

LOT 41.

A FREEHOLD DWELLING HOUSE ADJOINING,

CONTAINING

Two Sitting Rooms, Shop, Warehouse, Two Best Bed Rooms, Two Attics, Kitchen, Wash and Coal Houses, Stable,
Cowshed and Garden,

With Right of Way to Well in rear of Premises.

In the Occupation of Mr. James Wright.

N.B. The Tenant claims the Cow Shed and Summer House.

LOT 42.

A VALUABLE FREEHOLD DWELLING HOUSE,

ADJOINING,

WHICH MIGHT EASILY BE CONVERTED INTO TWO HOUSES,

AND CONTAINING

Entrance Hall, Dining, Drawing, and Breakfast Rooms, Office, with Fire Proof Safes, Store Room, Pantry, Wash and
Coal Houses, and Water Closet.

On the First Floor are Four Best Bed Rooms, Dressing Room, Laundry, Nursery, and Four Attics.

Detached—Three Stall Stable and Coachhouse with Loft over, Cow House, Summer House, and Garden.

IN HAND.

But of the Estimated Annual Value of £50.

LOT 43.

A VALUABLE FREEHOLD ESTATE,

CONSISTING OF

THAT OLD ESTABLISHED AND WELL KNOWN INN, CALLED

" The Mistley Thorn,"

OCCUPYING A VERY CONSIDERABLE SITE OF GROUND

IN THE CENTRE OF THE TOWN OF MISTLEY,

AND CONTAINS

On the Ground Floor—Bar, Bar Parlour, Coffee Room, Captain's Room, Store Room, Kitchen, Washhouse, and Larder.

First Floor—Three Front Sitting Rooms, commanding a beautiful View of the River Stour (these Rooms when thrown
together form a Handsome Ball Room), Seven Bed Rooms, Five Attics, and Water Closet.

ALSO,

EXCELLENT CELLARING, WITH BREWHOUSE,

Stabling and Standing for Thirty-two Horses, Large Loose Stable and Spacious Lofts over,

LOCK-UP COACH-HOUSES, GRANARY, CHAISEHOUSE, YARDS, AND WALLED GARDEN.

These Premises are in full Trade, and are in the Occupation of Mr. John Abbott, at a Rent of £   per Annum.

LOT 44.

A FREEHOLD DWELLING HOUSE,

Upon the Margin of Mistley Park, and having a beautiful View over that Property,

And adjoining Lot 43,

Occupying a Large Site of Ground,

AND CONTAINING

Two Attics, Four Bed Rooms, Dining and Drawing Rooms, Breakfast Room, Kitchen, Arched Wine and Beer Vaults, and Store Room,

Lawn and Flower Gardens, Kitchen Garden &c.,

Three-stall Stable, Coachhouse, Harness Room, and Hay House,

In the Occupation of Mr. John Ayles.

LOT 45.

A FREEHOLD PROPERTY,

Adjoining Lot 44,

COMPRISING

A Blacksmith's Shop, Shoeing Forge, and Counting House,

In the Occupation of Messrs. J. and W. Disney.

All Buildings erected and now standing on the Boundaries of the respective Lots (as shown on Plan), are to be considered as party walls. The respective Lots are all staked out, but should any dispute arise, after this sale, upon questions of boundaries, division fences, or buildings, the same shall be referred to Mr. Gilbert, Land Surveyor, Colchester, whose decision in all cases thereon shall be binding upon the vendors and purchasers. And it is further stipulated that the purchasers at this sale shall sign their approval of the Ground-plan which has been made by Mr. Gilbert, and which shall be binding upon them in the formation of the intended New Road, within the red dotted lines, and in the requisite removal of those buildings now standing, which otherwise would prevent the proposed arrangement being carried into effect.

ACKNOWLEDGEMENTS

Essex County Council - Records Office
Our Story - Local Publication
Once Upon a Tide by Harvey Benham
Maldon Salt Co. Ltd.
Joseph Glass - 19th Century poet
Horace Walpole - Letters
Alexander Pope - 19th Century poet
The Dolphin's Skin by James Turner
Mistley in Days Gone By - 19th Century Parish Magazine
David Garrick - Letters
The Curator - Woburn Abbey
Irmins - 18th Century journalist
Sir G.O.Travalyan writer
The real character of Richard Rigby by General Bernard Hale
Sir Nathanial Wraxall - writer
The Architecture of James and Robert Adams - Hammond
National Arts Museum - Stockholm
A Frenchman's Year in Suffolk by Norman Scarfe
Mrs Mullins of Old Hall, Mistley.

A special thanks is extended to Ian C. Rose for his photographic
contribution to this publication, and also to the many friends and colleagues of
Ivan's family for all their help and assistance.
Additional images - Lucas Books.

In years long gone, 'twas often said
If Mistley's moonlit lanes you tread.
A sound of music is faintly heard.
A ripple of laughter, the cry of a bird.
And sometimes, if you quietly stand,
See a couple walking hand in hand.
One with a dress of radiant hue,
Will pause to enjoy the glorious view,
Of tower below, with shining Stour so clear,
Who would doubt, 'twas the Rigbys strolling here?